THROUGH WESTERN EYES

For my family

THROUGH WESTERN EYES

Images of Chinese Women
in Anglo-American Literature

Mimi Chan

Orchid Press

Mimi Chan
THROUGH WESTERN EYES:
Images of Chinese Women in Anglo-American Literature

First published by Joint Publishing, Hong Kong, 1989.
Second edition, revised & expanded, 2011.

ORCHID PRESS
PO Box 1046,
Silom Post Office,
Bangkok 10504, Thailand
www.orchidbooks.com

ISBN: 978-974-524-134-3

Contents

Acknowledgments

Whatever reception this volume receives I can say with conviction that I shall not have any regrets about the time and effort I have spent on it. In the first place it represents the fulfillment, partially at least, of an academic ambition I have cherished virtually from the beginning of my career as a university teacher. Secondly in the course of my study I have had the opportunity to experience the genuine kindness of so many fellow academics, who have given unstintingly of their time and knowledge. The topic of the representation or, more often, of the misrepresentation, of Chinese women in literature written in English was first suggested by a colleague, Amelia Sun—truly a paragon of Chinese womanhood. To her I am very grateful. Although other research interests diverted my attention from this fascinating subject for many years I shall never forget the absorbing discussions Amelia Sun, another colleague, Helen Kwok, and I had about the topic, and how indignant we waxed over what we felt to be gross injustices done to Chinese women by Western writers. For her stimulation and insightful contributions to these early discussions and for her subsequent unfaltering interest in my project I also owe Helen Kwok a debt of affectionate gratitude.

In 1985, another colleague, Wong Tak-wai, urged me to present a paper at a conference on Hong Kong Literature which he was helping to organize. I agreed and the result was, in an unrevised form, my present Chapter V. For rekindling my interest in the literary presentation of Chinese women at a time when my research interests were almost exclusively linguistic I am very grateful to Wong Tak-wai, and to Leung Ping-kwan, another of the conference organizers. Leung Ping-kwan encouraged me to expand my research and incorporate my findings in a book. He also put me in touch with the Deputy Editor-in-Chief of Joint Publications, Poon Yiu-ming.

I wish also to thank most sincerely yet another colleague, Kingsley Bolton, who gave many useful suggestions as well as unfailing moral support. He introduced me to Judy Young, South China Morning Post librarian, who very kindly gave me access to the newspaper's files of photographs. I am grateful to L.Y. Chiu and C.Y. Sin of the Department of Chinese, who provided respectively much-needed information on Chinese History and Chinese Etymology. I was truly impressed by the promptness and thoroughness of their responses. I must also acknowledge the assistance of the Department of Comparative Literature, Pennsylvania State University, under whose auspices I gave a seminar on my work in progress in 1986. I was able to gauge popular response to my work. I am particularly grateful to Earl Moser of Penn. State's Department of Spanish for his charming and vocal appreciation of my early efforts and for his information about Spanish writers. Grateful thanks are also due to T.L. Tsim, Publisher, Chinese University of Hong Kong, for drawing my attention to the very pertinent and interesting work of Hsiao Ch'ien. I am deeply grateful to Ada Lee, who typed the early drafts of my manuscript and Susanna Lew, who labored over a wordprocessor for weeks on weeks, typing and re-typing the final drafts, Beryl McKenzie, the best and most conscientious proof-reader that any writer could ask for, Samantha Chan and J.C. Lai, who undertook the arduous task of making my manuscript camera-ready. If mistakes are still present they are the result of my own carelessness, not theirs.

A record of my indebtedness would certainly be incomplete without a mention of David Pollard, Professor of Chinese at the School of Oriental and African Studies, University of London, who has written a foreword as gracious and elegant as the man himself, and of John Preston, my Head of Department from 1984 to 1988 and a very good friend. He has been unfailingly supportive and encouraging. He read the entire draft and wrote a blurb during his last hectic days with the Department before proceeding on retirement. To both I am profusely grateful.

Last, but certainly not least, I must thank my colleague and friend of many years, Piers Gray, who was infinitely helpful and patient during my months of research and writing up, passing on to me all kinds of relevant books, articles, and photographs, and reading through the early drafts of each essay. Without his unwavering—possibly misplaced—faith in my ability I would probably not have completed this book.

Mimi Chan
Dept. of English Studies and Comparative Literature
The University of Hong Kong
July, 1988

Foreword

I was introduced to the Chinese language and the academic study of China without the benefit of prior education in popular works on that country and its people, and the first images of Chinese women I can now recall with any sharpness of definition were derived from ocular observation in Hong Kong in the late 1950s. Both the pampered sylph-like beauties and the wicked empresses, in which guise Chinese womanhood, as I learn from these pages, had been represented to the West for generations and even centuries, had simply passed me by, or had not seemed real enough to leave any trace on my memory. The Hollywood 'vamp', Anna May Wong, might have made an impression, but, alas, I was born at the wrong time, and she was only a name to me. In the light of this book's matter, how Anna May went about her vamping would have been of interest. The activity itself is practiced the world over, but modi operandi differ, and one hopes for the sake of those who did get to see her that Hollywood did not require her to be too obvious and heavy-handed. I suppose from the word yaojing that the Chinese did have their "come up and see me sometime" model, but the combination of "apparent delicacy and fragility on the one hand, and knowing coquetry on the other", as Mimi Chan puts it, has culturally been more typical. Native Chinese fiction suggests that seclusion and reticence also help make attraction fatal: what sets the man's heart fluttering is usually a glimpse fleeting of a woman at a window or behind the curtains of a sedan chair; and bashfulness is pretended even by courtesans. It is questionable how far foreign representations of Chinese seductresses, however richly adorned and admiringly described, could prove seductive when shorn of this dimension of bearing and behavior.

However, whatever sins of commission or omission Western writers have perpetrated in portraying Chinese women, in general the Chinese literati were there ahead of them. When they were not picturing lonely wives fading away while waiting for their men's return, they were reveling in dressing up the famous women of their history in finery and exciting themselves by extravagantly picturing their allure, while at the same time enjoying the luxury of condemning them—for it was the bad girls, self-destructive and destructive of great men and mansions, who most appealed to the Chinese male imagination. At the same time, there was no doubt a sound factual basis for presuming conquering charm: if only matrons were accorded a legitimate sphere of authority, lesser-women had to cultivate the arts of seduction in order to secure a position of influence for themselves. For those who made it the top, and became ruling empresses, again it was China's own scholars who supplied the makings of scurrilous stories for the Westerners to elaborate and retail—with what relish this book describes.

Both Mimi Chan's personal interest and the relative weight of material have determined that the twentieth century should dominate her study, especially the period since the Second World War, which destroyed Western "master race" notions and put an end to seeing the East simply as a source of curiosities, human and otherwise. Though of course fantasies of female submission to male domination survive, the meeting of Chinese woman and Western man has since then been more and more based on the presumption of equal relationships, which nevertheless does not lessen the power of refashioned old models such as Richard Mason's Suzie Wong, who in her film portrayal was responsible, so I am informed, for attracting more than one young man into Chinese studies.

But I should not give the impression that this book is all about the fate of Chinese women at the hands of male writers. Indeed, on balance women writers probably come in for more attention, from Americans like Pearl Buck through half-Chinese like Han Suyin to wholly Chinese like Bette Bao Lord and Nien Cheng (though the last two were still educated abroad). With them and their writing, since more or less intimate knowledge did not lack, the emphasis is on literary presentation.

Particularly in regard to the "Hong Kong novel", Mimi Chan's reactions to the works she discusses are as interesting and often more interesting than the works themselves, for implicitly she represents the real woman against whom the images in literature are measured. Fortunately she does not relentlessly maintain academic detachment. But wisely she does not roundly assert what the reality is, either. Plainly that would be impossible to describe in all its variety. Present-day Chinese women can freely pick and choose their own cultural models. The hypersensitive Lin Daiyu of The Story of the Stone does not seem to have entirely lost her grip, but any number of other, including Western, models have crowded in to contend for domination. And there is the added complication that the same person can assume a different personality according to whether she is speaking Cantonese, Mandarin, or English. But then the same is true of men, and to try to develop this line of thought would lead me into greater and greater confusion, so I should at this point pass the reader into the safe hands of the author, who as adumbrated above is not only an interested party, but also an experienced teacher of English literature, and is used to dealing with subtleties.

David E. Pollard
Professor of Chinese
School of Oriental and African Studies (SOAS)
University of London
January, 1988

Preface to the Second Edition

Ten years before the first publication of this volume, as a mark of the leveling off of the Cultural Revolution two colleagues and I were invited to visit Zhongshan University in Guangzhou, the premier university in the south. I made rigorous preparations for the trip. The preparation of lectures took time and energy, but no more than what it took for me to find appropriate attire for this ground-breaking trip. I tried to replicate my image of the typical Mainland Chinese woman at the time: I wore a shapeless cotton shirt, baggy grey trousers and nondescript black flat-heeled shoes, straightened my hair and flattened it down with a clip on the side. This way I thought I would inconspicuously merge with the masses.

Now, twenty years post-book the stereotypical image of Mainland Chinese woman has changed dramatically; it has multi-dimensional facets. One common one is an habitué of upscale fashion malls and other major shopping centres of the world; we see them—and hear them—in every shopping mall in Hong Kong, in queues in front of top name brand boutiques—Hermes, Chanel, Louis Vuitton. At their best, they are tall, fair and togged out in the latest and most chic; at their worst they are walking fashion *faux pas*, but nobody would call them plain or shabby. At the same time the media brings out the disparity of wealth, the extreme poverty of some areas and a large sector of the population, and—very sensationally—the barbarity of the infanticide of girl babies.

The media gives images of Chinese American women holding important office in the United States; of Chinese women divers and other sports luminaries, of glamorous film stars, singers, moguls' wives; it also gives the world images of the destitute, the overworked on farm and factory, the downtrodden; of those devastated by the forces of nature. In short, the whole spectrum of Chinese women is visible for those who have eyes to see.

The research in this book follows the evolution of the West's literary images of Chinese women from the time of Marco Polo to the late twentieth century. It records and analyses the influences and possible sources leading to these images and discusses the merits of literary depictions, with some emphasis on the vexed issue of "verisimilitude". Briefly put, in the over four centuries covered, although more Chinese woman characters have found their way into the literature of the West, up to around the mid-twentieth century, the images, though superficially varied, can almost always be reduced to three: the sexpot, the door-mat and the dragon lady. The image of the sexy seductress is in line with the generalized picture of the Chinese women of ill repute who found their illegal way to the United States during the time of the Exclusion Act. This type is epitomized by the screen vamp, Anna May Wong, with her fringed bob and slanty eyes; the subservient stereotype by the character O-lan from *The Good Earth*, Pearl Buck's novel about rural China in the 30's and its stereotypical chauvinistic men. The film version added insult to injury by using a Caucasian cast, made up to superficially suggest Chinese-ness. Their Caucasian features were still very much in evidence in order to ensure they would not alienate the audience. The dragon lady stereotype generated many representations of termagant wives and especially mothers-in-law and was probably inspired by historical characters like the Empress Dowager Tz'u-hsi (Cixi) of the Qing Dynasty.

The period of the Second World War and its aftermath brought new interest in China as a Western ally. In spite of this, the range of portraiture did not broaden appreciably. Even the Soong sisters, with the exception of Madam Sun, fell loosely into the dragon lady category.

The mid-twentieth century saw the growth of "Chinese American" literature, one of the earliest and best-known exponents being Maxine Hong Kingston. She and other Chinese American writers, notably Amy Tan and Jish Jen, tried to explore the conflict in their minds resulting from the pull of two very dissimilar cultures. In spite of their apparent sincerity, their efforts have largely resulted in "new stereotypes"—the conflicted Chinese-American daughter, the pushy immigrant mother and the (usually flawed) White American husband. The inclusion of the experiences of the first generation gave scope for age-old stereotypes like the dragon lady mother-in-law and the door-mat victim of her superstition or simply cruelty. In spite of such failings, the portrayal of Chinese women has definitely taken a step forward. A 2010 publication, *Girl in Translation* by Jean Kwok (New York: Riverhead 2010) shows a leap forward in the sensitivity of its portrayal.

This volume also traces the rise and decline in popularity of "Hong Kong" fiction. Pre-1997, the colonial ethos of this British colony provided a unique setting for what usually amounted to a cast of stereotypical representations of the colonizers— usually male, insensitive and vile, and the colonized—with some exceptions, female, servile, inferior and despicable. A relatively early example of such a setting and characters can be found in Somerset Maugham's *The Painted Veil*, (London, 1925; recently released (2006) as a film directed by John Curran). The image of Western male superiority strengthened with the growth in proximity of the return of sovereignty to China and the perceived need for a foreign passport and refuge from the Chinese communists.

Focus shifted to China itself after the handover and a number of Chinese writers won considerable attention for their accounts of experiences in the chaos in China before, during and immediately after the 1949 revolution. Nien Cheng's *Life and Death in Shanghai* and Jung Chang's *Wild Swans: Three Daughters of China* became international bestsellers. Both authors are educated and highly literate and the approach in both works is autobiographical. The images of Chinese women presented by both the authors and the characters have come a long way from "the dragon lady", "the door-mat" or "the sexpot" stereotypes. Less groundbreaking are a continuous stream of autobiographies of early years spent in China, usually written by women married to American men and living in the West. China does not yet boast writers like Nabokov or Murikami but writers like Ha Jin are approaching the stage of being internationally recognized.

Images of China and the Chinese have evolved and grown in diversity and complexity from the time Leigh Hunt wrote mockingly in 1833:

> "China, sir, is a place very unknown to us—in one sense of the word unknown; but who is not intimate with it as the land of tea, and China and *ko-tous* and mandarins and Confucius and conical caps, and people with little names, little eyes and little feet?"[1]

This book traces the long and tortuous road which has brought us to the more complex and "human" rendering of Chinese women characters. The developments which have brought us to this relatively sophisticated stage are interesting and worth recording and analysing. On this journey I have also discovered little-known information and texts which are of interest not only to the literary historian but to the general reading public as well.

Greater knowledge, absence of bigotry and determination are helpful in the creative process, but, as in the delineation of all characters, not just Chinese women, talent, genius—whatever we choose to call it—is indispensable, Having long been a critic of stereotypical images of Chinese woman characters, I decided to try my hand, The result of my endeavour—a work of historical fiction entitled *All the King's Women*—was published in 2000 by Hong Kong University Press. I approached the delineation of the eight major woman characters with a sincere desire to do their multifarious characters full justice. But there is considerable distance between intention and achievement.

But now, in the first decade of the "Pacific Century", there is sufficient knowledge of China and its people; there is generally less prejudice and sufficient good will to aid and abet a more "realistic" portraiture of Chinese women—indeed, of course, of women in general. The slinky, slitty-eyed image becomes a cute and lovable one in the cartoon version of the story of the Chinese warrior heroine, Fa Mulan. Lucy Liu, Chinese features very much in evidence, was seen regularly in high profile film and television roles as a self-assured, sophisticated woman of the world. And Connie Chung was a much-admired anchor woman.

There have also been some recent setbacks emanating from unexpected quarters. One cannot help but cringe at times at the exaggerated depiction of Chinese motherhood in Amy Chua's *Battle Hymn of the Tiger Mother* (Penguin Press 2011) wherein the Dragon Lady once again rears her scheming and manipulative head.

However, in balance the picture steadily improves. Among those chosen by *Time* magazine as the one hundred most influential persons in 2009 is not a single person but a group, namely Chinese woman factory workers. It did not name Hu Jintao or Wen Jiabao, but the women who contribute towards China's economic boom. Nor are we left to see the young women as a collective mass of humanity. Leslie T. Chang's book, *Factory Girls* (New York: Spiegel and Grau, 2008) is a poignant and powerful illustration of writers depicting with truth and compassion the thoughts, feelings and aspirations of today's Chinese women.

Mimi Chan
Hong Kong
January 2011

Preface

I. A Chinese Woman Speaks

This book contain a number of essays on the delineation of Chinese women in Western literature, primarily in literature written in English. Together they give a picture of the evolving image of Chinese women. Until the early years of the twentieth century few writers of literature in English attempted portraits, or even cameo sketches, of Chinese women. And for this reason the main focus of my research will be on twentieth century works. In my essays I bring in sociological and historical information, but my approach is principally literary. I want, and, to lend credibility to my research, *need* to grapple with the whole question of "accuracy" of portrayal. This question is beset by dangers and difficulties. How does one safely assess "accuracy" in literary characterization? When one is dealing with portraits of Chinese women of the past, historical documents and actual case studies throw light as least on general conditions and the plight of women at given periods of time. For example, Jonathan Spence's *The Death of Woman Wang* (London, 1978), a rare case study in English of a peasant woman in seventeenth century China, is an invaluable work. Comparisons with women delineated in Chinese literature dealing with a comparable period are also of great value. And, as a Chinese woman, though one is inevitably bound to a particular time and environment, I have on occasion fallen back on my own powers of perception and interpretation.

But the whole concept of verisimilitude in art is fraught with imponderables, and "images" are unstable and changing. And the same object can be seen as different images according to perspective. When I was young, two Western journalists, unbeknown to me, took photographs of me to illustrate stories about glimpses of Hong Kong women printed in two separate journals. In one I presented the image of the young mother, with two toddlers at the beach; in another, replete with business suit and briefcase in the Central District, I represented "the Hong Kong Career woman".

I have tried to "anchor" my discussion by the more tangible analyses of the literary techniques used by the writers in their portrayal of Chinese women: their use of narration, description, comment and dialogue. Dialogue is particularly interesting in this context. The conventions used by an author in formulating the dialogue of his Chinese women characters can be very illuminating in terms of his/her intentions and of the reader's response to the characters. With this brief preamble let me now begin, as it were, from the beginning.

II. Brief Historical Survey of Contacts between the West and China

(i) The West Comes to China: Marco Polo

The activities of navigators, travelers and missionaries of the sixteenth, seventeenth and eighteenth centuries brought the West into contact with China. The name which immediately comes to mind when one thinks of early East-West contact is that of Marco Polo (1254-1324). Marco Polo was the son of Niccoli Polo, a Venetian merchant. His father and uncle had already made one visit to China in 1260 when Marco joined them for the second journey in 1271. They spent the next twenty years travelling in the service of Kubilai Khan. He was allowed to return home to Venice in 1295. In 1298/9 Marco was a prisoner of war at Genoa. It was probably in prison that he met Rustichello of Pisa, a Romance-writer. Together they wrote *The Travels*. *The Travels* is the product of an observant merchant and a professional romancer. In *The Travels* Marco Polo described and area from the Polar Sea to Java and from Zanzibar to Japan and in so doing revealed a world almost wholly unknown to western civilization. In particular the West was enthralled by the splendours of the Mongol court.

Certainly the earliest presentations of Eastern women of any widespread currency appear in *The Travels*. There is no doubt that Polo was not immune to feminine pulchritude. In *The Travels* there are no less than ten specific references to the beauty—and in one case (of the women of Zanzibar) lack of beauty—of women. It was he who brought to the attention of the West the beauty of Chinese woman. As Polo travels east on the road to Cathay he keeps up a continuous commentary on the appearance of the women he encounters. He also includes "exotic" accounts of Middle Eastern and Eastern customs and mores in connection with women. One description may well be seen as encapsulating for future Western readers all the beguiling qualities associated with Chinese women in her stereotypical representation. Polo describes the genteel life of rich merchants of Kinsai (Hangzhou)

> As for the merchants they are so many and so rich and handle such quantities of merchandise that no one could give a true account of the matter: it is so utterly beyond reckoning. And I assure you that the great men and their wives and all the heads of the workshops of which I have spoken, never soil their hands with work at all, but live a life of as much refinement as if they were kings. And their wives too are most refined and angelic creatures, and so adorned with silks and jewellery that the value of their finery is past compute... Men as women are fair-skinned and good-looking. Most of them wear silk all the time, since it is produced in great abundance in all the surrounding territory, not to speak of the great quantity continually imported by traders from other provinces. (*Travels*, Penguin, 1982, pp.217-200)

Marco Polo gives a detailed account of the polygamous habits of Kubilai Khan and, without comment, relates at once the splendours of his harem and the servitude of women. We can see how the detailed account of how concubines were chosen would certainly have satisfied the fantasies of the most chauvinistic Western male.

> Kubilai has four consorts who are all accounted his lawful wives; and his eldest son by any of these four has a rightful claim to be emperor on the death of the present khan. They are called

empresses, each by her own name. Each of these ladies holds her own court. None of them has less than 300 ladies in waiting, all of great beauty and charm. They have many eunuchs and many other men and women in attendance, so that each one of these ladies has in her court 10,000 persons. When he wishes to lie with one of his four wives, he invites her to his chamber; or sometimes he goes to his wife's chamber.

He also has many concubines, about whom I will tell you. There is a province inhabited by Tartars who are called Kungurat, which is also the name of their city. They are a very good-looking race with fair complexions. Every two years or so, according to his pleasure, the Great Khan sends emissaries to this province to select for him out of the most beautiful maidens, according to the standard of beauty which he lays down for them, some four or five hundred, more or less as he may decide. This is how the selection is made. When the emissaries arrive, they summon to their presence all the maidens of the province. And there valuers are deputed for the task. After inspecting and surveying every girl, feature by feature, her hair, her face, her eyebrows, her mouth, her lips, and every other feature, to see whether they are well-formed and in harmony with her person, the valuers award to some a score of sixteen marks, to others seventeen, eighteen, or twenty, or more or less according to the degree of their beauty. And, if the Great Khan has ordered them to bring him all who score twenty marks, or perhaps twenty-one, according to the number ordered, these are duly brought. When they have come to his presence, he has them assessed a second time by other valuers, and then the thirty of forty with the highest score are selected for his chamber. These are first allotted, one by one, to the barons' wives, who are instructed to observe them carefully at night in their chambers, to make sure that they are virgins and not blemished or defective in any member, that they sleep sweetly without snoring, and that their breath is sweet and they give out no unpleasant odour. Then those who are approved are divided into groups of six, who serve the Khan for three days and three nights at a time in his chamber and his bed, ministering to all his needs. And he uses them according to his pleasure. After three days and nights, in come the next six damsels. And so they continue in rotation throughout the year.

While some of the group are in attendance in their lord's chamber, the others are waiting in as ante-chamber hard by. If he is in need of anything from outside, such as food or drink, the damsels inside the chamber pass word to those outside, who immediately get it ready. In this way the Khan is served by no one except these damsels. As for the other damsels, who are rated at a lower score, they remain with the Khan's other women in the palace, where they are instructed in needle-work, glove-making, and other elegant accomplishments. When some nobleman is looking for a wife, the Great Khan gives him one of these damsels with a great dowry. And in this way he marries them all off honourably.

You may be inclined to ask: 'Do not the men of this province regard it as grievance that the Great Khan robs them of their daughters?' Most certainly not. They esteem it a great favour and distinction; and those who have beautiful daughters are delighted that he should deign to accept them. They reason thus: 'If my daughter is born under a good planet and happy auspices, the Khan will be better able to satisfy her than I; he will marry her to a noble husband, which is more than my means would permit of.' And if she does not behave well or it does not turn out well for her, then the father says: 'This has happened to her because her planet was not propitious.'   (Marco Polo, ibid., pp.122-3)

(ii) China through English Eyes: Eighteenth and Nineteenth Century Writings

Marco Polo's *Travels* was and is widely read. Penguin books, for example, published its first English translation in 1958, and since then it has been reprinted many times—twice in 1982 alone. For some five hundred years or so after Marco Polo's travels China and its women remained essentially remote and mysterious to the West, though the continued activities of navigators, travelers and missionaries of the sixteenth, seventeenth and eighteenth centuries brought the West into contact with China. Until the collapse of their order in 1760, the Jesuits were an important bond between the East and the West. By the latter part of the seventeenth century they held first place as authorities on China. They were also China's best apologists, and gave favourable reports of the Chinese, markedly different from some of the unfavourable reports of traders.

Interest in China was increased by the Macartney embassy. This was the first official embassy, although there had been unsuccessful Elizabethan ventures and an earlier embassy which had to turn back because of the illness of the ambassador. The Macartney embassy, which set sail in September 1792, was for trade purposes. From the standpoint of trade no substantial objective was achieved, and China's Emperor Chien Lung rejected a request to have a British minister resident in China.

In spite of its failure to attain concrete commercial objectives, the embassy had a tremendous influence in that it generated great interest in China. On his return to England, Earl George Macartney wrote an account of his travels, during which he had seen a great deal and had been impressed by many aspects of Chinese civilization. His work appeared in 1807, a year after his death. But before that details of the embassy had been published as early as 1795 by Aeneas Anderson, body servant to Macartney. These accounts enjoyed great popularity. The interest in tales of China and travel resulted in many more publications. Among the works brought about by popular enthusiasm was John Barrow's *Travels in China*, published in 1804 after a short sojourn in the Celestial Kingdom. He described the splendours of the court, examined Chinese philosophy and religious beliefs, eulogized nature and attempted as well scholarly analysis. The second embassy to China, headed by Lord Amherst in 1816 was dismissed summarily because of the failure of Amherst to *kowtow* to the Emperor. It did not, like the first embassy, generate a wealth of travel literature. Possibly this was because scenes and events had already been made familiar by members of the earlier mission.

Vague and romantic notions of China prevailed and China and Chinese themes appeared not infrequently in the literature of the eighteenth and first half of the nineteenth century. On a material level, tea was becoming more and more popular as a beverage. The bulk of the cargo of the East India Company was tea. Samuel Pepys relates in his *Diary* how he drank tea for the first time on September 25th, 1661 (London, 1906, p.101). With tea came porcelain ware—china—also brought by the ships of the East India Company.

The vogue of hoarding porcelain started in the late seventeenth century. Also imported from China and much coveted were paintings, wallpaper, lacquered ware and *objets d'art*. Samuel Pepys' home at Chapham was "wonderfully well furnished, especially with Indian and Chinese curiosities". (John Evelyn, *Diary*, July 23rd, 1700)

A superficial fascination with China and things Chinese developed. But in spite of the "Chinese vogue" there was no real attempt to understand or to know about China and Chinese. The craze for Chinoiserie was a case in point. It was all the rage for the first three-quarters of the eighteenth century but there was little genuine knowledge of the symbolism of Chinese art, and Chinoiserie was often merely a hybrid of Chinese and other elements. When Boswell[1] suggested to Samuel Johnson that China had arts, he answered "They have pottery"; when Boswell spoke of the vast vocabulary of the Chinese language, the great lexicographer replied, "It is only more difficult from its rudeness; as there is more labour in hewing down a tree with a stone than with an axe."

Pre-twentieth century works clearly show unreal, unfair and very inaccurate presentations of both China and its people. What seems more infuriating is the apparent complacent refusal to find out more. Even Goldsmith, supposedly an admirer of the Chinese, was essentially exploitative in his use of them for satirical purposes and in his flippant obliviousness to fact in his *Citizen of the World* (1762). Examining China in English literature of the seventeenth, eighteenth and nineteenth centuries we can hardly find any find any attempt to delineate the Chinese as a race of human beings, let alone an individual man or woman as human being. In the late seventeenth century Milton's geographical imagination rove over the land of "the Chineses" (*Paradise Lost*, III, 1.438). Samuel Johnson in the eighteenth used China to indicate the farthest reaches of humanity: observation was to view mankind from "China to Peru" (*The Vanity of Human Wishes*, 1.2)

Daniel Defoe included a "Chinese" part in his *Robinson Crusoe* (1719). His knowledge of "Nanquin" and "Pekin" seem based on no more than hearsay and prejudice as well as a smug chauvinism. As witness this description:

> ... nothing was more awkward to see, than to see such an haughty, imperious, insolent people, in the midst of the grossest simplicity and ignorance; for all their famed ingenuity is no more... As for our mandarin with whom we travelled, he was respected like a king; surrounded always with his gentlemen, and attended in all his appearances with such pomp, that I saw little of him but at a distance; but this I observed, that there was not a horse in his retinue, but that our carriers' pack-horses in England seem to me to look much better...

One passage, in particular, is interesting from my point of view in that it relates to the servile status of Chinese women and the hateful male chauvinism of gross Chinese men—a Western view which seems, as we shall see, to have been perpetuated to the days of "Hong Kong" fiction exemplified by a work like *The World of Suzie Wong*:

> (This gentleman was), under a tree, something like the palmetto tree, which effectually shaded him over the head, and on the south side; but under the tree also was placed a large umbrella, which made that part look well enough: he sat lolling back in a great elbow-chair, being a heavy opulent man, and his meat being brought by two women slaves: he had two more, whose office, I think, few gentlemen in Europe would accept of their service in, *viz*, one fed the squire with a spoon, and the other held the dish with one hand, and scraped off what he let fall upon his worship's beard and taffety vest, with the other; while the great fat brute thought it below him to employ his own hands in any of those familiar offices which kings and monarchs would rather do than be troubled with the clumsy fingers of their servants.

Oliver Goldsmith (1728-1774) does exhibit a broad humanism in his *Chinese Letters* subsequently republished as the *Citizen of the World* in 1762. Like Voltaire, Goldsmith tried to satirize Europe through a puppet Chinese, But there is no attempt to characterize the instrument of satire. Since the letters are essentially satires directed at human foibles in general, accuracy in matters of detail did not seem to worry Goldsmith. A cautionary tale relating to the faithlessness of husbands and wives and the emptiness of professions of eternal devotion is told in Letter XVIII "The Story of a Chinese Matron". In spite of the title Goldsmith unabashedly introduces the matron and her husband thus:

> Choang was the fondest husband, and Hansi the most endearing wife in all the kingdom of Korea...

There are one or two gestures to the Oriental background; Choang, for example "had early been taught wisdom in the school of Lao". But it seems inconsequential what country in the Orient when Goldsmith relates how Hansi tricked herself out in readiness for her second marriage he writes:

> ...the bride wore in her nose a jewel of immense price...

Certainly this has always been an Indian, rather than a Chinese custom but to Goldsmith, Indians, Koreans, Chinese—they were all the same!

The open polygamy practiced by Eastern men was a factor of Oriental civilization which struck the West, and it responded with varying emotions. In these early English literary works, the plight of the women involved was little considered. In Letter XCIV: *A visit from a little beau. The indulgence with which the fair sex are treated in several parts of Asia*, we find this passage:

> I lately received a visit from the little beau... Our discourse happened to turn upon the different treatment of the fair sex here and in Asia, with the influence of beauty in refining our manners and improving our conversation.

> I soon perceived he was strongly prejudiced in favour of the Asiatic method of treating the sex, and that it was impossible to persuade him, but that a man was happier who had four wives at his command, than he who had only one. It is true', cries he, 'your men of fashion in the East are slaves, and under some terrors

of having their throats squeezed in a bow-string; but what then, they can find ample consolation in a seraglio; they make indeed an indifferent figure in conversation abroad, but then they have seraglio to console them at home. I am told they have no balls, drums, nor operas, but then they have got a seraglio; they may be deprived of wine and French cookery, but they have a seraglio; a seraglio, a seraglio, my dear creature, wipes off every inconvenience in the world. Besides, I am told, your Asiatic beauties are the most convenient women alive, for they have no souls; positively there is nothing in Nature I should like so much as ladies without souls; soul, here, is the utter ruin of half the sex. A girl of eighteen shall have soul enough to spend an hundred pounds in the turning of a trump. Her mother shall have soul enough to ride a sweepstake match at a horserace; her maiden aunt shall have soul enough to purchase the furniture of a whole toy-shop, and others shall have soul enough to behave as if they had no souls at all.'

With respect to the soul, interrupted I, the Asiatics are much kinder to the fair sex than you imagine; instead of one soul, Fohi, the idol of China, gives every women three, the Bramines give them fifteen; and even Mahomet himself no where excludes the sex from Paradise…

No, Sir, continued I, the men of Asia behave with more deference to the sex than you seem to imagine. As you of Europe say grace, upon sitting down to dinner, so it is the custom in China to say grace, when a man goes to bed to his wife. '*And may I die,*' returned my companion, '*but a very pretty ceremony; for seriously, Sir, I see no reason why a man should not be as grateful in one situation as in the other. Upon honour, I always find myself much more disposed to gratitude, on the couch of a fine women, than upon sitting down to a sirloin of beef.*'[2]

Another ceremony, said I, resuming the conversation, in favour of the sex amongst us, is the bride's being allowed after marriage, *her three days of freedom*.[3] During this interval, a thousand extravagances are practiced by either sex. The lady is placed upon the nuptial bed, and numberless monkey tricks are played round to divert her. One gentleman smells her perfumed handkerchief, another attempts to untie her garters, a third pulls off her shoe to play hunt the slipper, another pretends to be an idiot, and endeavours to raise a laugh by grimacing; in the meantime, the glass goes briskly about, till ladies, gentlemen, wife, husband, and all are mixed together in one inundation of arrack punch.

'Strike me dumb, deaf, and blind,' cried my companion, 'but very pretty; there's some sense in your Chinese ladies' condescensions; but among us, you shall scarce find one of the whole sex that shall hold her good humour for three days together...'

There is much in the whole piece to disturb feminists but with its total disrespect for the truth and anything-for-a-laugh cavalier attitude to Chinese customs there is much more to disturb *Chinese* feminists.

De Quincey (1785-1859) engages in a lengthy and relentless diatribe against the Chinese—"this vilest and silliest amongst nations towards the household of man"—in his essay "China", but it is directed against the whole Chinese race, as is J.S. Mill's (1806-1873) criticism of the conformity of Chinese people to fixed norms and conventions of behavior which has resulted in total stagnation and lack of progress. ("On Liberty"). As far as Chinese women are concerned, what allusions we have discussed so far to them have to do with their being sex objects and sources of pleasure for men rather than as individuals. We recall that Marco Polo's references to Chinese women are flattering; his remarks on their fair skins and their silken costumes. The willowy Chinese beauty as a stereotype has persisted in Western literature to this day.

In the nineteenth century we have a few references, by no means profound, only merely sketched, to individual Chinese woman which play up the sense of daintiness and mystery. An example of this type of presentation can be found in the early nineteenth century. There were many kinds of hyson (from 禧春, Cantonese *hei tsoen*, Mandarin *xi chun*) tea imported to England in the nineteenth century. Charles Lamb speaks familiarly of "our hyson (which we are old-fashioned enough to drink unmixed still". (from "Old China", first published in the *London Magazine* in 1823) In 1826 Lamb's friend Thomas Hood wrote an essay called "Fancies on a Tea-cup". This parodies Lamb's "Old China". Lamb's beloved hyson (tea) is used as the name of the lady of the obsequious Chinese man, Hum. She is known as Hy-son. Hood's description of the dainty Chinese lady has a malicious streak, but it already pinpoints many of the physical attributes Western readers are to associate with Chinese women for a good many years to come:

> Lo! Here, how sedulously the blooming Hy-son is penciling the mortal arches, and curving the cross-bows of her eyebrows. A musical instrument, her secondary engagement, is at her almost invisible feet. Are such little extremities likely to be tasked with laborious offices?—Marry, in kicking, they must be ludicrously impotent,—but then she hath a formidable growth of nails. (*Works*, edited by his son and daughter, B. Moxton, London, 1870)

The Western imagination has been intrigued for virtually three centuries by S.T. Coleridge's portrayal in "Kubla Khan" of the mysterious woman "wailing for her demon-lover". Chinese women as dainty and exotic would appear to be the general impression. This makes the comments of Leigh Hunt, referred to in the Preface to this edition, worth repeating; they reinforce one's sense of perspective and flexible criteria in aesthetic judgment. In a letter written to *Tait's Magazine* in 1833 (collected in *The World of Books*) Leigh Hunt writes,

> China, sir, is a very unknown place to us—in one sense of the word unknown; but who is not intimate with it as the land of tea, and China, and ko-tous and pagodas, and mandarins, and Confucius, and conical caps, and people with little names, little eyes, and little feet, who sit in little bowers, drinking little cups of tea, and writing little odes?… With *one* China they are totally unacquainted, to wit the great China of the past and old travellers' Cathay, 'seat of Cathian Can', the country of which Ariosto's 'Angelica' was princess-royal; yes, she was a Chinese, 'the fairest of her sex, Angelica'. It shows that the ladies in that country must have greatly degenerated, for it is impossible to conceive that Ariosto, and Orlando, and Rinaldo, and King Sacripant, who was a Circassian could have fallen in love with her for having eyes and feet like a pig…

Certainly one aspect of Leigh Hunt's opinions is irrefutable; China was indeed in the nineteenth century "unknown" to the average Englishman, and to a lesser extent this is still true today.

Great Britain's contact with China in the nineteenth century was mainly concerned with trade, but there was also some missionary activities, and much scholarly and useful work was done by missionary scholars like Robert Morrison to make the Chinese language and Chinese culture accessible to Europeans. This was part of the effort to convert the "heathen" Chinese. Morrison felt that learning the language alone is inadequate and his dictionary of the Chinese language is supplemented by his *Views of the Chinese*, an introduction to Chinese history, geography and other aspects of Chinese culture. But in spite of his work and that of other missionaries like Joseph Edkins (*China's Place in Philology*, London, 1871) the language of the Chinese for the ordinary person was made up of just so many strange sounds, and Chinese people were quaint, remote and strange. The many travel books that appeared in the wake of first the Macartney embassy and then the aborted Amherst embassy (1816) aroused superficial interest among limited circles in the Celestial Kingdom, but the Chinese in general were not considered in human terms. The work which perhaps comes closest to the task of "interpreting" the mind of the Chinese people to the West is that of James Legge, who tried to make accessible to English readers the rich heritage of the Chinese classics. To those interested, through Legge's translation of *The Book of Rites* it became possible to be aware of the status—or rather lack of status—of women. Passages like this one from Legge may have helped form the opinions of those interested in the Chinese:

> Man is the representative of Heaven, and is supreme over all things. Woman yields obedience to the instructions of man, and helps to carry out his principles. On this account she can determine nothing of herself, and is subject to the rule of the three obediences. When young, she must obey her father and elder brother; when married she must obey her husband; when her husband is dead, she must

obey her son. She may not think of marrying a second time. No instructions or orders must issue from the harem. Woman's business is simply the preparation and supplying of drink and food. Beyond the threshold of her apartments, she should not be known for evil or for good. She may not cross the boundaries of the State to attend a funeral. She may take no step on her own motion, and may come to no conclusion on her own deliberation. (James Legge, *The Four Books*, Oxford, 1892, Chapter V, Section II, pp.103-4)

Meanwhile the scramble for trade privileges and concessions went on. One of the major commodities the British were trying to sell was "foreign mud" or opium. The first Opium War (1840-1842) ended with the Treaty of Nanking by which the island of Hong Kong was ceded to Britain. Today Hong Kong comprises the island of Hong Kong, the Kowloon peninsula, the territory leased to the British in 1899, known as the New Territories, comprising the large hinterland of Kowloon, as well as various outlying islands. For many years after the commencement of British rule, Hong Kong remained virtually unknown internationally. The British colonizers came for gain and for adventure, but unlike Malaya, generally speaking, Hong Kong was not favoured as a setting for stories until after 1949. Somerset Maugham did start his *Painted Veil* off in Hong Kong (though because of fear of libel suits he subsequently changed the name to a mythical one) but brought the main characters into the epidemic-infested interior of China. Apart from a rather peculiar pairing of an English customs officer with a Manchu princess, the novel certainly does not explore the mysteries of the "forbidden fruit", as women of the East—Malayans and so on—were called, nor the depravity of miscegenation as he does in his Malayan stories like "The Pool" or "The Force of Circumstances".

One Chinese woman figure certainly did force her way into the consciousness of a great many Westerners, Americans and Europeans, and this was the very formidable Empress Dowager, Tz'u-hsi, who reigned as regent over the declining Manchu empire, the power behind the throne in China from 1861 to 1908. The Western powers were busily carving out their spheres of influence during the last years of Chinese dynastic rule, and as the woman who was the *de facto* ruler of the effete Chinese empire she would have naturally elicited a great deal of interest. Histories, or at least stories, of the colourful Empress Dowager took hold of the collective imagination of the West in the last years of the nineteenth century and for a few decades after her death in 1908. In 1943 Maurice Collis's play about the exploits of the Empress Dowager, *The Motherly and Auspicious*, was acted on the London stage. Tz'u-hsi or "Orchid" holds centre-stage for virtually the whole play and must have contributed towards creating for the British audience a new concept of individualistic Chinese womanhood. The depth of this characterization, though it too is stylized in parts, far surpasses that of Lady Precious Stream, the heroine of Hsiung Shi-i's play of the same name. (*Lady Precious Stream*, London; Methuen, first published 1934). *Lady Precious Stream* enjoyed an underserved popularity in Britain in the 1930s, and although the play was written by a Chinese scholar, it panders to the desire of Westerners to see the Chinese race as quaint and backward, given to arranged marriages and with very little to identify them as individual members of the human race. The play hardly attempts realistic portraiture and the comic opera style and subject matter merely confirmed the impression, if any, in English minds, of the Chinese as rather ludicrous beings, full of aphorisms.

(iii) Chinese People Go to "the Gold Mountain": American Images of the Chinese

Migration of Chinese people to the United States in the last year of the nineteenth and early years of the twentieth centuries meant Americans were able to observe the ways and behavior of Chinese people, largely of the laboring classes, cut off from their roots and disadvantaged by being aliens in an alien land. The immigrants were regarded with contempt, suspicion and fear. Harold Isaacs, in an admirable work, traces all these attitudes in his *Scratches on Our Minds: American Images of*

China and India (New York, 1958). Men tended to go to "the Gold Mountain"; to seek their fortunes alone, leaving their women-folk in the old country. Later the American Exclusion Act (1882-1943) was to leave them no option but to do so. As a result the image the Americans had of Chinese women tended to be based on saloon hostesses and women of ill-repute. Bret Harte and Mark Twain's work gives only examples of evil and/or ridiculous Chinese men. The stereotypical image of Chinese woman was that of the sultry siren with sinister features and more sinister occupations. A picture postcard of Anna May Wong, the American Chinese film star, the picture dating back to 1929, is available in London bookstores to this day. The photograph shows her in the archetypical pose of super vamp. Chinese "dragon ladies" became popularized in American culture through books like Sax Rohmer's, about the evil, manipulative Fu Manchu and his bejewelled, befringed, slanty-eyed henchwomen.

Some thirty years after the appearance of Issacs's work on American attitudes to the Chinese, William F. Wu published his work *The Yellow Peril: Chinese Americans in American Fiction 1850-1940* (Archon Books, 1982). The book is the result of Ph.D. research undertaken in American studies at the University of Michigan. Dr Wu has concentrated on the early years of Chinese migration up to the eve of the Second World War. He deals with the "Yellow Peril" as a literary theme. He writes,

> The fear of the people of East Asia focuses on specific issues, including possible invasion from Asia, perceived competition to the white labour force from Asian workers, the alleged moral degeneracy of Asian people, and the potential genetic mixing of Anglo-Saxons with Asians, who were considered a biologically inferior race by some intellectuals of the nineteenth century. (p.1)

Dr Wu's work is highly informative and his research painstaking. He discusses the treatment of Chinese immigrants in American fiction dating from the 1860s and 1870s, and deals with Chinese characters as they appear in the work of Bret Harte, Jocquin Miller, Ambrose Bierce, Stephen Crane and Margaret Hosmer as well as less known writers who contributed to magazines and journals of the time. One becomes aware of how certain stereotypes had already developed in the American mind: the Chinese servant, the tong boss, the opium addict. Because of the Exclusion Act few Chinese women were in evidence in the United States. The women characters who do appear tend to be brides kidnapped or purchased either from some Chinese ghetto in the United States of from China. Wu states, "In 1860, the male-female ratio for Chinese immigrants in the United States was 1,858 to 1; by 1890, it was 2,678 to 9." (Wu, ibid. p.72) There are one or two exceptions of Chinese women who figure more prominently in short fiction which deals with love between Chinese immigrants. Notable is James Hanson's heroine in a story, "The Winning of Josephine Chang" (1920). Josephine is Chinese-American educated and socialized by American society. She is beautiful and has been educated in an American university. The picture is a sympathetic one but Josephine's values are contemporary American ones. And in general the writing about Chinese Americans of that period is biased and does not help in bringing about a sympathetic appraisal. It was not until much later that the American Chinese themselves—writers like David Henry Hwang and Maxine Hong Kingston—found their own voice and began to write of their own people trying to find their places in American society.

(iv) A Turning Point in the Depiction of Chinese Women: Apologists for China and the Chinese in the Twentieth Century

The turning point in the depiction of Chinese people in general—and Chinese women in particular—came with the arrival in China in the early decades of the twentieth century of a number of Westerners, mostly Americans—journalists and missionaries. They acquired first-hand information about China, then on the brink of tremendous historic changes, a land disrupted by civil war, student unrest and military oppression.

Women writers like Pearl Buck, Agnes Smedley, Emily Hahn and Helen Foster Snow (Mrs Edgar Snow) were particularly conscious of the conditions of women, who at that time were taking vast strides from their feudal past into the present. During the 1920s and 30s and into the 40s during the Sino-Japanese War many portraits of Chinese women, fictional, historical-fictionalized, appear in their work, which won varying readerships in the West. Pearl Buck, for example, had a tremendous readership in the United States and Europe. Her *Good Earth* in the book and film versions reached tens of millions of Americans and people all over the world. The work of Agnes Smedley, on the other hand, had an undeservedly small readership, and still does. Only her autobiographical novel, *Daughter of Earth*, has any sort of circulation in the United States and is included in some curricula of Women's Studies programmes. Throughout the late 20s translations of Chinese poetry, especially T'ang poetry, came into vogue among Western cognoscenti through the work of Ezra Pound, Arthur Waley, Witter Bynner, Florence Ayscough and Amy Lowell. And images of gorgeous women, resplendent in silk and jewels like those of Yang Kuei-fei and her family, as well as more subdued images of victims of the feudal discrimination against women, like the girl with the pipa immortalized for Chinese readers by the T'ang poet, Po Chu-i, began to impinge on the consciousness of at least a limited number of Western readers. Han palace poetry also gave many images of women in love and longing and under oppression, women as aesthetic objects. During the period of the Second World War China became the ally of the West, and the Soong sisters, Ai-ling, Ching-ling and Mei-ling, became almost legends—Mei-ling, wife of Chiang Kai-shek receiving the most exposure.

The year 1949 saw the beginning of what can be described as "Hong Kong literature", written in English, with few exceptions, written by Anglo-American men. But paradoxically one of the first "Hong Kong" novels to achieve international reputation is probably Han Suyin's *A Many-Splendoured Thing* (London, 1952), which gives the West a carefully delineated portrait of a Eurasian woman, but Han Suyin insists on her Chinese consciousness and attitudes. Rosalie Chu is Han

Suyin's real name; she falls between two worlds and her autobiographical novels from *Destination Chungking* show her perspective of the impossibly chauvinistic attitudes of Chinese men as represented by her Kuomintang militarist husband. Many more "Hong Kong novels" have appeared since 1952, the date of publication of *A Many-Splendoured Thing*. They are of varying degrees of merit and include many portrayals of Chinese women from many walks of life, with a broadening of the slanty-eyed *femme fatale* stereotype. With interest in Hong Kong and resurgence of interest in China, especially after the Nixon visit, a spate of novels about historical China pre-1949 began to appear around or just before the 1970s. The novels, of varying degrees of merit, or no merit at all, continue to appear. These include James Clavell's *Taipan* and *Noble House*, Robert Elegant's *Dynasty*, *Manchu* and *Mandarin*, Malcolm Bosse's *The Warlord*, Christopher New's *Shanghai*. These all attempt portraiture of Chinese women. Bette Bao Lord's *Spring Moon* elicited a great deal of interest in Hong Kong and the Chinese mainland. After having left China for the United States as a child, the author returned to her homeland in the 1970s with her husband, the present United States ambassador to China, Winston Lord, and her reunion with her family became the genesis of *Spring Moon* (London 1982), which traces the history of a beautiful, highly intelligent and "unconventional" Chinese woman from girlhood until her nineties; the delineation is done with sympathy. The interest in Chinese women and rituals associated with them, such as foot-binding, has also resulted in television programmes and films. Perhaps no single item connected with the making of *Taipan* received so much publicity as the search for the Chinese girl to play Mei-Mei, the beautiful mistress of the Taipan.

Meanwhile in the United States Chinese Americans usually of the second and third generations were becoming more vocal in expressing themselves in literary writings: short stories, novels and plays. Their works tend to focus on themes relating to alienation or integration, on their ethnic "roots". So numerous have works by Asian-American writers become that American literary criticism has come to recognize "Asian-

American" literature as a separate genre, of which literature about American Chinese is a part. This type of literature, perhaps best exemplified by the work of Maxine Hong Kingston, has received considerable critical study. Chinese immigrants to Britain are sketched in lively detail and with considerable sympathy by Timothy Mo in his 1980 novel *Sour Sweet*, a film version of which was released in 1988, with an almost all Chinese cast.

(v) Order in Apparent Randomness: An Explanation of My Approach

With every visit to a bookstore, with every perusal of a book review, one is aware of the proliferation of books about China, fictional or otherwise. Some deal with the China of the past, others with the China of today, and with the increased knowledge of, and interest in, China and the Chinese, there has been some increase—but this is by no means general to all fictional works of the genre—in the degree of sophistication in characterizing Chinese women. But I must repeat that this is by no means general. And that is unfortunate. But I feel that an interim study of the subject is called for. Instead of using a historical approach, I have chosen to throw light on the subject by means of a series of essays, which focus on what I think are landmarks in the creation of images of varying degrees of accuracy of Chinese women. The first deals with three historical characters who so fascinated the West that their exploits have been fictionalized and passed into literature which either directly or indirectly helped to shape Western ideas about Chinese women. Wu Tsertien, Yang Kuei-fei and the Empress Dowager, I am aware, are not the only Chinese historical figures who have captured the Western imagination. I am not forgetting the Soong sisters or Jiang Qing, and indeed they are referred to in more than one section. What is more, I think the combined elements which have gone into the genesis of the images of the three very dominant Chinese historical figures are, in varying proportions, the very elements which make up the images of the Soong sisters and Madame Mao. Of the three very formidable historical figures I have focused on, certainly the Empress Dowager, Tz'u-hsi, is the most important in terms of being really the first Chinese woman to impinge on a wide European consciousness as an individual, inspiring a whole range or emotions, from hatred and revulsion to awe and admiration. She is a character in works of historical fiction: for example she appears as a very humanized woman in as recent a work as Robert Elegant's 1983 novel *Mandarin* and her life is dramatized in Maurice Collis's *The Motherly and the Auspicious* which played to London audiences and was published in 1943. The literary, as distinct from historical, representations seem to be more numerous, and this, as well as the fact of her significance in placing as individual Chinese woman within the ambit, as it were, of the Western imagination, is the reason why I have devoted the longest part of my first essay to her.

As I have mentioned, a breakthrough in terms of attempts to "interpret" Chinese women in the context of their own homeland came with the arrival of Western missionaries and journalists. Two American women, of very different domestic and intellectual background and diametrically opposed political affiliations—Pearl Buck and Agnes Smedley—Buck on a much larger scale than Smedley—did a great deal to give the West images of Chinese women. The two used entirely different literary techniques and styles, but their work is equally indispensable to the study I have undertaken. In many ways they complement each other. Pearl Buck concentrates for the most part on peasant women or genteel women living in the rural backwaters of China in the 30s. There are only background glimmers of the national and international events which were to bring the old feudal structures crumbling down entirely. Agnes Smedley, as a journalist marching with Chinese in a China trembling on the edge of unprecedented change, writes of the suffering and the courageous women living through or working selflessly for these changes. Pearl Buck's contribution towards bringing images of Chinese women before a mass audience is well-known, but Agnes Smedley is a writer whose work on China has been undeservedly neglected and I feel my analysis of her work forms a vital part of my entire study.

Pearl Buck lived in China as the daughter of missionaries and studied the language and culture, but she was still not Chinese, not really part of the surging masses beside her. Agnes Smedley went to China as a mature, politically-conscious journalist and her contribution towards the delineation of Chinese women is that of an observer, who suffers and feels with them as a choice, as part of life's experience, but who also has a choice of leaving, which she finally does, reluctantly.

The writer whom I deal with in my fourth essay, Han Suyin, is one who, until she attained freedom of movement through education and intellect, was very much caught up in the turmoil and agonies of China in the 20s and 30s. Her father was a Chinese engineer educated in Belgium who had none of the privileges and immunities of his expatriate colleagues. Her Belgian mother was embittered and crushed by the hardships of a country that she could not accept and that would not accept her. Han Suyin grew up amid traumatizing domestic tensions and national unrest and civil war. She is a prolific writer, and a very controversial one. Yet, in spite of her European blood and—to many—her brazenly Western outlook and behavior (more stereotyping at work here), her work is vital in the development of the awakening of the Western awareness of Chinese women. She is also the writer of what I consider to be the first "Hong Kong novel" written in English to attain a wide international readership, namely, *A Many-Splendoured Thing*.

"The Hong Kong novel" is the subject of my fifth essay. After 1949, Hong Kong became a focal point of interest to the Western world. As it grew in wealth and international importance, and with its proximity to all the fascinations of China and its mixture of nationalities living in a small area, Hong Kong became a favoured setting for novels and stories of love or intrigue or both. The canvas in some of these "Hong Kong novels" broadens often to take in the Chinese mainland. It is in these novels that the Chinese women as heroine comes into her own, and best-sellers like Elegant's *Dynasty* and Clavell's *Noble House* have, for better or worse, caused a proliferation of images, which, as I shall try to establish, by strange turn of the kaleidoscope are, essentially, the same image.

The final essay of this book examines the role of speech by Chinese women in English language fiction, as writers employ the device of dialogue to simulate 'real life' situations and characters. Inevitably, once again, the words that are spoken by Chinese female protagonists provide the writer an opportunity to portray a nuanced view of Chinese womanhood—or, as has frequently occurred, to perpetuate old and simplistic stereotypes.

Note

In connection with China as seen through the English imagination I ought to cite the invaluable work of a Chinese writer and scholar of repute, Hsiao Ch'ien, who lived and taught in London for a good many years. He produced a very interesting anthology (notwithstanding the difficulties and privations of World War II) made up of pieces about China mostly written by Englishmen. He entitled it *A Harp with a Thousand Strings* (London: Pilot Press Ltd., 1944) and claims in his preface that he wants to give a picture of China "through the writers of today and yesterday, a panorama taking in confessions and observations, reports of revolutions and comments on butterflies." The section he calls "China Through the English Imagination" (China in English literature) is particularly pertinent to my research. He takes the anthology up to the Second World War.

Chapter I

Reality into Images: A Study of Wu Tsertien (624-705), Yang Kuei-fei (717-755) and Tz'u-hsi (1835-1908)

Part I : Preamble

How do images of human beings take shape in the mind? It is a cliché and an understatement to suggest that for people of the same race, different images of different classes take hold of the imagination. Thus, in Hong Kong, she looks and talks like an *amah*; here is a typical *tai-tai*, "a professional woman", "a secretary", "a market woman" and on and on. The stereotypical image differs in details for different people, and certainly external image and reality don't always coincide. We can have a legislator who superficially resembles an *amah* to the general public; a successful career woman who projects the image of a market woman; school marms who project the image of fashion models. And of course many women have more than one role, and it is distinctly difficult to associate one image with them. But the tendency to talk in terms of types persists, in spite of the basic fallacy inherent in generalizations. If this is so among members of one race, it is much more so when different races try to conceptualize one another. When geographical and other barriers are considerable, and when knowledge is gleaned at second or third or tenth-hand, from word of mouth or through the printed word, then so many misconceptions, or at least, generalizations and over-simplifications arise. This has been very much the case for many, many years with China and the West, and even now, with so much more being known of China, with travel to and fro relatively easy, China and the Chinese, for the average Western man on the street, is still mysterious and very little known, much less understood, a nation of slitty-eyed, yellow-skinned pygmies, images left from almost a century ago, from writings and from misconceptions drawn from a small sampling in the form of migrants to the West. Equally the average Chinese person, especially living in more rural areas, has hardly any conception of "foreigners" beyond rudimentary (and often unfavourable) superficial images of redness, hairiness, ungainliness, all embodied in terms like *fangui* and *gweilo*. Even among highly educated, Westernized *Hong Kong* Chinese, and I am most familiar with the Chinese in Hong Kong, unfair generalizations about Westerners prevail. Many have close Western friends and yet will heartily endorse at least in casual conversation, if not serious discussion, accepted stereotypical traits as being indeed typical of Westerners: that they don't ever take care of their aged parents, that they are promiscuous, that all their marriages end in divorce. Racial prejudice and intolerance seem to be, unfortunately, facts of life. And the human mind, confronted with a mass of people, as opposed to individuals, seems to prefer to think in terms of stereotypes. In this present chapter I shall first attempt to write a descriptive account of the "images" which exist in the Western mind of Chinese women and secondly to trace the process by which these images have come into being. In effect the two things are interrelated in cyclic movement: the "images" are generated from hearsay, from actual experience, through reading, then more recently through forms of the media other than the printed word. These images are absorbed by other image-makers—writers, artists, film-makers—who reinforce them by their presentation and interpretation. This is not to say that the images are not, in this process, also being renewed or added to or altered, not just reinforced.

When we talk about the qualities of any ethnic group of women, we enter into the realm of dangerous generalizations: French women are chic; Italian women temperamental; Japanese women servile and English women straitlaced; Chinese women are… These traditional classifications have, since the time they were promulgated, been updated in the minds of the better-informed and the better-travelled, but the prevailing image sticks, and possibly first originated from some tenuous basis of truth. Foolhardy writers have tried to pin down, within a context of a specific time, characteristics of *the* Chinese woman. Florence Ayscough, writing in China in the early decades of the twentieth century, simplistically compares Chinese women of today with those of yesterday, (*Chinese Women Yesterday and Today*, London, 1938). Today they are…, whereas yesterday they *were*… Her approach is naïve and optimistic. Reading her naïve work, which is laced with her translations of poems about the lives and loves and aspirations of Chinese women, mainly of yesterday, one is left totally unaware of the agonies of poverty and foreign invasion and civil war waging outside her happy enclosed world. Individual writers may have shaped and given focus to the images, but in many cases they have done so through a kaleidoscope of parts The kaleidoscope consistently yields two fragments, two contrasting parts, and these two parts keep recurring in literary presentations of Chinese women. One characteristic is submission coupled with gentle beauty which suggests passivity and the Confucian virtues; the contrasting characteristic is fierce ambition coupled with unscrupulous amorality and immorality, a rapaciousness that knows no bounds. Both parts of the image are associated with immense physical attraction, daintiness, small hands and feet, silk and brocades, jewels and perfume. There are variations and elaborations, but in its bare outlines, these two components account for the appearance in novels of Chinese women like Maugham's heavily made-up and bejeweled Manchu lady who hangs upon an unprepossessing middle-aged English customs official with utmost devotion, obedient to his every whim, quite prepared to live her entire life through him and for him. Here the first component: docility. In the Dragon Ladies of Sax Rohmer's work, the accomplices of Fu Manchu, we have the second component: rapacious amorality. In more recent works heroines like Su-mei of Christopher New's *Shanghai* (Futura, 1985) tend to show a combination, in a somewhat more subtle, humanized form, of both components: loyal, in many ways believing in old concepts of duty, and yet fiercely independent, with a will as strong as that of Tz'u-hsi, the notorious Empress

Dowager. And very delicate and beautiful.

How do we account for the persistent use of the image of docility and the counter image of ferocity? If we look at Chinese literature and Chinese history we can perhaps see some basis for this general impression of "Chinese Women". From primeval times women never received their due in Chinese society. Many historians attribute the inequality of women to the stranglehold that Confucianism had over Chinese thought and ethics for so many years.[1] But in fact as early as the time of *The Book of Songs*, which predates Confucius by centuries, we can find poems which give evidence of sexual inequality, for example we can find the lines:

> When a baby boy was born he was laid on the bed and given jade to play with, and when a baby girl was born she was laid on the floor and given a tile to play with. (prose translation by Lin Yutang, *My Country and My People*, Heinemann (Asia), 1977, p.131)

And the progressive subjection of women followed the increasing development of Confucianism.

Yet in spite of the rigours of Confucian doctrine in relation to the position of women, it must be remembered that China had been, before Confucianism, and was, even after it became the basis of the national ethos, a matriarchal society. The Chinese mother, especially after attaining a venerable age and the status of being mother-in-law, was the supreme arbiter of the household. This is borne out by the position of Chiamu in the Qing Dynasty novel, *The Dream of the Red Chamber*.[2] The strength and power of the matriarch provides the starting point for the other half of the generalized image: that of the dragon lady, the termagant. When Western people glibly speak of the wholesale suppression of Chinese women they are forgetting the historical examples of very dominant women. It is a peculiar facet of China's history that its greatest villains have often been women. The examples of the Empress Wu, the only woman to ever ascend the Dragon Throne and to proclaim her own Dynasty, and Tz'u-hsi, the Empress Dowager, readily come to mind. Women were excluded from power and important decisions, and had to practice the three obediences: that is, obedience to their fathers and elder brothers when young, their husbands when married, and their sons when widowed. Thus, their way to power was through men. When education and professional opportunities were totally deprived her, the ambitious Chinese woman had recourse to feminine wiles and sexual charms to gain advantage and power. Sex was then virtually the only route by which a woman could gain power. With the very significant exceptions of the Empress Wu and The Empress Dowager, to the end the woman's power could only be seen as an extension of the power of some man. The prostitute may enter the halls of power—as Chinese history shows—but the way she entered those halls is never overlooked by the image-makers. Thus, reinforcing the image of the dragon lady is that of the *femme fatale*, a treacherous opportunist of devastating beauty. And here devastating can in some cases be brought back to its etymological sense of destructive even of empires. The lovely Oriental lady with dainty hands and feet of English Romantic literature blends in with the *femme fatale* of Chinese history.

In Chinese history books the model emperors' wives always were those who refrained from becoming politicians in their own right, and those empresses who did wield power in one way or another were judged evil. And a peculiar aspect of these bad consorts—empresses or imperial concubines—was that they could only attain power through their husbands or sons. In Chinese history a handful of women attained effective power through this means, The Empress Wu, or Wu Tsertien, whose lifetime covered the greater part of the seventh century, is unique among these women in that she alone reached the throne. Of her the West—and I think this is a loss—knows very little. The rest were empresses dowager permitted to rule behind a screen when the emperor, either their husband, son, or close male relative like a nephew, was sick or mad or in his minority. Among the empresses dowager the great example was Tz'u-hsi (1835-1908). An emperor's concubine, she rose to be empress dowager because she happened to be the mother of the emperor's only son.

Apart from the empresses dowager another group of women sought places on China's political stage. These were the famous "wicked" concubines, the presupposition being that only wicked women sought power. The best known of these—to the Chinese and also the West—is almost undoubtedly the famous beauty Yang Kuei-fei of the T'ang Dynasty. Unlike Empress Wu or the Empress Dowager Tz'u-hsi these imperial favourites were not career politicians, merely meddling amateurs. They played upon the weaknesses of the flesh of their emperor-lovers and defied an angry and resentful bureaucracy. They were totally dependent on their husbands. Such is the prejudice against women that when things went badly for an emperor-plus-concubine team the judgment of Chinese history always went against the woman. The image of the concubine Yang has been made known to the West—albeit a rather restricted circle in the West—through translations of T'ang poems which celebrate her beauty and recount her story of early triumph and final tragedy.

In the rest of this chapter I shall attempt to trace the impact of these three women on the West, and the part they played in shaping or reinforcing images of Chinese woman. I have placed them in chronological order, but it will become clear that this order does not coincide with the order in which they started to impinge on the Western consciousness. Let us first consider the woman least known to the West of the three, namely Wu Tsertien, and then move in ascending order of celebrity or notoriety to The Empress Dowager, Tz'u-hsi.

Part II: Wu Tsertien

Marina Warner wrote in the preface to the Papermac edition (1984) of her 1972 work, *The Dragon Empress*, that if she were writing the book in 1984, when her knowledge of China had grown, she "would inquire further into other 'wicked ladies' in China history—the Empress Wu, Jiang Qing—and try to understand how Tz'u-hsi was perceived against a tradition of termagants". This "tradition of termagants" is a unique phenomenon of Chinese history. Isolated names from Western history come to mind: Elizabeth I, Catherine the Great, Catherine de Medici, but they are isolated instances and don't add up to a national tradition, as it were. Tz'u-hsi of the Manchu Dynasty, the last Imperial Dynasty, lived at a time when the West had gained inroads into China and was aware of China and the Chinese, and the fascination she inspired gave rise to varied and intriguing images of her. But the farther back into Chinese history we go the more we find facts, legends, myths unknown to the West.

It is true that the historical novel about China is in vogue among writers in English now, but the writers so far have inevitably focused on nearer periods of history—the Ming, the Ching, when China had already been opened to Europeans and, apart from any other advantage, it would be possible to introduce Europeans as major characters, and clearly the novelists (as, almost to a man or woman, with a few notable exceptions, the writers are European) found the task of writing about Europeans easier. Once the average person, as opposed to the sinologist, tries to come to grips with even the bare facts of Chinese history, he or she is at a loss. Chinese historians of the past were indefatigable in the recording and collection of facts, arranging these compendious materials in a manner which makes direct translation of the original texts a baffling and unrewarding task. Consequently Chinese history has been very little translated into any European language, and such scholarly works of this kind as exist are so packed with names of individuals and titles of office as to be wholly indigestible to the ordinary reader. Such direct translations, while invaluable to the student and the scholar, can never reach a wide public. The general reader is thus left without any other knowledge of Chinese history than can be provided by broad surveys in which a whole dynasty is barely granted the space of a chapter. (See C.P. Fitzgerald, *The Empress Wu*, published for The Australian National University by F.W. Cheshire, Melbourne, 1955, Preface) Thus for the general reader, Chinese history, except for those periods where there were extensive contacts with the West (as the Yuan Dynasty, with Marco Polo visiting the court of the Khans, the Mongol rulers who later conquered the Han and set up the Yuan

Dynasty, the Ming and the Ching, the period preceding and after the 1911 Revolution, and of course China today) is pretty much a closed book, yielding no images of any sort to the average Western person.

Wu Tsertien remained virtually unknown to the West. Naïve over-simplifications can be found in one or two early works. As early as 1913, Dr Lucinda Pearl Boggs, in a work entitled *Chinese Womanhood* (Cincinnati, New York) trying to foster good feelings between the American and Chinese peoples, writes a panegyric on "Illustrious Women of China"; she includes this statement about the Empress Wu, which would, no doubt, strike the average Chinese reader as quite outrageously naïve:

> The most celebrated lady of ancient times was the great Empress Wu, who reigned over a thousand years ago, strongly and brilliantly. Wedded to a weak Emperor, she first gained absolute control over him, and at his death she became the reigning sovereign in name as well as in fact. During her long period she extended the limits of the empire and contributed markedly to the welfare of her people. She favored the education of women, established colleges for them, and even granted them degrees, much to the disgust of some of the learned gentlemen. Women were allowed greater freedom than ever before and, indeed, the great Empress was severely criticized for a too great liberty of manner and morals. But she was great in State craft, and left her mark on the Chinese Empire as few men have done. It was only when weakened by age that she was forced by her son and ministers to retire at the age of eighty-one. (pp. 84-5)

Some years later, in 1938, the translator and sinophile, Florence Ayscough, in the introduction to her *Chinese Women Yesterday and Today* (London) writes very briefly of Wu Tsertien, using her as an example of "ladies more fair than virtuous" famous in Chinese records. She couples her with Tz'u-hsi in the following quotation:

> Powerful Empresses, Regents such as Tz'u-hsi, the Manchu Ruler, or Usurpers like Wu Tsertien, who for twenty-five years and more interrupted the rule of the T'ang, have issued Edicts from the Dragon Throne. (p.x)

which would interest the Western reader. His avowed purpose is given in his Preface: "I have written this biography of Lady Wu, who is more commonly known simply as Wu Tsertien rather than empress, as the study of a unique character combining criminality with high intelligence, whose ambitions reached truly maniac proportions, but whose methods were cool, precise and eminently sane." (Lin Yutang, ibid., p.viii)

But the story as told is not riddled with psychological inquiry but told as a gripping story of an individual's ascent to power, supposedly narrated by the Prince of Bin. Perhaps at this juncture it is necessary to provide the reader with an outline of this fascination woman's life and times.

In the 1970s the image of the Empress Wu received considerable notice in China and to a lesser extent in the West because of the political activities of Jiang Qing or Madame Mao Zedong. According to her best known and possibly most widely read biographer, Ross Terrill (*The White-Boned Demon*, Heinemann, London 1983, pp.307 ff) Jiang Qing took Wu Tsertien as her model, her justification. In describing Jiang Qing's establishment of a *raison d'etre* for her political manoeuvres through a glorification of the Empress Wu, Terrill gives a readable and succinct (possibly controversial in places) account of her history, in its way as full of glory as of infamy.

Wu Zetian's (Wu Tsertien's) rise from toy to stateswoman thirteen hundred years ago resembled Jiang Qing's. The tough, pretty Wu began as a concubine—the only route to power for a woman of old China—and became China's Catherine the Great.

One day during concubine Wu's service to Emperor Tai Zong, (Tai Tsung) the crown prince left the emperor's presence to go to the bathroom. As he emerged into the antechamber of the washing room, the heir to the throne was burrowing deep between the thighs of his father's most magnetic concubine.

Emperor Tai Zong (Tai Tsung) soon died, and as custom dictated, his women of the night were sent off to a convent for a change of pace as Buddhist nuns. But the crown prince, upon becoming Emperor Gao Zong (Kao Tsung) did not forget Wu. He already had an empress, Lady Wang, who had stepped up to the position from her previous post as senior concubine, first class. But he found an excuse to visit Wu's convent, and another to bring Wu back, against all the rules, to a modest post at his own court.

(In the words of a historian) 'She [Wu] had...made her first great move, to return to the Palace; now she had still to win the emperor's lasting favor, to give birth to a possible heir, and to achieve the downfall of the reigning empress.'

Wu proved as good at imperial affairs as she had been on the silken couch. After hair-raising plots—apparently Wu framed Lady Wang by suffocating her own infant in its bed and pointing a finger (to the emperor, an irresistible finger) at the innocent empress—the concubine retrieved from the convent supplanted the worthy Lady Wang as empress, the First Lady of a promising administration in a distinguished dynasty.

Wu's position was buoyed by the birth of two sons and by her systematic removal of elder statesmen who objected to her rising influence. She soon eclipsed the emperor, an irresolute character who spent much of his limited physical energy upon seductions (his list included Wu's sister and niece). It was Wu who masterminded a difficult war in Korea, filled the kingdom with shrewd appointments based on merit, and eliminated all opposition to the administration. Her influence upon Gao Zong was all the greater because she did not hesitate to cater to his prodigious and unusual sexual demands; the sober official historians observed that she 'abased herself'... When the emperor gave an audience, Wu sat beside him on a throne equally elevated but, in deference to the tradition that women should keep out of politics, hidden by a screen. The official histories reluctantly noted the real situation: 'The whole sovereign power of the Empire passed into her hands; life or death, reward or punishment were decided by her word. The Son of Heaven [emperor] sat on his throne with folded hands, and that was all.' Emperor Gao Zong died in 683.

Wu, by then fifty-five years old, should have become empress dowager and faded into dignified retirement. But as a result of quiet, fierce struggle, during which Wu coolly disposed of two crown princes (her own sons) and others who threatened her bid to be number one in name as well as in fact, she made herself in 690 Emperor (Empress) of China—the true 'Son (Daughter) of Heaven', the first woman ever to be such.

She gave herself the title 'Holy Mother Divine Imperial One' and founded a dynasty of her own, the Zhou, which provided a remarkable interregnum within the span of the Tang dynasty. The Buddhist clergy busied their pens with a lofty justification for the rise of a woman to a position hitherto reserved for men; they produced a sutra called the Great Cloud Classic, which praised Wu as the greatest blessing ever to fall upon China and 'revealed' that she was an incarnation of Maitreya sent by Yama to rule the earth.

Wu not only benefited from her sexual charms in her rise to power, but she also used the power she attained to bring an array of handsome men to her bed...

Allowing for the fact that intrigue was endemic to the imperial system... Wu ruled with success and a degree of enlightenment until she, and her one-woman dynasty, came to an end when she was eighty-one. She had in essence ruled China for fifty years. (Ross Terrill, ibid., pp.308-311)

I have quoted part of Terrill's 1983 account because he has summed up so pithily and racily the essential elements of the story which both Fitzgerald and Lin Yutang tell in the late 1950s.

Fitzgerald and Lin Yutang use two entirely different approaches to the story of Empress Wu. Fitzgerald gives the account as scholar and historian, with very close footnoting and every evidence of meticulous scholarship. He is not concerned with sensational effects. Consider this passage of commentary which follows the account of what is certainly one of the high points of Wu Tsertien's cruelty—the murder of her own infant daughter.

The story as given by the historians is treated as if the guilt of Wu Chao in this murder was proved beyond question; yet these historians are always hostile to the future Empress Wu and one may be inclined to wonder whether the account as they give it does not require further consideration. It is suggested that Wu Chao perpetrated this crime as the only way of bringing the Emperor to the point of deposing Empress Wang, and that nothing less than the conviction that the Empress had murdered his child would have roused him sufficiently. Yet Wu Chao already had a son, Li Hung, whose existence is ignored in the story of this murder, and the fact that she, the Emperor's favourite, had a son while the Empress had not, already gave her an immense advantage. It will be seen that it was on these grounds, not on that of the alleged murder, that the Empress was to be deposed.

To murder a child, only a few minutes, at most an hour or so after the birth, argues that Wu Chao must have been both exceptionally strong physically, and also that she had the opportunity, in an Imperial birth chamber, of committing the crime unperceived. This is already a considerable assumption, to which must be added the still more difficult assumption that none of her attendants, who must have known the truth, was prepared to reveal it, while all of them were unanimous in declaring when questioned, 'that the Empress had just been there', meaning that she was responsible. Wu Chao was certainly ruthless, yet in later life the one small group whom she spared, even when she had grounds against them, were her own children. On the whole it seems more probable that, infant mortality being high in that age, the child died naturally and Wu Chao seized the opportunity to incriminate the Empress Wang… (Fitzgerald, ibid., pp.22-23)

His scholarly restraint does not prevent Fitzgerald from telling a very vivid story, replete with direct quotations translated from the Chinese sources. The image of rapacious cruelty is established for the general reader. The passage recounting the terrible revenge on the fallen Empress Wang and the Pure Concubine will serve to support my point.

Wu Chao had now achieved her ambition, she was Empress, and mother of a son who was soon to be declared the heir of the Empire; there seemed no obstacle to the quiet enjoyment of her honours, but she was not prepared to leave any remnant of the opposition to watch for a chance of bringing about a change of fortune. The fallen Empress Wang and the Pure Concubine still lived imprisoned in the side apartments of the Inner Palace. One day Kao Tsung, remembering their existence, happened to pass unexpectedly into the part of the Palace. He found their prison, with the door blocked up leaving only a narrow hole through which food could be passed, Kao Tsung was shocked, and felt a twinge of remorse; he called out to the prisoners, saying, 'Empress and Hsiao Liang-ti, are you both well?' They answered, in tears, 'We poor concubines for our crimes are now Palace slaves, why does Your Majesty still address us with titles of honour?'

Then they said, 'Your Majesty has fortunately recollected former times, changing death into life for us, so that we many once more see the sun and moon. We beg you to change the name of this place to "Court of Remembrance".' The Emperor, moved, replied, 'It shall be done at once.'

Slight though this act of consideration seemed to be, the new Empress, when she heard of it, was filled with rage and suspicion. She at once sent executioners, who after beating the two unfortunate women with a hundred blows, cut off their feet and hands, and then threw them, bound, into a brewing vat. Wu Chao exultantly remarked, 'Now these two witches can get drunk to their bones.' After several days of agony the two victims died, and their corpses were then cut to pieces, and decapitated.

When the Empress Wang heard her fate, she bowed several times to the ground and said, 'Long life to His Majesty; Wu Chao has obtained favour, death is my lot.' Hsiao Liang-ti showed less submissive resignation: when she was told her sentence she cursed aloud, saying, 'Ah Wu is a treacherous fox who has brought me to this. I pray that in my future lives I shall return as a cat, and Ah Wu will be a mouse, and then from life to life I shall tear out her throat.' In consequence, Wu Chao ordered that henceforward no cats should be kept in the six palaces. (ibid., p.31)

High drama and a sense of present experience also characterize Fitzgerald's account of the Empress's final fall from power. The conspirators, the Empress and her weak son, the Crown Prince Chung Tsung, come alive through their utterances, which are rendered in straightforward colloquial English, with fairly natural syntax and only that degree of archaism in word choice as not to render the dialogue ludicrously inappropriate:

When the conspirators appeared, Chung Tsung, always irresolute, had his doubts about the whole enterprise, and at first refused to come out. One of the officers attending on Li To-tso then said to Chung Tsung, 'The Late Emperor bequeathed the Throne to Your Highness, but you have suffered oppression, imprisonment and deposition for twenty years. Today heaven has taken pity on your distress; the garrisons of the North and South (the Palace Guards) are both on your side, ready to slay the evil rogues and restore the altars of the Li family. We wish Your Highness to proceed to the Yuan Wu Gate to satisfy the hopes of all men.'

Chung Tsung was not able to make up his mind. 'The rogues should certainly be destroyed,' he said, 'but as Her Majesty is not well we should not alarm her. I think you gentlemen should postpone the plan.' This was an unexpected, and possibly fatal hitch. The conspirators had already gone too far to draw back or delay with safety. Li Chan turned to the Crown Prince and said, 'All the generals and ministers have taken no thought for themselves or their families in order to protect the state. Are they willing to jump into the cauldron of boiling water? If Your Highness wants to postpone the plot, I request that Your Highness himself should ride to the Yuan Wu Gate and tell them to stop.'

Chung Tsung was taken in by this trick. He came down and was at once mounted by one of the officers, who took his bridle and conducted him, surrounded by the others, to the Yuan Wu Gate. There he was given no time for explanations, for as soon as he appeared, which was the agreed signal without which the guards would not be prepared to act, the soldiers broke open the gate, and the whole force poured into the Palace. It was now too late for Chung Tsung or anyone else to arrest the course of events.

The Empress, attended by the two Changs, was then residing in the apartments on the western side called the Ying Hsien Palace—Palace Where the Immortals Are Welcomed. The conspirators, who knew where she was to be found, went straight there, and caught the two brothers Chang I-chih and Chang Ch'ang-tsung in the court-yard of the Ying Hsien Hall. Chang Chien-chih gave orders that these two should be decapitated forthwith, which was done on the verandah of the hall. The conspirators then forced their way into the court where the Empress was sleeping, and rounded up and bound the eunuchs in attendance.

Hearing the uproar made by the slaying of the Changs, the Empress rose and came out, asking 'Who is making this disturbance?' There Wu Chao saw the conspirators and their soldiery with the Crown Prince in their midst. She knew that her long reign was ended. They answered her, ceremoniously, saying, 'Chang I-chih and Chang Ch'ang-tsung were plotting rebellion; we ministers received orders from the Crown Prince to execute them. As it was feared that there would be a leakage, we didn't dare to inform Your Majesty in advance. Yet for committing the crime of bringing armed men into the Palace we deserve to die ten thousand deaths.' It was a singularly untruthful explanation of what had occurred, but Wu Chao did not deign to refute it in detail. She caught sight of Chung Tsung, standing among the others in the torchlight. 'So you!' She exclaimed. 'Well, the two boys have been killed; you can get back to the Eastern Palace.'

Whether Wu Chao still really hoped that the conspiracy had no other aim than the elimination of her favourites, or whether she hoped that the lifelong habit of submission which she had imposed on her son would still work, this last fling failed. Chung Tsung, it would seem, was almost prepared to do her bidding, certainly it was not he who now stepped forward and made the facts plain to the Empress. Huan Yen-fan came up and said, 'How can the Crown Prince return to the Eastern Palace? The Late Celestial Emperor entrusted his beloved son to Your Majesty. Now he is no longer young, and has for long been living in the Eastern Palace. The will of Heaven and the hearts of men have inclined towards the Li family. The whole body of officials has not forgotten the virtue of Tai Tsung and the Late Celestial Emperor. Thus, now that the Crown Prince has ordered the execution of those scoundrels, we ministers wish Your Majesty to abdicate and transmit the Throne to the Crown Prince, in conformity with the will of Heaven and mankind.' (ibid., pp.190-192)

I find Lin Yutang's style and narrative method more artificial, indeed pretentious. The preface is full of the author, as it were, his experiences, his opinions, his political views. He is determined to impress on his readers the uniqueness of the fabulous Lady Wu. He tries to focus the image by comparisons.

> Lady Wu, as a woman, was an anomaly. It is difficult to compare her with some other notable woman. Not Cleopatra, not Catherine the Great; a bit of Catherine de Medici, the strength of the former and the ruthlessness of the latter combined. And of course she was the antithesis of Maria Teresa. She defied moralists and perplexed historians who have not quite known how to call her reign, which itself is an anomaly, or what to call her by title.
>
> Because she was mistress, usurper, empress, and—what is still more confusing—'female emperor', I have here used the term Lady Wu, corresponding to the Chinese *Wu She*. She shattered more precedents, created more innovations and caused more upsets than any male schemer in history. If Madame du Barry were to kill Marie Antoinette and the King's three aunts, imprison Louis XVI for fifteen years while she proceeded to murder and exterminate all the Bourbons, thinking the Dubarrys a better race than the Bourbons, and send a dozen Richelieus to the gallows, we should have a comparable parallel. (Lin Yutang, p.ix)

He claims to have written his book not as fiction but as a strictly historical biography and to have included only what is based on T'ang history. He underlines this with the rather typical Lin Yutang style aphorism: "…the facts would be incredible if told as fiction. The incredible is always true, and the true often incredible." Lin Yutang chooses a somewhat cumbersome first person narrative method. The point of view is that of the Prince of Bin, "to give", according to the author, "a sense of immediate experience" and also because it is "a family story", a story of the feud of the two families, the princes of T'ang (family name Li) on the one hand, and the Wus, the family of the empress, or the other. The Prince, living from the age of twelve to twenty-seven in strict confinement in the palace along with his Uncle Dan and his children, played the passive role of the persecuted. He saw his own two brothers flogged to death and his aunts, the wives of Prince Dan, secretly murdered and other daughters-in-law of the empress persecuted to death. But he survived to see the extinction of the Wus, living in peace and honour after the restoration of the T'ang House, for twenty-nine years under the Emperor T'ang Minghuang. The Prince of Bin was born in 672 and died in 741, at the age of seventy.

In spite of Lin Yutang's repeated assertions that he has based his account on historical fact, he relates the facts as "fiction" with a strong sense of "drama" (p.x.) The first-person narration is coupled with a rather irritating "personal", almost childish style. The sentences are, apparently deliberately, almost always short and simple, compound or multiple, hardly ever complex.

The reader is struck by the rather jarring mixture of lexis. Lin Yutang seems overly fond of the set "idiom", such as one finds in old-style idiom books for English learners. A cursory glance reveals "no stone unturned", "find loopholes" (p.22), "the fair sex" (p.12), "caught red-handed" (p.24), "was it a frame-up?" (p.25). He also exhibits a propensity toward the "original" but rather forced comparison, for example "the empress was unimaginatively moral and proper like a starched clean sheet" (p.22). But for all its failings the story of Lady Wu makes for easy and fairly pleasant reading, and for those who avail themselves of it, it gives a sharply focused image of the fabulous "female emperor". I have deliberately quoted a passage parallel to the Fitzgerald one relating to the murder of her own child. We see the greater elaboration and addition of dialogue which the narration of "facts" using a fictional mode seems to require. And yet I think the loss of terseness detracts from, rather than adds to, the horror of the event.

At last her chance came. She gave birth to a baby girl. She had a brain-storm when it was told her that the child was a girl. But Heaven knows that grandmother was not a woman to be put out; she knew how to turn a bad situation into her advantage. We must not be surprised by what Lady Wu did, for from now on we must get used to the idea that she was a very unusual woman who did very unusual things. The gods were kind to her; they could not have done better than send her a baby girl.

One day, when the baby was hardly ten days old, the empress, who had no child of her own, came to see the baby. She took her up in her breast, fondled her for a while, and laid her back in the cradle. Lady Wu had gone away on purpose when the empress's visit was announced. She came in after she left, strangled the baby and covered it under the quilt. She knew the emperor would come and see her after court duties.

Gowtsung came. Lady Wu was the happy mother who could not help talking about her wonderful baby.

'Take the baby out for His Majesty to see. And wrap her up well,' said the happy mother to one of her favourite maids.

The maid came out with the baby, and the mother went to receive her in her arms. To her consternation, the baby didn't open her eyes, didn't move, didn't breathe. She was dead! Lady Wu was terrified, or looked as if she was, and beside herself with grief.

'What happened? She was well and lively this morning' she asked in utter despair, frantic with unbelief, and all but sobbing out loud as this sudden loss of her dear child. 'We thought she was quietly lying asleep,' said the well-coached maid.

Drying her tears, the mother, who had not quite broken down, asked, 'Has anyone been in the room when I was away?'

'The empress was here. She came to see the baby, fondled it for a while and put it back.'

Lady Wu's and the emperor's eyes met. It was incredible; such a heinous thing to do!

Gowtsung said, 'The empress has lately been very jealous of you. But I never thought she could do such a thing!' The empress denied it of course. But to what avail? Why hadn't she cultivated friendship with the maids? She was the only one who had touched the baby in the last hour.

Gowtsung, never very fond of his wife, was now completely disgusted with her. She was now as jealous of Lady Wu as she had been of Siowfei. But this was beyond the bounds of decency for one who was expected to be an example to all wives and mothers of the land. And poor suffering Lady Wu, who only shed silent tears mourning for her dead child—his heart warmed toward her.

'I have a mind to depose this despicable woman. She is no longer fit—no longer worthy...'

'Don't ever think of such a thing. What's done is done,' replied Lady Wu with considerable magnanimity. (Lin Yutang, ibid., pp.12-13)

The use of a style almost appropriate to fairy tales of wicked step-mothers lends a softening patina which shields the readers, as it were, and diminishes the stature of the wicked mother. The same is true of the following extract. The grisly subject matter is attenuated by the "fairy tale" style. The repetition, like the refrain in children's stories—of the horrible command in the form of a question—truly takes away from the deep sense of malevolence and cruelty of the speaker.

Gowtsung should have left the deposed Empress Wang and Siowfei alone in their confinement. It was his mistake. Soft-hearted and bitten with remorse, one day he went to visit them when Lady Wu was on a visit to her relatives. Alone, he sauntered along to the back court, with a bad conscience and almost a feeling of guilt. He was shocked to find the door securely locked, with only a hole on the side permitting servants to bring in food. A court lady falling under disfavor was usually relegated to a back court, under house detention at the most. But this was real imprisonment.

He called through the hole, 'Empress, Siowfei, where are you?'

After a while, he heard shuffling feet and soft, faint, distressed voices from within.

'We have been disgraced. We didn't think you would still call us by our former titles… For old times' sake, let us out, we beg you. Just set us free. We shall call this place the Hall of Mercy in gratitude.'

Gowtsung was deeply touched. 'Don't worry. I will do something about it.'

The emperor did not know his wife yet. For she had her spies everywhere who reported everything the emperor did to her. He did not know that he had been shadowed. When Lady Wu returned, the emperor's stolen visit was reported accordingly. It was evident that he was still thinking of those two women! She would take no chances. Before the emperor had the opportunity to speak to her she spoke to him. He had been to see the two convicts, she was told. Was it true?

The emperor quickly denied it.

'Oh, I'm glad you didn't.'

Time and again, we are to see a decision reversed and the course of events changed by the confronting of a dull, nervous, average man and a determined, alert, forceful woman.

The emperor had as good as admitted the he had been wrong to see them. Lady Wu gave orders to her servants to have the two women whipped a hundred lashes. Then she had their hands and feet cut off, and, with their arms and legs crooked behind them, had them thrown into wine vats.

'Let these wenches' bones and marrow melt in drunken ecstasy,' she said. The phrase was a reference to sexual pleasure.

After a couple of days, the two women died, as was to be expected. Their death was reported.

'Have their bones and marrow melted in drunken ecstasy? She asked with an idle smile.

'Yes, they have, Your Majesty,' answered the servant. (ibid., pp.40-41)

In the next extract I quote, the author, through the narrator, tries to sum up the horror which confounded the nation when Wu Tsertien succeeded in supplanting the Empress Wang. We find the same rather naïve style. The whole sense of heroic scale is undercut by the word "bitch"; all the details of her crimes build up to the rather ludicrous—"Clearly she was a 'bitch'" (p.36). But still the subsequent paragraphs do give to the Western reader a sense of her grandeur and the pomp and circumstance of a Chinese imperial coronation. I am not by any means setting out to belittle Lin Yutang's contribution towards the presentation of images of Chinese women to the West, here, and in other works. The West in general was—and is still—in many ways so ignorant of China and her people that any effort at illumination is to be lauded.

The decision was made. An edict was issued. Empress Wang had perpetrated a crime and was dethroned, to be punished by confinement inside the palace. Lady Wu was to become Empress Wu. it was a scandal. The dethronement of Empress Wang and promotion of Lady Wu made sensational news and afforded the public a much relished subject for gossip. The new empress was a mistress of the king's father. What was worse, she was a nun. And what was worse, she had a child by the king while still a nun. Clearly she was a 'bitch'. The nation's sense of decency was outraged. Why didn't the veteran statesmen stop it? But they did.

Suiliang had resigned on this account and was exiled. The king had gone wrong, the public felt, but it had happened before. When the king had gone wrong and was in the power of a scheming woman, nothing could be done about it. The courtiers, no less than the people, felt it like a blight upon the throne, something sinister, unwelcome, but unavoidable. The tea-houses buzzed with gossip.

The date for the coronation was set for November, only one month away. Lady Wu was not one to be crowned apologetically or surreptitiously. Not Wu Tsertien! The coronation was to be a grand affair, celebrated with more pomp and circumstance than that of an emperor, that the world might know that Lady Wu was rightfully and properly their queen. And it must be said that lavish pomp and grandeur suited her well, were her very life. She simply loved it. She wanted to impress and knew that common people loved to be impressed... A thousand things had to be done and the time was short—the coronation gown, the carriage, the new seal to be given the empress, the songs and music and dancers and entertainers, the reception, and the preparations of all the princes and princesses and the members of the court and their wives for the great occasion.

The day came. The music of drums and bells was sounded. The hall was crowded with members of the court and officials of the highest ranks. Assisted by her maids, Lady Wu came in, her head-dress glittering in gold and pearls, fully decked out in the formal *weiyi*, the formal gown of an empress worn on grand occasions such as the annual worship of Heaven and Earth. It was navy blue satin, hand-painted with phoenixes on the wing in rainbow colours, with a broad red band coming down the centre to the edge of the skirt, with gold-embroidered shoes and belt and hangings similar to those of the emperor. Calm and dignified, with a well-proportioned chin and large, bright eyes, she looked indeed every inch an authentic and authoritative empress. Probably on that day, during the coronation hour, the least flustered person was Lady Wu herself. The empress's seal was formally handed to her in a jade box by Archduke Liji— the man whose corpse was to be mutilated by her years later. She ascended the queen's throne. The imperial scroll was read, other congratulatory poems in pompous four-word lines were declaimed, the solemn classical music was played, and the formal ceremony ended. (ibid., p.36-37)

In discussing my findings about the Empress Wu with friends, Chinese and European, the inevitable question they asked was: What did she look like? The average Western person has vague physical images of Elizabeth I, of Catherine the Great. Many even have in their mind's eye an image of the Empress Dowager—from the portrait painted in her old age. It is clear from the way she gained power and her history of debauchery after gaining power that Wu Tsertien was a very sexy, desirable woman. That is the assumption. Fitzgerald relates her presentation to the Emperor when she went to the palace at the age of thirteen with the rank of Concubine of the fifth grade.

When Wu Chao was presented to the Emperor he was delighted and called her Beauty Wu. (Fitzgerald, ibid., p.3)

And history tells us that as Crown Prince, the Emperor Kao Tsung "saw and admired" Wu Chao when attending on his father. But of her actual physical attributes Fitzgerald gives no account. Lin Yutang gives a rather disillusioning description of her looks. In Fitzgerald we are told she returned to the palace from the convent at the age of twenty-five. Lin tells us that she was twenty-seven already before she managed to get anywhere by seducing the twenty-two-year-old Kao Tsung. The description of her appearance is certainly at variance with the stereotypical set-piece that we have more or less come to associate with descriptions of Chinese beauties:

To Tai Tsung, she was merely one of the many king's maids, and her flat, squarish face and wide forehead rather put him off, for his favourites were delicate, fair-skinned women, entertaining, attractive and not always burdened with a sober sense of responsibility. (Lin Yutang, ibid., p.13)

"Flat, squarish face and wide forehead"! Rather off-putting. But there is the insistence on her intelligence and coolness of mind. Let us now turn to Yang Kuei-fei, whose beauty is not in dispute.

Part III: Yang Kuei-fei (717-755)

I have mentioned that the general image the West has of Chinese women tends to be one of great physical attraction, usually with emphasis on daintiness, small hands and feet, immense delicacy, smooth pale skin; narrow "moth eyebrows", this being an abbreviated way of referring to the thin curved antennae of moths, garments of richest silk, brocade, perfume and, of course, an abundance of gorgeous precious gems. Consider the following extracts from works of the twentieth century by writers in English: the same components keep appearing in the descriptions of beauties. If the work is set in period times, then the daintiness of the feet reach the point of being "golden lilies", bound to an unnaturally small size.

He remembered, for instance, that the corners of Golden Orchid's eyes had shadows—those were the phoenix eyes about which he had heard and read so much in poetry, but it was the first time he had actually seen them. They were luminous and moist, and full of feeling. Her hair was combed straight back and was tied into a tight, becoming knot, ornamented with pearls. A neat fringe hung just above her delicate eyebrows, which arched like new moons on either side of her face. He had even noticed that she wore ear rings inlaid with kingfisher feathers, and their deep, almost iridescent, blue contrasted beautifully with the soft and delicate whiteness of her skin.

But then, the girls in Soochow, Ping-mo thought, are famous for their smooth and lovely complexions.

A dainty and small mouth showing a set of perfectly formed teeth, which he had seen as she gave him that last smile, completed what Ping-mo thought was one of the most divinely beautiful faces he had ever had the good fortune to see (Chang Hsin-hai, *The Fabulous Concubine*, first published 1956, p.32)

Her face was oval, her eyes almond-shaped and her eyebrows perfect crescents. A perfume surrounded her now, and her long, flowing robe was of the finest blue silk brocade. Her hair was dressed in crescents on the top of her head and adorned with jade pins. She was tall for a Chinese and her skin so white as to be almost translucent. She was from the province of Soochow. (James Clavell, *Taipan*, 1966, p.114)

Nonetheless his eyes were drawn by the mystery—and the beauty—of the first nubile Chinese maiden he had ever met...

Marta's underskirt was turquoise, contrasting with Candida's tangerine. The turquoise shawl-collar of her primrose overtunic revealed only a small triangle of her soft throat beneath her rounded chin. Even her slender fingers, glowing with jade-and-pearl rings, darted from flowing, concealing sleeves. But the wide lavender sash that girded her tunic thrust her high, small breasts forward; and the fragile silk outlined her rounded hips and legs. Francis had never been as stirred by the form within a European dress that displayed half the bosom.

Marta's face, he rhapsodized to himself with Elizabethan lyricism, was a soft petaled flower amid the glossy foliage of her hair. Her dark eyes, set aslant above delicate cheekbones, glowed within the thicket of her black-kohled eyelashes when she smiled. Her nose was short and delicately arched above a generous mouth. Her molded lower lip, slightly open even in repose, displayed small white teeth. Her skin glowed translucent pink-and-gold, matte-smooth and almost poreless. (Robert Elegant, *Manchu*, 1980, p.85)

Kitty shook hands with her. She was slim in her long embroidered gown and somewhat taller than Kitty, used to the Southern people, had expected. She wore a jacket of pale green silk with tight sleeves that came over her wrists and on her black hair, elaborately dressed, was the head-dress of the Manchu women. Her face was coated with powder and her cheeks, from the eyes to the mouth, heavily rouged; her plucked eyebrows were a thin dark line and her mouth was scarlet. From this mask her black, slightly slanting, large eyes burned like lakes of liquid jet. (Somerset Maugham, *The Painted Veil*, 1925, p.165)

In the first interval I talked with my neighbor, who mistook me for a Frenchwoman she had met. To my good fortune, because from the moment she came in with her husband, I had been fascinated by her. Slender, fragile, elegant in a plain black *chi-pao*, with long jade ear-rings, waved grey hair, patrician face the texture of old ivory, small proud mouth, eyebrows like a moth's antennae above narrow jet eyes. Beautiful by any standard, at any age...

She smiled across the slow, graceful movements of her gold-embossed fan, the jade ear-rings catching the light. (Dymphna Cusack, *Chinese Women Speak*, 1985, p.20)

The stereotypical physical images seem to owe something to the picture of the legendary Chinese beauty, Yang Kuei-fei, celebrated in Chinese literature and made known to the West by some of the best known poets of the T'ang Dynasty, notably Po Chu-i in "The Song of Everlasting Grief". In the preface to his *Selections from the Three Hundred Poems of the T'ang Dynasty*, Soame Jenyns gives a survey of the history of the T'ang Dynasty, stating that "The apex of the T'ang culture was reached in the reign of the Emperor Hsuan Tsung (715-756)—he abdicated and died in 762—known as Ming Huang, when Li Po, Tu Fu, Wang Wai, Meng Hao-jan and Ts'en Ts'an were writing poetry. The chief events of his reign are continuously referred to in poems." In two long footnotes Jenyns relates the event of Ming Huang's reign which has most caught the imagination of the Chinese from that time onwards:

He was a great patron of the arts. He founded the famous Academy of Music called the Hua Lin Yuan. When they played to him, if any note was out of tune the Emperor recognized it and corrected it. He even composed himself an air called 'Orioles in Spring' and ninety-two pieces for the drum. He also played on a reed pipe. His court was full of rope-walkers, butting experts, performing horses, 'who threw up their heads and switched their tails and pranced in rhythm to the air of "Inverting the wine-cup"; their bridles of gold and silver, their manes plaited with pearls.' Elephants and rhinoceroses, we are told, were brought into the arena and made to perform to music. Ming Huang was also passionately fond of polo and cockfighting. He played polo with his harem on horses decorated with tassels and bells and mirrors, with balls of vermilion wood.

The story of the Emperor's infatuation for the Lady Yang is as famous as that of Helen of Troy and has been celebrated ever since in play and ballad. It was a sordid story, for she entered the palace as a concubine to his son, Prince Shou, and was transferred to his father's harem when the Emperor was already over sixty. This plump beauty acquired a domination over the ageing monarch. It was the extravagance of this woman and her creatures that brought about the rebellion of An Lu-shan, who was a Khitan general. He is said to have been captured as a boy in Liaotang (S. Manchuria) and sold to an officer in the Chinese northern garrison as a slave. He seems to have coveted both her person and the kingdom. He is described as 'very fat, his stomach overhanging his knees'; he looked simple, but was crafty and ready for a reply before his majesty. When the Emperor pointed to his stomach and jokingly asked what he kept there, he replied, 'Nothing but a red heart.' When seated with the Emperor and the Lady Yang, whom he had before begged to adopt him as a son, he first saluted the lady; when ordered to give a reason he said it was a foreign custom to salute the mother first and then the father, he himself being a T'u-chuch (Turk).

In 751 the Emperor built him a palace regardless of expense and ordered the premier and the imperial princes to attend him on his birthday, when he and the Lady Yang gave him rich presents. However, in 755 he rose in rebellion at the head of 150,000 men, seized Ch'ang-an and assumed the title of Emperor while the real emperor fled to Szechwan. At Hangyang the Emperor's troops mutinied and killed Yang Kuo Chung, Yang Kuei-fei and her sisters. Meanwhile Fang Kuang, who had been sent against An Lu-shan, was defeated at Chen T'ao Hsien, in Shansi, where the whole imperial army was destroyed. Two years later An Lu-shan, now blind was murdered by his own son, An Ching-hsiu. (Soame Jenyns, selections from *The Three Hundred Poems of the T'ang Dynasty*, London, 1952, pp.17-18 Note)

These are the bare facts (plus most likely fictions passed off as fact). Jenyns refers to her as "the plump beauty". This is perhaps the irony. Those Westerners who know of her are usually not aware that she is other than the stereotypical sylph-like creature who conforms to conventional standards of Chinese feminine pulchritude. She is established as one of the

"Four Great Beauties" in China, the only one who departs from the slender "norm". One other of the four, Flying Swallow of the Han Dynasty, is reputed to have been so ethereally slender that she was able to dance on a man's palm, a phenomenon which scholars have tried to explain today by reference to ancient dances on trays hoisted aloft by strong men. Yang Kuei-fei is well-known to virtually every Chinese person, her fame being based on poems, stories, plays. A few years ago two rival television stations in Taiwan simultaneously produced versions of the life of the fabulous Kuei-fei, and a great deal of excitement was roused in the popular press in the contest for ratings. Both actresses chosen for the part were well-endowed and quite amply proportioned.

Yang Kuei-fei first became known to English-speaking readers on a very limited scale—and indeed I have noted the general ignorance in any case of Westerners about things and persons Chinese—in the early years of the twentieth century, through the translations of T'ang poetry, especially through the work of Li Po, Tu Fu and through Po Chu-i's "Song of Everlasting Grief". An interesting little volume in English on the famous beauty is a book called *The Most Famous Beauty of China: Yang Kuei-Fei* by one Shu Chiung, published in London (Bretano's Ltd.) in 1924. On the title page the authoress's married name, "Mrs Wu Lein-teh", is given demurely in brackets. Harold Levy included a study of her in his *Harem Favourites of an Illustrious Celestial* (Tai Chung: Chung-tai Printing Co., 1958), and a very interesting work appeared in 1984 as a Columbia University Ph.D. thesis. It is entitled *Yang Kuei-Fei: Changing Images of a Historical Beauty in Chinese Literature* by Fan Pen Li Chen. In her abstract Chen states that literary representations of Yang Kuei-fei (717-755) reflect both traditional Chinese prejudice against, and sympathy for, beautiful women who played a part in history. Because T'ang Hsuan-tsung's reign ended with the rebellion of An Lu-shan, official historiography as represented by the *Tzu-chih t'ung chien* of Ssu-ma Kuang (Sung Dynasty) blames her as a major cause of the rebellion and alleges that she had an affair with An. Yet the Emperor's evident love for Kuei-fei even though he had no alternative but to punish her with death to appease his army has also made her a tragic figure of romance in Chinese literature.

Chen's dissertation examines Yang Kuei-fei as a character in history and studies the more important literary works about her from the middle T'ang (circa 756) to the early Ch'ing (1688). The evolution of the image of the historical beauty makes for fascinating reading. Throughout, the dichotomy between censure and sympathy exists. Yang's literary poses are fairly typical of traditional Chinese attitudes towards famous beauties, but the fact that she is capable of arousing both negative and positive reactions makes her something of a rarity. She lacks the imperious grandeur of both Wu Tsertien and Tz'u-hsi, who would have made a splash in history no matter at what period they began to wield power. Yang Kuei-fei's notoriety might be attributed to the fate of her lord. She belongs to the same category of beauties as the favourite wives of the last rulers of dynasties, such as Pao-ssu (褒姒). In the eyes of traditional Chinese scholars, such beauties are a source of national misfortune because they are capable of toppling states and cities. (See Chen, ibid., pp.1-2)

I have mentioned the English language sources for information on Yang Kuei-fei. Apart from the T'ang poems in translation, none of the works have enjoyed a wide circulation—indeed Chen's work remains unpublished. As for Shu Chiung's rather naïve and genteel account of *The Most Famous Beauty of China*, it hardly achieved the status of a bestseller. The content and style, indeed (as I have mentioned) the use of the married name in parenthesis on the title page, and Herbert Giles's gentlemanly foreword give another image of *genteel* and educated Chinese womanhood of the 1920s. Giles ends his preface with this recommendation:

> Not one, it may safely be said, of the beauties of China has ever left such an indelible impression on the hearts of the Chinese people as Yang Kuei-fei, the Honourable Mistress Yang, of the 8th Century AD; and to those who would read the moving story of her triumphs and her tragedy, I venture to commend the fascinating work of Mrs Wu, wife of His Excellency Wu Lien-teh, the eminent physician who, by the energy and skill of his efforts in China and

Mongolia, succeeded in staying the plague. (Shu Chiung, ibid., p.viii)

The Chinese woman, in the sinologist Giles's view, seems to rely on her husband for any reflected luster. By chance I got hold of a copy presented by her husband in Hong Kong on March 10th, 1930 to the then Governor of Hong Kong, Sir William Hornell, with "compliments". Evidently Dr Wu was very proud of his accomplished literary wife and of her little volume on the beauty celebrated in Chinese history and literature.

The one T'ang poem on which Yang Kuei-fei's reputation in the West—what reputation there is—rests is Po Chu-i's "Song of Everlasting, Grief (Sorrow)", 長恨歌. Po Chu-i (白居易 – AD 772-846) ranks with Tu Fu and Li Po as one of the greatest poets of the "golden age of Chinese poetry"—the T'ang. The first literary works on Yang Kuei-fei are Ch'ien Hung's (circa 806) *Chu'an-chi'i* story, "Tale of Everlasting Sorrow" and Po's poem. (See Chen, ibid., p.49) Neither is a historical record but are attempts at preserving a story which occurred about two generations before the writers' time. Parts of Ch'ien's "Tale" have been translated by Harold Levy in his *Harem Favourites*, but of course, Po Chu-i's work is infinitely superior in artistry and was by far the more popular of the two pieces. Arthur Waley is well-known to be a great admirer of Po's work. Waley writes in an account of Po's life:

> No poet in the world can ever have enjoyed greater contemporary popularity than Po. His poems were 'on the mouths of kings, princes, concubines, ladies, plough-boys and grooms. They were inscribed on the walls of village-schools, temple and ship-cabins.' A certain Captain Kao Hsia-yu was courting a dancing-girl. 'You must not think I am an ordinary dancing-girl,' she said to him, 'I can recite Master Po's "Everlasting Wrong."' And she put up her price. (*One Hundred and Seventy Chinese Poems* translated by Arthur Waley, London, first published 1918, p.89)

But Po Chu-i's contemporary popularity was confined to the long, romantic poems like "The Everlasting Sorrow" and "The

Lute Girl" and the *lu-shih* or regulated verse, or conventional lyric verse, and yet Po himself did not value these poems, but rather favored his satires and reflective poems. "The world," writes Po to Yuan Chen "values highest just those of my poems which I most despise." Although Waley translated a great many poems of Po, he did not translate "The Song of Everlasting Sorrow". But others did, and the various versions have made the poem certainly one of the best known of Chinese poems among such readers as read Chinese poetry in English translation.

I have tried to established the popularity of the poem in Chinese. What is really pertinent to this study would be the popularity of the poem in English translation. *Twenty Five T'ang Poets: Index to English Translations*, compiled by Sydney S.K. Fung and S.T. Lai (A Renditions Book, Chinese University Press, Hong Kong, 1984) gives a list of translations of Po's *Ch'ang hen ko*. It contains no less than sixteen different versions, and this does not include, because it was published in a journal, not a book, a version "The Song of Everlasting Grief" done by a colleague, Piers Gray and myself and published in *Renditions* in autumn, 1980. Many of the sixteen versions have appeared in more than one anthology, and more than one of these anthologies have been reprinted more than once. (See Fung and Lai, ibid., pp.211-12) The "Song", then has been, again relatively speaking, widely available to Western readers. Whatever its demerits, and his critics are many, Witter Bynner's version, first published in his *Jade Mountain* (New York: Knopf) in 1929, has appeared in the greatest number of anthologies. W.J.B. Fletcher's translation has considerable popularity, first appearing in 1914 and in subsequent anthologies mainly compiled by Chinese scholars. The earliest published version is that of the eminent sinologist, Herbert Giles. The translation which Giles entitled "The Everlasting Wrong" appeared in his *A History of Chinese Literature*, first published in New York by D. Appleton and Company in 1901.

Po Chu-i's intentions were ostensibly moralistic. According to Ch'ien Hung's postscript to his "Tale of Everlasting Sorrow" both his tale and Po Chu-i's "Song" were meant to be warnings against the allure of women and to be "instruments for punishing the beauty", Yang Kuei-fei. (See Chen, ibid., pp.49-50) But as it turns out, neither quite achieves its avowed purpose. The works do start with condemning Yang Kuei-fei, but half-way through, the point of view shifts and the authors end up admiring her instead. It seems these two T'ang scholars were too romantic not to sympathize with her. Po Chu-i lamented the fate of another woman in his other famous long poem, "The Lute Girl" or "Ballad of the Lute". According to Chen (ibid., p.51) the dictates of the genre chosen also complicated the contrast between the author's intent and what is actually written. It is not my intention here to go into the vexed questions of accuracy and elegance in the translation of Chinese poetry since my main concern is with image-creating through the translated versions. The best-known translations reflect fairly faithfully the mood and motifs of the original. I shall use as a basis for discussion Giles's version of 1901, complete with his footnotes (reproduced in the Endnotes section of this book).

THE EVERLASTING WRONG

Poem by Po Chu-i (AD 772-846),

Ennui—His Imperial Majesty, a slave to beauty,
      longed for a "Subverter of Empires";[1]
For years he had sought in vain to
      secure such a treasure for his palace…

Beauty—From the Yang family came a maiden,
      just grown up to womanhood,
Reared in the inner apartments,
      altogether unknown to fame.
But nature had amply endowed her
      with a beauty hard to conceal,
And one day she was summoned to a
      place at the monarch's side.
Her sparkling eye and merry laughter
      fascinated every beholder,
And among the powder and paint of the harem
      her loveliness reigned supreme.
In the chills of spring, by imperial mandate,
      she bathed in the Hua-ch'ing Pool,
Laving her body in the glassy wavelets
      of the fountain perennially warm.
Then, when she came forth, helped by attendants,
      her delicate and graceful movements
Finally gained for her gracious favour,
      captivating His Majesty's heart.

Revelry—Hair like a cloud, face like a flower,
      head-dress which quivered as she walked,
Amid the delights of the Hibiscus Pavilion
      she passed the soft spring nights.
Spring nights, too short alas! for them
      albeit prolonged till dawn, -
From this time forth no more audiences

in the hours of early morn.
Revels and feasts in quick succession,
    ever without a break,
She chosen always for the spring excursion,
    chosen for the nightly carouse,
Three thousand peerless beauties adorned
    the apartments of the monarch's harem,
Yet always His Majesty reserved his attentions
    for her alone.
Passing her life in a "golden house",[2]
    with fair girls to wait on her
She was daily wafted to ecstasy on the wine
    fumes of the banquet-hall.
Her sisters and her brothers, one and all,
    were raised to the rank of nobles.
Alas! for the ill-omened glories which she
    conferred on her family.
For thus it came about that fathers and mothers
    through the length and breadth of the empire
Rejoiced no longer over the birth of sons,
    but over the birth of daughters.
In the gorgeous palace piercing the grey
    clouds above,
Divine music, borne on the breeze,
    is spread around on all sides;
Of song and the dance to the guitar and
    flute,
All through the livelong day,
    His Majesty never tires.
But suddenly comes the roll of the fishskin
    war-drums,
Breaking rudely upon the air of the "Rainbow
    skirt and Feather Jacket".

Flight—Clouds of dust envelop the lofty gates
    of the capital.
A Thousand war-chariots and ten thousand
    horses move towards the south-west.

Feathers and jewels among the throng,
    onwards and then a halt.
A hundred li beyond the western gate,
    leaving behind them the city walls,
The soldiers refuse to advance;
    nothing remains to be done
Until she of the moth-eyebrows perishes
    in sight of all.
On the ground lie gold ornaments with no
    one to pick them up,
Kingfisher wings, golden birds,
    and hair-pins of costly jade.
The monarch covers his face,
    powerless to save;
And as he turns to look back,
    tears and blood flow mingled together.

Exile—Across vast stretches of yellow sand
    with whistling winds,
Across cloud-capped mountain-tops they
    make their way.
Few indeed are the travelers who reached
    the heights of Mount Omi;
the bright gleam of the standards glows
    fainter day by day.
Dark the Ssuch'uan waters,
    dark the Ssuch'uan hills;
Daily and nightly His Majesty is consumed
    by bitter grief.
Travelling along, the very brightness of
    the moon saddens his heart,
And the sound of a bell through the evening
    rain severs his viscera in twain.

Return—Time passes, days go by, and once again
    he is there at the well-known spot,
And there he lingers on, unable to tear
    himself wholly away.

But from the clods of earth at the foot
of Ma-wei hill,
No sign of her lovely face appears,
only the place of death.
The eyes of sovereign and minister meet,
and robes are wet with tears,
Eastward they depart and hurry on the
capital at full speed.

Home—There is the pool and there are the flowers,
as of old.
There is the hibiscus of the pavilion,
there are the willows of the palace.
In the hibiscus he sees her face,
in the willow he sees her eyebrows;
How in the presence of these should tears
not flow, -
In spring amid the flowers of the peach
and plum,
In autumn rains when the leaves of the
wu-t'ung fall?
To the south of the western palace are
many trees,
And when their leaves cover the steps,
no one now sweeps them away
The hair of the Pear-Garden musicians
is white as though with age;
The guardians of the Pepper Chamber³
seem to him no longer young.
Where fireflies flit through the hall,
he sits in silent grief;
Alone, the lamp-wick burnt out,
he is still unable to sleep.
Slowly pass the watches,
for the nights are now too long,
And brightly shine the constellations,
as though dawn would never come.
Cold settles upon the duck-and-drake tiles,⁴

and thick hoar-frost,
The kingfisher coverlet is chill
    with none to share its warmth.
Parted by life and death,
    time still goes on,
But never once does her spirit come back
    to visit him in dreams.

Spirit-land—A Taoist priest of Lin-ch'ung,
    of the Hung-tu school,
Was able, by his perfect art, to summon
    the spirits of the dead.
Anxious to relieve the fretting mind
    of his sovereign,
This magician receives orders to urge
    a diligent quest.
Borne on the clouds, charioted upon ether,
    he rushes with the speed of lightning
High up to heaven, low down to earth,
    seeking everywhere.
Above, he searches the empyrean;
    below, the Yellow Springs,
But nowhere in these vast areas
    can her place be found.
At length he hears of an Isle of the Blest
    away in mid-ocean,
Lying in realms of vacuity,
    dimly to be descried.
There gaily decorated buildings rise up
    like rainbow clouds,
And there many gentle and beautiful
    immortals pass their days in peace.
Among them is one whose name sounds upon
    lips as Eternal,
And by her snow-white skin and flower-like
    face he knows that this is she.
Knocking at the jade door at the western
    gate of the golden palace,

He bids a fair waiting-maid announce him
    to her mistress, fairer still.
She, hearing of this embassy sent by the
    son of heaven,
Starts up from her dreams among the
    tapestry curtains.
Grasping her clothes and pushing away the
    pillow, she arises in haste,
And begins to adorn herself with pearls
    and jewels.
Her cloud-like coiffure, disheveled,
    shows that she has just risen from sleep,
And with her flowery head-dress awry,
    she passes into the hall.
The sleeves of her immortal robes are filled
    out by the breeze,
As once more she seems to dance to the
    "Rainbow Skirt and Feather Jacket".
Her features are fixed and calm,
    though myriad tears fall,
Wetting a spray of pear-bloom,
    as it were with the raindrops of spring.
Subduing her emotions, restraining her grief,
    she tenders thanks to His Majesty,
Saying how since they parted she has missed
    his form and voice;
And how, although their love on earth
    has so soon come to an end,
The days and months among the Blest
    are still of long duration.
And now she turns and gazes
    towards the abode of mortals,
But cannot discern the Imperial city
    lost in the dust and haze.
Then she takes out the old keepsakes,
    tokens of undying love,
A gold hair-pin, an enamel brooch,
    and bids the magician carry these back.

One half of the hair-pin she keeps,
    and one half of the enamel brooch,
Breaking with her hands the yellow gold,
    and dividing the enamel in two.
"Tell him," she said, "to be firm of heart,
    as this gold and enamel,
And then in heaven or on earth below
    we two may meet once more."
At parting, she confided to the magician
    many earnest messages of love,
Among the rest recalling a pledge
    mutually understood;
How on the seventh day of the seventh moon,
    in the Hall of Immortality,
At midnight, when none were near,
    he had whispered in her ear,
"I swear that we will ever fly like the
    one-winged birds,[5]
Or grow united like the tree with branches
    which twine together."[6]
Heaven and earth, long-lasting as they are,
    will some day pass away;
But this great wrong shall stretch out for ever,
    endless, for ever and ay.

(Translated by H. A. Giles, *A History of Chinese Literature*, New York, 1901)

There are points of accuracy of detail and some infelicitous expressions that I would quarrel with, but as I have noted, it quite effectively does the work of image-creation for the Western reader—except that there is an almost Victorian restraint in the description of Kuei-fei's sensuality. The physical image is unequivocally alluring, but the moral attitude to her inconsistent and ambiguous. Scholars as a consequence have held different views concerning the "theme". (See Chen, ibid., p.52) Three different views have emerged as to the motif in "Song". One group of scholars consider it to be an exposition of the debauchery at Ming Huang's court. These scholars maintain that Yang Kuei-fei is depicted as a "toppler of the state whose evil influence is what constitutes the "everlasting sorrow" of the title. Other scholars are of the view that "Song" is a celebration of romantic love. Yet others combine these two views and suggest that while the first part of the piece warns against the danger great beauties present to the stability of the state, the part after the death of Kuei-fei emphasizes the undying love between Ming Huang and his famous consort. I would suggest that in spite of the overt moral sentiments of the first part the complimentary, indeed amorous, dwelling on Kuei-fei's sensuality and beauty makes the whole poem a tribute to the power of feminine beauty and romantic love. Because of the dictates of the form he had chosen, Po had little space for details and concentrates on dramatizing situations. History records that Kuei-fei was first married to Prince Shou, son of Ming Huang, a fact considered most unspeakable even in the irregular liaisons of the time, but this fact is not mentioned at all in "Song". The effect of elaborating one idea at a time and of concentrating on the relationship between Ming Huang and Kuei-fei focuses the readers' attention more forcefully on the romance. Kuei-fei dies a third of the way into the poem, and until her death she is consistently shown to be a disruptive influence upon the emperor, and hence the state. Her seduction is such that he ceases to hold morning audiences.

Reading Po's version of the events and unaware of the sordid aspects of the story, the Western reader would no doubt see as quite heart-rending the account of the intensity of the Emperor and Kuei-fei's mutual longing after her death. If historical records are to be believed, the Emperor was well over sixty when Yang entered the palace as a consort and she dominated his affections for something like twenty years before he was forced to order her death. The playing up of the Romeo and Juliet aspect of the separation, the evocation of the legend of the cowherd and the spinning maid who are only allowed to see each other for one day (the seventh day of the seventh moon) may seem a little discordant in the context of reality. But be that as it may, what the reader of "Song" is left with is an indelible impression of a most seductive, fascinating, passionate and (ironically) faithful Chinese woman of great beauty. There is no specific reference to the plumpness which is so much a part of her legend among the Chinese.

Part IV: The Empress Dowager Tz'u-hsi (1835-1908)

For all the impact Wu Tsertien and Yang Kuei-fei have had on the Chinese consciousness they are virtually unknown to the West.

The woman in Chinese history who probably made the earliest and possibly the greatest mass impact on the West is the Empress Dowager, Tz'u-hsi. She was, and is still, clearly an object of fascination and controversy. The Western powers were busily carving out spheres of influence during the last years of Chinese dynastic rule, and as the woman who was the *de facto* ruler of the effete Chinese empire she would have naturally elicited a great deal of interest. What added to the intrinsic interest of a person in this position was the intriguing story of her ascent to power and the force of her powerful and flamboyant personality. The bare outline of her life is given in the introduction to the Hamish Hamilton Paperback edition of popular historian, Marina Warner's book, *The Dragon Empress: Life and Times of Tz'u-hsi 1835-1908 Express Dowager of China*, (1984; first published in great Britain by Weidenfeld and Nicolson Ltd., 1972), the latest of many full-scaled works on Tz'u-hsi's life:

> The Empress Dowager Tz'u-hsi, born the daughter of a minor mandarin, was the power behind the throne in China from 1861 to 1908. She bore the Hsien-feng Emperor his only son, and after her husband's death in 1861 her position as mother of the new Emperor T'ung-chih gave her enormous status in the Confucian system. During his minority she became co-regent and acquired then her taste for power.
>
> While she was a child the British defeated China in the First Opium War, and during her early years at court the British and French were again victorious. These events strengthened Tz'u-hsi's conservatism and xenophobia, and her later politics only

deepened the problems of foreign exploitation, poverty and civil strife in China.

In 1875, her son died, and she again became Regent; when her nephew the Kuang-hsu Emperor came to the throne and began sweeping reforms, Tz'u-hsi staged a successful *coup d'etat*. Her government's conservatism gave heart to the Boxers, who in 1900 rose against the foreigners, and laid siege to the Legations in Peking. While Tz'u-hsi wavered fatally, an international force crushed the uprising. The court fled. When Tz'u-hsi died, the last imperial dynasty of China survived her a bare three years.

From this bare outline a great deal of what is history, quasi-history, myth, and literature has been generated both in China and in the West. Let us briefly consider the image of Tz'u-hsi in China before looking at the process of her literary idealization in Western writings. Until very recent times the popular Chinese view of Tz'u-hsi, and here I am talking about her image in the minds of the man and woman in the street and of the traditional Chinese historian, is not ambivalent or equivocal: the view is that she is unequivocally bad. She has become a symbol of the evil, ambitious self-indulgent and incredibly cruel woman. The fact that she was a woman has perhaps made her more outstandingly monstrous to the Chinese mind, bred on feudal ideas. Her name Tz'u-hsi, ironically meaning "benevolent and auspicious", or Empress of the West, 西太后, has become synonymous with "an ambitious termagant", and is a favoured nickname for women exhibiting qualities of petty tyranny at home and especially in the workplace. After her death, many "wild" histories sprang up about her evil ways, and, as is always unfortunately the case with all Chinese women who come to power, a great deal of censure was directed towards her lasciviousness. The Confucian double standards for men and women seem to have subtly left its imprint on our powers of judgment. Virtually every Chinese woman, and I am here thinking even of some whose power is not even a tithe of a fraction of the power enjoyed and abused by Tz'u-hsi, is charged, openly or in whispered gossip, with selling sexual favours to attain power, and of general licentiousness. When young they are "on the make"—from the Empress Wu, through Yang Kuei-fei and Tz'u-hsi to Jiang Qing and later. When old they become "dirty old women". I have noted that Chinese historians record with relish the sexual excesses of Empress Wu; and yet it has been recorded that she felt she was only behaving as a true emperor. She was an early feminist. Tz'u-hsi is, of course, associated with the last years of the decaying Manchu Dynasty and with repeated national humiliation by foreign powers greedy to exploit China's weakness. Her willfulness and egocentric extravagance are outstanding characteristics. The usual image of Tz'u-hsi in the Chinese mind is when she is already an elderly woman, "the Old Buddha", who forced the Pearl Concubine, her nephew's favourite, to jump into a well, and aided and abetted by her gang of incredibly wicked and greedy eunuchs led by the Grand Eunuch, Li Lien-ying, would do the most unbelievably cruel and terrible things to those who plotted against the Manchu Empire.

The image has been created for the younger generation, reinforced for the older, by television melodramas which periodically appear on Hong Kong screens. A formidable part of the image consists in her famous "nail guards", on display now in the Forbidden City, in Beijing. The worst productions are very poor on historical research. A cursory glance at extant historical photographs and texts will indicate that Li Lien-ying was a very tall, gaunt, almost ascetic-looking man, but he has been played at least once by an oily, obese, short and pudgy actor. Two films, out of a projected series of six, were produced by a noted Chinese director, with the cooperation of the Chinese government and gave the public a new popular image of Tz'u-hsi. They deal with the early years of her life, up to her co-regency and she is presented as beautiful, desirable, indeed very human and winning. The West seems to have, from its first knowledge of her, had an image of great complexity, and the general tendency in writing in English about her is one of literary idealization. But more of this later.

The West has always regarded the Empress Dowager with awed fascination. There is no doubt that hers is a more complex and sophisticated personality than the simple sadist often exhibited in second-rate Cantonese films or television programmes. It would probably not be too foolhardy to venture the assertion that, with the possible exception of the Soong sisters, she is the one woman figure from Chinese history who has most strongly impressed the West as a whole. She was the *de facto* ruler of the Manchu Empire for forty-six years, and the Manchu Dynasty was the one under which China had captured the imagination of "enlightened" Europe. The work which was regarded as a crucial source for events relating to Tz'u-hsi's reign was J.O.P. Bland and Edmund Backhouse's biography, *China Under the Empress Dowager* (London, 1910), published just two years after her death. The "secret" documents which provided the essential material for the work were furnished by Edmund Backhouse, a rather mysterious figure, a sinologist who lived and worked in Peking until his death in 1944.

He became highly notorious and the centre of a historical controversy relating to the authenticity of his materials when Sir Hugh Trevor-Roper was given, in 1973 at Basel airport, Backhouse's autobiography, which Trevor-Roper then described in *Hermit of Peking: The Hidden Life of Sir Edmund Backhouse*, (first published by MacMillan, London, 1976; published by Papermac, 1986). Backhouse's phantasmagoria about the love affairs of the Empress makes the reader retrospectively doubt his credibility. To the subject of Backhouse and the Empress Dowager's alleged lasciviousness I shall return a little later. Meanwhile it may be worth reflecting on yet another example of the illusiveness of truth, the fluidity of "images", even those drawn specifically from recent, not ancient, history. And this seems particularly the case with a woman who deliberately created different images for herself at different stages of her career to fit her changing situation vis-à-vis her own people— and, even more important, vis-à-vis the West. Trevor-Roper gives reasons for the success of Bland and Backhouse's book, *China Under The Empress Dowager*, which went into eight impressions in the first eighteen months of its release. The Empress Dowager had doubtlessly captured the imagination of the West and she was a total enigma to them, more so than even to the ordinary Chinese peasant from whom she was indeed very, very distant. The "strange language" and "contemptuous secrecy" of the Chinese formed virtually impenetrable barriers which made the "true" story of the Empress even more titillating to the West, and what Bland and Backhouse supplied was the first documented and readable account of the whole reign. The authors claimed they were using authentic Chinese sources, supplied and translated by Backhouse. One of the features of the book which most excited well-informed readers was the diary of Ching-shan. The published parts of the diary, which run mainly from May 1900 until a few hours before Ching-shan's death on August 15th, 1900, give a vivid account of the reactions of the imperial court to the Boxer rebellion directed against Westerners and the varying attitudes of the Empress and her advisors. Historically the diary's chief contribution relates to the attitude of Jung-lu, the Empress's most constant military and political supporter. According to Ching-shan, Jung-lu constantly opposed the Boxers and tried to curb their influence and to protect foreigners against them. He appears as a persistent advocate of moderation and cooperation with the West. This is in effect a new image for Jung-lu. In subsequent Western works the idealization of his person takes place alongside the idealization of the Empress Dowager. Jung-lu is to become in future fiction the dashing and frustrated lover to the beautiful but ambitions Tz'u-hsi. The cult of romance requires a hero to be paired with the heroine, and Jung-lu becomes such a figure. It was a literary idealization which took place after both Jung-lu and Tz'u-hsi were dead. It became a fixation almost, a formalized cult which grew in intensity as the real persons so idealized receded into historical time.

I shall now go back to the image which became most familiar to Westerners who came into personal contact with Tz'u-hsi, an image which the flamboyant woman apparently consciously cultivated for their benefit. The Boxer uprising of 1900 which had shaken the Western World with the siege of the legations and the mass slaughter of Europeans and its equally bloody retributions on the Chinese had focused a great deal of attention on China and its Empress Dowager. The

Empress by 1900 had dominated the political scene in China for thirty-nine years. She had made and unmade puppet-emperors and emerged victorious from many intrigues. After the Boxer Uprising she ruled by the sufferance of the great powers which she had challenged but which could not find a substitute for her monarchy, feeble and corrupt though it was. In the last decade of her reign she did make some concessions to modernity. She opened up her court and, at least in theory, supported the reforms advocated by her nephew, the Kuang-hsu Emperor. Western diplomats and their wives, who had trembled for their lives in the barricaded legations during the Boxer Uprising, were now received in the palace. One wife, Lady Susan Townley, wrote how difficult it was to realize that "this friendly little woman with the brown face of a kindly Italian peasant was the mysterious and powerful autocrat who had deliberately debased and degraded the unfortunate emperor sitting beside her; the fiend who had egged on the Boxers to nameless outrages." (Sergeant, *The Great Empress Dowager of China*, London: Constable, 1965) Indeed, "There is no art to find the mind's construction in the face." An American lady, Katherine Carl, was allowed to paint her portrait for an exhibition in St Louis. It was during this period, when her multitudinous crimes were being buried by a sort of collective public relations exercise under the patina of a graceful old age, that the spate of Western biography and fiction about the Empress Dowager started. Some of the work which emerged from what assumed almost the proportions of a cult is not great writing worthy of criticism from the academic angle. The writers of the history, fiction, historical fiction centring on the Empress Dowager were aiming for the "best seller list" if only for a transient place on it. The impulse behind the writing of the "genre", if I may call it a "genre", is comparable to the motivating forces behind the virtually endless stream of works on China and Hong Kong, ancient historical, recent historical and contemporary, of every level of merit—from the critically acclaimed like Timothy Mo's *Insular Possession* through the readable and successful, like Elegant's *Dynasty*, to the truly terrible and instantly forgettable, like *Flagrant Harbour*. (Indeed

47

I have already conveniently forgotten the author's name.) The chroniclers of the Empress Dowager were obviously cashing in on a demand for such exotica to write "best sellers" in the Queenie Leavis sense; this attests to the avid interest in the unusual Manchu woman who held centre stage in the Chinese empire for so many decades.

Those who wrote about her in the early decades of the twentieth century were usually exploiting some advantage—writing as it were from the privileged position, real or assumed, of having insider information, or at least experience, of China, like Edmund Backhouse and the self-styled "princess" Der-ling or Te-ling, otherwise the wife of Thaddeus White, an American. She wrote a series of books on imperial court life, which she claimed to know intimately as "First lady-in-Waiting" to the Empress Dowager. Although later scholars, like Sir Reginald Johnston, attacked her claims to intimacy with the imperial family, her account of her *Two Years in the Forbidden City*, first published in 1911 by Dodd Mead, New York, was widely read and her detailed descriptions of the splendours of court life and court dress, the magnificence of her Imperial Majesty's person and her capriciousness were avidly read by Western readers. I.T. Headland who wrote *Court Life in China* (London and New York, 1919), too, had good sources: his wife was, for over twenty years, physician to the ladies of the imperial court. The American lady, Katherine Carl, commissioned to do Tz'u-hsi's portrait, put her sojourn at the Manchu Court to good use. She produced not only the painting, which the Empress Dowager, unused to Western principles of light and shading and perspective, found very displeasing, but also a book, *With the Empress Dowager of China*, London, 1906. The "cult" of the Empress Dowager was growing in the West, not just in the English-speaking West. Daniele Vare, an Italian diplomatist, arrived in Peking in 1912 as secretary to the Italian Legation and stayed there till 1920. Nearly twenty years later Vare wrote a popular biography in Italian of the Empress Dowager which was heavily based on Bland and Backhouse's *China under the Empress Dowager*. When the English edition of the work, *The Last of the Empresses*

(John Murray, 1983), appeared, he declared that his work had been inspired by that of Bland and Backhouse, and in his work the trend towards idealization continues, and this related in particular to the person of Tz'u-hsi's favourite courtier, Jung-lu. Sir Reginald Johnston's *Twilight in the Forbidden City*, 1934, is an exception in that Johnston, far from idealizing her, was extremely critical of the Empress Dowager. Johnston had come to China in 1898. He was an administrator who acquired an intimate knowledge of China, its language, its history, its philosophy. He had close contacts with the imperial family and the Manchu aristocracy. In 1918 he was appointed European tutor to the last Ch'ing Emperor, P'u-i, known as the Hsuan-t'ung Emperor, and lived for six years in the Forbidden City, since the abdicated imperial family continued to live in their palace, and enjoy their titles privileges and ceremonies until the *coup d'etat* which evicted and dispossessed them in 1924. Through his imperial friends as well as through his own experience Johnston must have known a great deal of court history. *Twilight in the Forbidden City*, written some years later, is a record of that history. It is critically regarded as nostalgic and partisan towards the imperial family, although he was prejudiced against the Empress Dowager.

So much that is fiction has become intermingled with the facts of Tz'u-hsi's personality and life that "those confused seeds which were impos'd on Psych as an incessant labour to cull out, and sort asunder were not more intermixt." Her more recent biographers, Marina Warner, and Charlotte Haldane (*The Last Empress of China*, London: Constable, 1966), who do not have any of the advantages of time and location of many of their forerunners, are very much aware of the problems of disentangling fact from myth. Charlotte Haldane gives an acknowledgement of sources which emphasizes the difficulty of extracting the "truth" from masses of material:

> At an early stage in my research it became clear how few were the reliable sources on the life of the empress Dowager Tz'u-hsi. The Annals of the Ching dynasty are in several instances as unreliable as the libels published by the Empress's enemies. Very few of her subjects came into direct contact with her Majesty. With the

exception of the American painter Miss Katherine Carl, almost none of the foreigners who wrote about the Empress Dowager did so, and then only after 1900. I therefore endeavoured as far as possible to use as sources only those who, like Der Ling, Li Hung Chang, and Sir Robert Hart, were in her personal or political service, and the works listed below by other biographers and historians who approached the problem of her mysterious personality and existence without accepting, even if referring to, the many legends about her. An exception had to be made in the case of R.F. Johnston, who, although violently prejudiced against the Empress Dowager, did have an intimate and scholarly knowledge of the Forbidden City and its administration. (C. Haldane, *The Last Empress of China*, Preface)

Other biographers and chroniclers would probably disagree with Miss Haldane's principle of selection. Marina Warner has an interesting comment on the blending of truth, half-truths and fantasy. She writes in the Foreword to the paperback edition of *The Dragon Empress*:

When Marco Polo's stories of China began circulating, people did not believe what they heard was true, but on verification by later historians and archaeologists, Marco Polo has largely been vindicated. The thirteenth century was a more skeptical age than ours, contrary to what one might expect; we live in credulous times, when the irrational and the mythic have gained acknowledgement as fundamental forces over our lives. Tz'u-hsi, the monstrous and powerful empress of so many millions is perhaps, a bit of '*une fable convenue*' as Voltaire said of history itself, since the chief sources reporting her statements and her character may have found in her the realization of their own fantasies.

One is struck by the justice of her final comment. Marina Warner is a self-confessed sinophile, not a sinologist nor a specialist in Chinese history, but, she tells her readers, ever since she was a child "China: the ancient civilization of the Far East existed for [her] as some kingdom of fantasy, so civilized and refined did it appear, with its language written in symbols, its immeasurable antiquity, its scholar-poets writing with brushes to wise rulers with pavilions wreathed in clouds." Being born in as age when the "vogue" of the Empress Dowager had passed in England, it was not until 1964 that she heard, from the first Chinese she had ever met, of Tz'u-hsi. She wrote her *Dragon Empress* (first published 1972) as an outsider, "without an insider's skills". (Hamish Hamilton Paperback, London, 1984, p.ix)

She drew a great deal from the two volumes of memoirs of the Princess Der-ling, whose credentials are somewhat dubious. Hugh Trevor-Roper, in *Hermit of Peking*, records the efforts of sinologists to discredit her claims to being First Lady-in-Waiting to the Empress Dowager. J.O.P. Bland and Reginald Johnston were outraged by the latest work of her series on imperial court life entitled *Son of Heaven: A Life of the Emperor Kuang-hsu* (1935). According to Johnston, "The Emperor himself denied that she was a princess, and this denial was corroborated by Shao Ying, head of the household department, who would certainly have known. She held no high position as court but was brought in to help to interpret when foreigners were presented. She never appeared at court functions during the years I was attached to the court, though she was certainly in Peking during part of the time, and I feel pretty sure she never entered the Forbidden City during those years." (H. Trevor-Roper, p.245) So the controversy raged among learned scholars and insiders. Meanwhile Der-ling's work reached a wide and eager readership. Indeed Marina Warner was not to raise the question of the credibility of Der-ling's memoirs until 1984, and this is only "after conversation with Hugh Trevor-Roper". Ghosted, forged, either partially or totally, we can see Der-ling's memoirs as not just total or partial fantasies about the Empress Dowager, but also as the realization of her own fantasies. In presenting a magnificent and yet human image of the Empress Dowager she also presented the image to the West of another Chinese woman: herself, the perfect blending of delightful delicate Chinese beauty and traditional virtues and Western education, *savoir faire* and French chic, together with a touch of spunk in the good old American tradition of "woman of spirit". In her account it is her superior beauty and intelligence which invariably allow her to be preferred to her sister. This is to be refuted by the sister, Roung-ling, years later, after 1949, in a record of Chinese women after the overthrow of the Kuomintang government, by the Australian writer Ellen Dymphna Cusack entitled *Chinese Women Speak* (London: Century Hutchinson Ltd., 1958). The work contains vignettes of life under the new regime, and one chapter is devoted to "The Empress Dowager's Lady-in-Waiting"; this is the notorious Der-ling's sister, Yu Roung-ling, a very youthful seventy-eight, a woman, according to the author, of the most extraordinary elegance and charm: "Slender, fragile, elegant in a plain black *chi-pao*, with long jade earrings, waved grey hair, patrician face the texture of old ivory, small proud mouth, eye-brows like a moth's antennae above narrow jet eyes." (Cusack, p.14) The archetypical Chinese beauty, although the writer adds, "Beautiful by any standard, at any age." And this beautiful woman—creating partial fantasies of herself and her past perhaps—recounts how *she* was the chic beauty and the pampered favourite of the Empress Dowager, *not* Der-ling. She recalls:

> When we used to go shopping in the *Galeries la Fayette*, buying the most enchanting clothes, people used to turn and look at me and say, *'Qu'elle est gentile cette petite chinoise!'*
>
> She giggles at the sixty-year-old memory. 'They never said it of my sister and she used to get awfully angry. Once she slapped my face! My sister was a strange girl. She married an American.' She pauses. 'She is dead now... Today, I sometimes wonder...' (Cusack, ibid., p.20)

And we are led to wonder, too—about where the truth lies, and of the mechanism of fantasizing and of image creation.

The Princess Der-ling, whatever her credentials, wrote in an intimate, conversational style, a style reminiscent of that of women's magazines in its minute attention to details of furniture and dress, to the minutiae of everyday life and conversation, all these being made intriguing by the fact of the central character, the Empress Dowager. The circumstantial, child-like nature of the narrative contributes to the sense of truth and first-hand knowledge, which led Haldane and Warner to quote extensively from her in the conviction that Der-ling could only have been writing from personal experience. I shall cite one passage out of many which give details of the intricacies of the Empress Dowager's toilet, rituals of bed making and the splendor of her apparel and jewels. The use of direct speech, translated into what may well strike the reader as English of highly inappropriate style, seems a little ludicrous and yet is in keeping with the overall rather naïve tone of the narrative.

Then she arose and started to dress. She put on her white silk socks first, having slept in her pantaloons as is the custom, and tied them at the ankle with pretty ribbon. I must tell you here that although she always slept in her clothes, she changed them for clean ones every day. Then she put on a pale pink shirt of soft material and over that a short silk gown, that was embroidered with bamboo leaves, as she always wore low heeled shoes in the morning and consequently could not wear her long gowns. After she had dressed she walked over to a window in front of which were two long tables covered with toilet articles of every kind and description...

As she was washing her face and dressing her hair, she said to my mother that she could not bear to have the servant girls, eunuchs, or old women, touch her bed, that they were dirty, so the Court ladies must make it. When she said this she turned to my sister and myself, we were standing a little to one side, and said: 'You two must not think for a moment that the Court ladies do servants' work, but you know I am an old woman and could easily be your grandmother and it will do you no harm to work a little for me. When it comes your turn, you can superintend the others and don't have to do the work with your own hands.' Then Her Majesty said to me: 'Der-Ling you are a great help to me in every way and I make you my first lady-in-waiting. You must not work too much for you will have to make all the arrangements for the audiences for foreigners and you will have to interpret for me. I also want you to look after my jewels and don't want you to do rough work at all. Roon Ling (my sister) can choose what she likes to do. I have two more besides you, Sze Gurgur and Yuen Da Nai Nai, making four altogether and you must all work together.

It is not necessary to be too polite to them and if they are not nice to you, you let me know.' Although I was very happy at receiving this appointment, I knew that according to custom I must refuse it, so I thanked her Majesty very kindly for the honor she had given me and said that I did not know enough to hold such an important position and would prefer to be just an ordinary Court lady, and that I would learn as quickly as possible to be useful to her. She hardly let me finish what I was saying, when she laughed and said: 'Stop! don't say anything like that; you are too modest, which shows you are very clever and not a bit conceited. I am surprised to see what a perfect little Manchu lady you are, knowing even such small etiquette as this, although you have spent many years outside of China.' She was very fond of making fun and liked very much to tease, and said that I could try and if she saw that I could not do the work, she would scold me and put someone else in my place. After all this that she had said, I accepted the appointment and went over to her bed to see how it was made, and I found that it was very easy work to do. As this would be one of my duties, I watched while the bed was being fixed. First of all, after Her Majesty had risen, the bedclothes were taken out into the courtyard by the eunuchs and aired, then the bed, which was made of beautifully carved wood, was brushed off with a sort of whiskbroom, and a piece of felt placed over it. Then three thick mattresses made of yellow brocade were placed over the felt. After this came the sheets made of different colored soft silk, and over the whole thing was placed a covering of plain yellow satin embroidered with gold dragons and blue clouds. She had a great many pillows, all beautifully embroidered, which were placed on the bed during the daytime; but had a particular one stuffed with tea leaves on which she slept. It is said that stuffing the pillow on which you sleep with tea leaves is good for the eyes. In addition to all these, she had another very curiously shaped pillow about twelve inches long in the middle of which was a hole about three inches square. It was stuffed with dried flowers, and the idea of the hole was that when she lay on it she could place her ear in this hole and in this way hear any and every sound. I suppose in that way no one could come on her unawares.

Besides this last yellow embroidered cover, there were six

covers of different colors, pale mauve, blue, pink, green and violet, and were placed one on top of the other. Over the top of the bed was a frame of wood handsomely carved and from this frame white crepe curtains, beautifully embroidered, hung, and numerous little gauze silk bags filled with scent were suspended from the carved work of the frame. The odor from these bags was very strong and made one feel sick until they became used do it. Her Majesty was also very fond of musk and used it on all occasions.

It took us about fifteen minutes to make the bed, and when I had finished, I turned around and saw that Her Majesty was dressing her hair. I stood beside Her Majesty while the eunuch was dressing it and saw that, as old as she was, she still had beautiful long hair which was as soft as velvet and raven black. She parted it in the center and brought it low at the back of her ears, and the back braid was brushed up on the top of her head and made into a tight knot. When she had finished doing this, she was ready to have the Gu'un Dzan (Manchu headdress) placed on and pinned through the knot with two large pins. Her Majesty always dressed her hair first and then washed her face. She was as fussy and particular as a young girl and would give it to the eunuch if he did not get it just to suit her. She had dozens of bottles of all kinds of perfume, also perfumed soap. When she had finished washing her face, she dried it on a sort towel and sprayed it with a kind of glycerine made of honey and flower petals. After that she put some kind of strong scented pink powder on her face.

When she had completed her toilet, she turned to me and said: 'It must seem to you quite funny to see an old lady like me taking so much care and pains in dressing and fixing up. Well! I like to dress myself up and to see others dress nicely. It always gives me pleasure to see pretty girls dressed nicely; it makes you want to be young again yourself.' I told her that she looked quite young and was still beautiful, and that although we were young we would never dare compare ourselves with her. This pleased her very much, as she was very fond of compliments, and I took great pains that morning to study her and to find out what she liked and what she didn't.

After this Her Majesty took me into another room and showed

me where her jewels were kept. This room was covered with shelves on three sides of the room from top to bottom, on which were placed piles of ebony boxes all containing jewels. Small yellow strips were pasted on some of the boxes on which was written the contents. Her Majesty pointed to a row of boxes on the right side of the room and said: 'Here is where I keep my favorite everyday jewels, and some day you must go over them and see that they are all there. The rest are all jewels which I wear on special occasions. There are about three thousand boxes in this room and I have a lot more locked up in my safety room, which I will show you when I am not busy.' Then she said: 'I am sorry you can't read and write Chinese, otherwise I would give you a list of these things and you could keep a check on them.' I was very much surprised at this and wondered who had told her I couldn't. I was anxious to know, but did not dare to ask her, so I told her that although I was not a scholar, I had studied Chinese for some time and could read and write a little, that if she would give me a list I would try and read it. She said: 'That is funny, someone told me the first day you were here, I forget now who it was, that you could not read or write your own language at all.' While she was saying this, she was looking all around the room and I was sure she knew who it was that had told her, but she would not tell me. Then she said: 'When we have time this afternoon, I will go over this list with you. Bring me those five boxes on the first row of shelves.' I brought the boxes to her room and placed them on the table. She opened the first one and it contained a most beautiful peony made of coral and jade and each petal trembled like a real flower. This flower was made by stringing the petals which were made of coral on very fine brass wire, also the leaves which were made of pure jade. She took this flower and placed it on the right side of her head-dress. Then she opened another box and took from it a magnificent jade butterfly made in the same way. This was an invention of her own and it was done by carving the coral and jade into petals and leaves and boring holes in the lower ends through which brass wire was run. The other two boxes contained bracelets and rings of different patterns. There was a pair of gold bracelets set with pearls, another pair set with jade, with a piece of jade hanging from the end of a small gold chain, etc. The last two contained chains of pearls, the like of which I never saw before, and I fell in love with them at once. Her Majesty took one which was made into a plum blossom string by winding a circle of five pearls around a larger one, then one of single pearls, then another circle of five pearls around a large one, and so on, making quite a long chain, which she suspended from one of the buttons of her gown.

At this juncture one of the Court ladies came in carrying several gowns for Her Majesty to select from. She looked at them and said that none of them suited her, to take them back and bring more. I had a look at them and thought they were perfectly lovely, such pretty colors and so beautifully embroidered. In a short while the same Court lady came back carrying more, and from these Her Majesty selected a sea-green one embroidered all over with white storks. She put this gown on and looked at herself in the mirror for a while, then took off her jade butterfly. She said: 'You see I am very particular about little details. The jade butterfly is too green and it kills my gown. Put it back in the box and bring me a pearl stork in No.35 box.' I went back to the jewel room and fortunately found No.35 box and brought it to her. She opened the box and took from it a stork made entirely of pearls set in silver, the bird's bill being made of coral. The pearls making the body of the bird were so cleverly set that the silver could not be seen at all unless one looked at it very closely. It was a most magnificent piece of workmanship and the pearls were of perfect color and shape. Her Majesty took it and placed it in her hair and did look very graceful and pretty. Then she picked out a mauve-colored short jacket, also embroidered with storks, which she put on over her gown. Her handkerchief and shoes were also embroidered with storks and when she was entirely dressed she looked like the stork lady. (Der-ling, *Two Years in the Forbidden City*, London, 1912, pp.60-68)

The association of the Manchu Empress Dowager with fabulous jewels creates and reinforces the idea of the Orient and the fabled gems "of Ormus and of Ind". I wonder if this type of image of capricious self-indulgence coupled with, and expressing itself in, incomparably magnificent jewels did not influence the perception of one half-Chinese author, namely

Han Suyin. In the first volume of her history and autobiography, *The Crippled Tree*, she devotes a section to recalling childhood friends. In the description of her friendship with one Suchen (in real-life Lydia Dan) she describes Suchen's mother, a Manchu Princess, in the most bizarre terms, in many ways a character so like the stereotypical cruel Chinese beauty that one can either gasp at the eccentricity or, more likely, the exaggeration of fantasy. The latter seems to be not an unlikely possibility, judging by a letter which Suchen, many years later wrote in protest to *Asiaweek*. But more of that in Chapter IV. Now I just want to show how strong was the impression left by pictures like Der-ling's, linking power and capriciousness—especially Manchu power and capriciousness—with jewels. I quote the pertinent part of Han Suyin's description of the Manchu Princess, Princess Dan, mother of Suchen, a lovely lady with "a delicate oval face like a melon seed, very purely drawn, a small nose, thin, slightly hooked as some Manchus have, eyebrows sweeping away, very very dark hair". The long nails are enhanced by nail guards, ornaments which have been made familiar by photographs of the Empress Dowager. Indeed Tz'u-hsi's nail guards are on exhibit in the Forbidden Palace. Han Suyin's Princess Dan "wore long nails, the ring and the last finger nails were about two inches long". Han Suyin combines the two components which I have suggested go into the conceptualization and characterization of Chinese women: fragility and cruelty. Her capriciousness and absorption with self on the occasion of the narrator's visit, if indeed a figment of the narrator's imagination, may well have been borrowed from, at least inspired by, the image of the Empress Dowager and her legendary love of precious ornaments:

> The Princess laughed. 'All women want be men,' she said. 'When I was young I also wanted to be a man, a boy, so that I should not be oppressed.' Her mouth twisted its thin lips into a curve, one side up and one side down, again a lovely movement to watch, and so expressive, like a theatre bitterness, so much more real than real people who are often silly when bitter. The Princess affected one all the time, she played on one's nerves and brain as on her flute, easily, negligently. She looked so fragile and lovely, and Rosalie knew she

must be very cruel, capriciously cruel, like so many lovely, fragile looking women are.

And then the princess said: 'I will show you something,' and gave an order, not turning her head, and almost instantaneously two servants came running in, and she said: 'My baskets,' and they said: 'Yes Lady, yes Lady,' precipitately, and ran away and soon ran back with other servants, bringing in baskets of lacquered wood and bamboo close-woven, covered with red brocade silk, blue and orange brocade silk, their lids topped with knobs encrusted with coral. And when the princess lifted the lids there were marvels to see, turquoises, pearls, jade, gold, and other stones of which Rosalie did not know the names. Jades of all kinds, pale or deep, light apple-green, tender bamboo jade, and deep dark-green jade like emeralds, some near-black, some pieces carved, others uncarved, rings and bracelets and necklaces, brooches and earrings like drops of green light, and others like round moons. There were turquoises, sky-piercing blue and with wonderful names like Wing of Morning, See the Sun, Frozen Delight; pearls, baskets and baskets of them, seed pearls so small, pearls mounted by the thousand on head pins and diadems, bigger ones like tears, with downward droop, large round ones. There were rubies and aquamarines and sapphires, but there were few diamonds, perhaps because there are no diamonds in China; only some diamonds that the Princess had bought at Cartier's in Paris on her trips, solitaires unmounted, which she kept, and now playful she rolled them on the carpets, and they flashed sleepily. (Han Suyin, *The Crippled Tree*, pp.390-91)

The same imperiousness; servants running in terror to do her bidding. Der-ling's tone seems uncritical, indeed deferential, as she narrates the events of her years with "Her Majesty" and yet not a little that is frighteningly cruel in the Empress's character is divulged in the same even, apparently bland tone. For example, there is the relatively well-known episode relating to the loss of a few strands of the Empress Dowager's hair:

I can never forget the fifteenth day of the fifth moon as long as I live, for that was a bad day for everyone. As usual we went to Her

Majesty's bedroom quite early that morning. She could not get up and complained that her back ached so much. We rubbed her back, in turns, and finally she got up, though a little late. She was not satisfied. The Emperor came in and knelt down to wish her good morning, but she scarcely took any notice of him. I noticed that when the Emperor saw that Her Majesty was not well, he said very little to her. The eunuch who dressed her hair every morning was ill, and had ordered another one to help her. Her Majesty told us to watch him very closely to see that he did not pull her hair off. She could not bear to see even one or two hairs fall out. This eunuch was not used to trickery; for instance, in case the hair was falling off, he could not hide it like the other one did. This poor man did not know what to do with any that came out. He was frightened, and Her Majesty, seeing him through the mirror, asked him whether he had pulled her hair out. He said that he had. This made her furious, and she told him to replace it. I almost laughed, but the eunuch was very much frightened and started to cry. Her Majesty ordered him to leave the room, and said she would punish him later. We helped her to fix up her hair. I must say it was not an easy job, for she had very long hair and it was difficult to comb.

She went to the morning audience, as usual, and after that she told the head eunuch what had happened. This Li was indeed a bad and cruel man, and said: 'Why not beat him to death?' Immediately she ordered Li to take this man to his own quarters to receive punishment. (Der-ling, ibid., pp.167-8)

Der-ling relates also how Tz'u-hsi would indulge her love of rain by watching it under the shelter of a huge umbrella, while her eunuchs and ladies stood by miserably soaked to the skin. Der-ling comments blandly: "It was a characteristic of Her Majesty's, to experience a keen sense of enjoyment at the troubles of other people." (Der-ling, ibid., p.260) We are also given many accounts of the violent punishments inflicted on the maids and eunuchs until the punishments became so commonplace that all sense of human dignity was taken away. Der-ling reports the pride the Empress Dowager took in her capriciousness and her devilish power over others. After an account of a day of fiendish moodiness and ill-temper, Der-ling notes rather sycophantically:

> I was told that when once Her Majesty got angry, she would never finish. On the contrary, she talked to me very nicely, just as if there had been no troubles at all. She was not difficult to wait upon, only one had to watch her moods. I thought how fascinating she was, and I had already forgotten that she had been angry. She seemed to have guessed what I was thinking, and said: 'I can make people hate me worse than poison, and can also make them love me. I have that power.' I thought she was right there. (Der-ling, ibid., p.171)

Sumptuous clothes, fabulous jewels, unparalleled largesse in giving gifts, but capricious and malevolent cruelty and dangerous vanity all add together to convey an image that the West found most intriguing. I have noted that the Tz'u-hsi took care to "clean up" her image as she entered middle age, sending away Jung-lu, whom gossip alleged to be her lover. Der-ling, in her strangely prim Victorian prose, does not touch on these matters, especially since Der-ling's account deals with the time when the Empress had entered into a venerable old age.

The contribution of Der-ling in forming the image of the Empress Dowager in the minds of English-speaking people is considerable. The controversy surrounding the authenticity of her pretensions does not detract from this contribution, although it supports the contention that a great deal of what is reported as "historical fact" may actually be the realization of fantasies. It is to Der-ling that we owe the well-known quotation from the Dowager: "Do you know I have often thought that I am the cleverest woman who ever lived and that others cannot compare with me. Although I have heard much about Queen Victoria and read a part of her life... still I don't think her life is half as interesting and eventful as mine. Now look at me, I have 400 million people all dependent on my judgment." (Quoted by Marina Warner, ibid., frontispiece)

If Der-ling was at least partially feeding her own fantasies in her accounts of the Empress Dowager, this must have been more blatantly the case with Edmund Backhouse and his manuscript of the second volume of his memoirs handed over to Hugh Trevor-Roper in 1976 entitled "Décadence Mandchoue". Facts would suggest the record was actually written during the Second World War when Backhouse was spending his last years in China, but it seems with Backhouse, whose multiple and amazing frauds are documented by Trevor-Roper, it is impossible to separate fact from fantasy.

The memoirs have remained unpublished until very recently because of the scandalously pornographic nature of their contents.[3] Viewed as history they are not to be thought valuable records, but as "literature", according to Trevor-Roper, they have verve and vigour, and include entertaining conversation pieces which give the appearance of authentic experience. Yet he admits that Backhouse's "memoirs" are not an edifying work. "They are a pornographic novelette. No verve in the writing can redeem their pathological obscenity." (Trevor-Roper, ibid., p.335) The Empress Dowager plays a leading role in his Walter Mitty style sexual fantasies. Backhouse, collaborating with the respected journalist and sinologist, George Bland, on *China under the Empress Dowager*, had been meticulously circumspect about excluding anything offensive, but there is little doubt that for some years he had been fabricating or imagining a romantic autobiography. Backhouse gives an image of the Empress Dowager as a sort of super Mae West of the Eastern world, lascivious beyond description, and Backhouse was her European lover. Trevor-Roper gives us an account of Backhouse's highly detailed, deliberately circumstantial narrative, the inclusion of details being a device he repeatedly uses to bolster up the sense of authenticity. We are told by Trevor-Roper the "Décadence Mandchoue" opens in a high-class homosexual brothel patronized by the Manchu aristocracy. Backhouse had been introduced to it by Prince Ch'ing, an imperial clansman. The readers then are initiated, in great detail, into every practice, every refinement, of the institution. In the next chapter we are told how Backhouse first came to the notice of the Empress Dowager.

According to Backhouse, during the period of the Boxer uprising, he was responsible for saving the Chinese imperial treasures housed in the Summer Palace from European looters. With the help of a group of "trusty Manchus" he removed 600 pieces of *objet d'art* and 25,000 volumes, and sixteen months later, when the court returned to Peking, Backhouse tells us, he got in touch with the Chief Eunuch, Li Lien-ying, in order to arrange for the return personally of the Empress Dowager's property. This led to the first meeting between Backhouse and Tz'u-hsi in the Forbidden City and the restitution of the imperial treasures of China. Trevor-Roper records with skepticism Backhouse's story:

...Having thus unexpectedly recovered the treasures of her Empire, the Empress graciously received her benefactor, and Backhouse, who now found himself in the presence of his fourth Empress, was thanked and rewarded... These rewards were to be increased later, for further services of a different kind...

In the course of his interview, Backhouse, he tells us, enjoyed some interesting private conversation with the grateful and bountiful Empress, whose personality he set out almost in the terms ascribed by him, in his letter to Bland, to the memoirs of Li Lien-ying, adding that she reminded him, particularly, of that famous Victorian *grande dame* and Lady Bountiful, the Baroness Burdett-Coutts. She too dwelt on the recent Boxer troubles and rattled away indiscreetly about the actions of her ministers at that time...

This interview, says Backhouse, marked the beginning of his close relations with the Empress Dowager. Soon afterwards, he tells us, he was summoned for a no less interesting interview with the most powerful politician at her court, the man who, in political matters, ruled both the Empress and the Empire: the Viceroy and Grand Secretary Jung-lu, 'the father-in-law of the future Regent and grandfather of the present emperor of Manchukuo'. Already, he tells us, his admiration for Jung-lu knew no bounds: 'I had already idealised him, partly from Chingshan's diary and partly knowing that, but for him, every alien in North China would have been massacred...'

If only Jung-lu had lived! sighs Backhouse, he would have prevented the dismissal of Yuan Shih-kai in 1909, and perhaps there would have been no revolution in 1911... But alas, by 1904 he was dead, and by his death he left a void in the Empress's heart. No doubt this explains, in part, the next striking episode in Backhouse's life. For in August of that year Backhouse (he tells us) received a message from the eunuch Li Lien-Ying commanding him to come to the Summer Palace. He was to leave his chair at a discreet distance and arrive at the palace in a closed palanquin 'so as to attract less attention'. He had no doubts what this meant. As the palanquin was carried 'along the waterlogged country by-paths, some eight or nine miles distance, to the Wan Shou Temple's imperial road', where two eunuchs met him to escort him on foot for the rest of the journey, he felt himself a second Konigsmarck or Potemkin. His doubts were solely about his performance. 'Was I sexually adequate for Her Majesty's overflowing carnality?' Might he be so unfortunate as to 'present to the Old Buddha a *telum imbelle sine ictu*, a tool unwarlike and devoid of thrust, like the faltering sword of Priam, slain by Pyrrhus at the fall of Troy?' He need not have worried. Although Her Majesty's demands, in her seventieth year, were both exacting in number and unusual in form, delicious refreshments, sophisticated devices, well-tempered aphrodisiacs, supplied any defect of strength in her partner; and in the intervals of action he was able to enjoy intimate conversation about Queen Victoria and John Brown (a subject to which the Empress continually returned), the Jewish origin of the Prince Consort ('a court secret of which my family have sure and certain cognizance'), the unfortunate circumstances of the death of the French President Felix Faure, the English laws against homosexual practices, and Backhouse's intimacy with the Queen's lifelong friend, 'Sir John Clark, baronet, of Tillypronie (near Balmoral)'.

Ex uno disce omnes, as Backhouse is fond of quoting, though he does not often follow his own precept. The rest of the book consists largely of an alternation of two themes, tediously and minutely reiterated: homosexual relations with eunuchs, professional catamites and Manchu *jeunesse dorée*, and command performances for the Empress Dowager. At one point the two threads are intertwined. In conversation with Backhouse, the Empress expressed an interest in a fashionable homosexual *hamam*, and turning to the eunuch Li Lien-ying said 'after our return to town, you must arrange for me to go there in disguise: it would amuse me to see all you dissolute young men diverting yourselves.' As she ordered, so it was done. The young men were indeed diverting themselves, when 'a peremptory voice shouted from the foot of the short flight of stairs, "Kuei Hsia, kneel down"', and who should enter the reception room but Her Majesty, 'who had disguised herself with a Feng Ling or windproof cape round her head and was wearing a yellow riding jacket and masculine trousers and wadded shoes'. Her Majesty ordered the diversion to continue while she engaged in light badinage with those not immediately occupied. Backhouse, as always, described the diversion in revolting detail, but the badinage reads well. When the Empress had gone, 'Prince Kung asked me if my queen would have come out incognito on such a visit. I replied that customs differ and that such spectacles, though existing in London and Paris, were concealed from publicity by the cloak of hypocrisy, though equally libidinous.' In counting up his experiences, Backhouse concluded that he had in Peking 'many hundred (perhaps a thousand) love affairs' with his own sex and 150 to 200 with the Empress Dowager. We need not seek exactitude in such matters, nor follow Backhouse in his indefatigable reiteration... (Trevor-Roper, ibid., pp.304-312)

This account of the lascivious side to Tz'u-hsi's personality comes as a surprise as it is almost entirely absent in her English biographies written earlier. In a note on p.459 of Sir Reginald Johnston's *Twilight in the Forbidden City* (1934) he refers to what he calls "the scandalous stories once current in Chinese and foreign circles about the Empress Dowager's private life," and adds "I do not believe the stories to be true." He even ventures the opinion: "It seems possible that the warping of her character, so far from having had anything to do with sensual pleasures, was due in part to an inner conflict arising from sex-repression." The Chinese sources give no support to this view regarding her sexual repression. Indeed, as I have indicated earlier, the image of licentiousness almost inevitably accompanies, in the Chinese mind, the image of female power. But up to a good many years after her death her image in the West remained free from suggestions of rampant sexuality. Backhouse's autobiography, after all, did not get into print, and it only came to the knowledge of readers through Trevor-Roper's account of it in his *Hermit of Peking*, which was not published until 1976.

More than three decades before the publication of Trevor-Roper's work, Maurice Collis, traveller to the East and author of works like *Foreign Mud* and *The Great Within*, wrote a play on the life of Tz'u-hsi which was published in 1943. This play represents a volte-face as far as Western attitudes to the Empress Dowager are concerned. To my knowledge this is the only extant play in English on this subject. The play is called The *Motherly and the Auspicious*, this being the literal translation into English of the Chinese characters Tz'u-hsi, 慈禧. It was a title the Manchu adventuress assumed when, as mother of the boy Emperor, she became Empress Dowager and Co-Regent with the Empress on the death of the Emperor Hsien Feng. Collis provided a lengthy introduction and notes which filled in details such as the dramatic form he had chosen made difficult to include in the text. Collis represents her as a charming, unscrupulous, totally self-seeking pragmatist, brilliant but totally amoral. Collis claims that he could never have constructed his drama on the basis of the information provided in the English biographies of Tz'u-hsi. Nor would he "have attempted to write of Tz'u-hsi had there not been placed at his disposal private translations of Chinese works. The most important of these is *The True Records of Chung Ling* by Yun Yui-Ting. This man is actually a character in the play, being the Grand Historiographer in Scene 3 of Act III." (Collis, p.12) The *Records* were printed after the establishment of the Republic in 1911. They deal with the whole life of Tz'u-hsi and the play draws heavily upon him from first to last. Collis accepts his version of the deaths of the Emperor Tung-chih and the Co-Regent, Tz'u-an, that is they were murdered by Tz'u-hsi, and also the evidence of foul play in the death of the Emperor Kuang-hsu. Thus Collis's play presented to the English-speaking world the Empress Dowager as a total monster, capable of cruelty different in intensity and kind to the capricious cruelty suggested by Der-ling. Collis also includes in his play passages which hint at Tz'u-hsi's moral licence. For many English readers this would, as he acknowledges, "cause surprise, for in her English biographies no such reflection on her character is to be found". (Collis, p.25)

Let us consider the literary merits or demerits of this play, which caused consternation to not a few sinologists. Collis has used a three-act structure, representing the three steps of Tz'u-hsi's accession to supremacy. The characters are all historical persons, with one exception. Wen-li, the Mentor, who appears before each scene, is a creation of the author's imagination.

This character serves the same sort of function as, say, the chorus, in Shakespeare's *Henry V* or that of Time at the beginning of Act IV of *The Winter's Tale*. He is a device for filling in the gaps between the scenes. His speeches are long monologues and go beyond that rudimentary function. From the point of view of practical stagecraft, Wen Li may have created a problem, but his monologues have a wider significance in that, according to Collis, he stands for the most conservative element in the China of the period. The Confucian ideas he represents had become fossilized and by the declining years of the Ching Dynasty members of the Literati like Wen Li were mainly intent on upholding a system to which they owed their privileges. Wen Li's commentary is meant by Collis to show how a biography of Tz'u-hsi would run, if it had been written by an official historian. There is always a marked contrast between Wen Li's judgment of Tz'u-hsi's conduct and philosophy and the judgment the playgoer or reader is almost bound to form through the playwright's presentation of them. Frequent contrast, too, of subject matter with style, as for example, in the opening lines of Wen Li's commentary following Act I, scene ii contributes to the ludicrous note, and indeed the whole question of writing dialogue, whether for a novel or a play, is one worthy of a great deal of research. (See, for example, Norman Page, *Dialogue in the English Novel*,

Longman, 1982, and my Chapter V and VI.) The semblance of verisimilitude is difficult enough with contemporary, English-speaking fictional characters. It is more difficult still when the characters are meant to be famous figures in real life. I, for one, am always slightly jolted at the appearance of, for example, John F. Kennedy—or to take things a little further back, Abraham Lincoln—among fictional characters in, for instance, a novel like Jeffrey Archer's *Shall We Tell the President?* or John Jakes' more recent best-seller *North and South.* When there is not only a time gap but also a very wide racial, cultural—and still more important, linguistic—disparity, then it is very easy for the novelist or playwright to fall into the ridiculous. Maurice Collis confronts the problem squarely and I think with a degree of success. While Wen Li speaks in a deliberately archaic and artificial way to reinforce the sense of his outmoded ideas and his hypocrisy, Collis steers a middle course in general with the other characters, and in the case of his central character has recourse to a racy idiomatic mode of speech which strikes a reader even of today as "contemporary" and befitting a cynical, hard-boiled lady "on the make".

It may be worthwhile looking at Act I scene ii of the play with its "Cinderella and the glass slipper" undertones—but what a sardonic and cynical Cinderella! This scene is set in the third year of reign of Hsien Feng, that is, 1853, and gives an account of how Tz'u-hsi, then Orchid, daughter of an impoverished Manchu widow, by using her superior taste, sense of style and insidious wiles, secures election by the eunuch Li Lien-ying into the Inner Palace as a "lady in waiting". The scene has a touch of the climatic scene in Cinderella, when the palace officials bring around the glass slipper to find the owner, with Chrysanthemum, Orchid's harmless but stupid and overdressed sister playing the part of Cinderella's "ugly sister". But Orchid is no Cinderella; rather, she is an infinitely cunning operator. A very "slick operator" indeed. Let us now consider this scene more carefully.

Tz'u-hsi's speech is surprisingly "incongruous", given the usual expectations readers have of a historical Chinese woman character's mode of utterance. The scene opens with a description of the genteel poverty of Orchid and her family. The year is the third of the reign of Hsien Feng, that is, 1853. After the over-dressed, over-made-up Chrysanthemum is rejected, Orchid emerges and plays her cards carefully. She bargains with the imperial eunuchs; she cunningly strengthens her position by feigning nonchalance at this point in the scene. She finally comes out after repeated expressions of indifference and astounds with her beauty:

LI. [*exclaiming*] Heavens, what a beautiful girl! And what taste in dress!

SERVANT. Certainly she is not over-dressed like her sister, sir.

LI. Nor over-rouged and over-powdered. Sit down, please.

ORCHID. I prefer to stand until the honourable visitor has resumed his chair.

LI. And not ill-bred, either. Thank you. [*He sits down.*]

ORCHID. [*taking a seat some distance from the men, but in a calculated and seductive pose*] You needn't thank me for that. The courtesy was paid not so much to you as to His Majesty, in whose service you have come.

LI. [*with an uncomfortable grin*] Smart! [*to his man*] I perceive we have met our match! [*to Orchid*] Now that I've seen you, it breaks my heart to reject you. But you see, we eunuchs have to live. Isn't there any chance at all of your managing some money ...?

ORCHID. [*demurely*] We needn't bother about that! I do not want to go.

LI. [*staggered*] What! Do you really not want to go into the Palace?

ORCHID: What is the use? If people realized that their own promotion depended on what a favourite might whisper into Imperial ears, one could make a bargain. But as it is what can one do if they are so shortsighted as to prefer a trifling fee in cash.

LI. [thinking] A-hem! I can take the hint. But even were I to enter you, it would mean you'd be only one of the Ladies-Constant-in-Waiting who are no more than servants, and most of them remain so until their hair is grey.

ORCHID. You said "most of them". Then there are exceptions?

LI. Yes, some may become Imperial Concubines, and rank next to the Empress. That is why this business is generally called the Selection of Imperial Concubines. But not more than two out of over a hundred girls are ever given that rank.

ORCHID. I would like to hear the details. How are they all selected?

LI. I see you are ambitious!

ORCHID. [*charmingly*] Is there any objection to that?

LI. No, on the contrary! Well, our Lord of Ten Thousand Years is to have an Empress, two Imperial Concubines, twelve lesser Consorts, thirty-two Noble Ladies, and sixty-four Ladies-Constant-in-Waiting. As soon as the girls I select come into the Palace, the Chief Eunuch examines them carefully and the Empress Dowager promotes some of them to the rank of Noble Ladies, leaving sixty-four to be Ladies-Constant-in-Waiting. Later she will pick from among the Noble Ladies some to be promoted as Lesser Consorts.

ORCHID. [rather alarmed] And does the Emperor himself have no say in the matter at all?

LI. No, not at first. But not all the vacancies for the Lesser Consorts will be filled at once. As time goes by the Lord of Ten Thousand Years may favour some of the girls and have them promoted. Of course, when the Empress Dowager mounts on high in her Phoenix Carriage, then the Lord of Ten Thousand Years may even name his own Empress.

ORCHID. [thoughtfully] How old is the Empress Dowager?

LI. Not very old, though she is getting on. But don't dream, my girl. People from families like yours seldom get promotion. Besides, you must have the eunuchs on your side, and they all have to live.

SERVANT. Yes, sir, they all have to live.

ORCHID. Then, is money everything in the Palace?

LI. I should say that the eunuchs' backing is everything. And you can't get it without paying.

ORCHID. But there are various ways of paying!

SERVANT. His Honour prefers cash down…

(Collis, ibid., pp.49-54)

And the bargaining goes on. The rest of Act I scene ii gives us more examples of Orchid's pragmatic attitudes which are reflected in her terse, "hard-boiled" mode of speech. We can see that Collis does not affect the almost Biblical rhythms and un-English cadences, absence of contractions and inflated lexis the reader has come to associate with representations in English of Chinese speech, especially of a past period; instead, always with the exception of Wen Li, the characters for the most part speak as English speakers would, with the occasional evocation of "Chinese" expressions like "My humble father". Indeed Collis deliberately mixes registers on occasion, and puts "inappropriate" phrases into the mouths of his characters; for example, the Eastern Empress, Tz'u-hsi's co-Regent, Tz'u-an, surprises with the phrase "in the family way".

Each scene opens with the entry upon the stage of one of the principal characters, who makes to the audience, or, if you prefer, the readers, in an aside, some remark of "a sententious or improving character". This, according to Collis, is "in accordance with the invariable custom of Chinese theatre". He has employed the device sparingly, seeking "a middle course in the belief that this small departure from English stage technique will not be found too stiff, while it may also harmonize with those numerous passages where the matter and sentiment are so wholly Chinese as to be completely alien to English ways of thought". (Collis, ibid., p.17) Tz'u-hsi's mother, Madame Hui Ching, opens the scene with the repeated lamentations of Chinese parents in a feudal society. (And yet, one is sometimes not a little astonished to find this sentiment, unfortunately, universal and timeless rather than specifically feudal or Chinese.)

> To bring up daughters is a miserable job. As soon as you've done everything for them, sedan chairs are waiting outside your gate to take them away from you.

Apart from the reference to sedan chairs, the language, as we can see, is not artificially contorted to fit any preconception or fulfil any expectations of "Chinamen's English".

Through her own lips Collis tries to destroy the image of the kindly old lady the West had of her in her last days. The "kindly old lady" discloses her contempt for the "Barbarians" who are untutored, stupid and easily taken in by her pretended gentleness and kindness. Collis replaces the image of the gentle and kind old lady with that of a monster—of licentiousness, greed, cruelty and ambition. Yet for all her crimes Collis's Tz'u-hsi is cast in a heroic mould. And she rises to a height of heroic grandeur in a finale that clearly owes something, significantly perhaps, to Shakespeare's *Cleopatra*. Kind old lady or Monster—which image more nearly reflects the reality? Perhaps neither?

Collis's play did not appear to have enjoyed the popular success as the more trifling earlier play about Chinese people, *Lady Precious Stream*. It was published in 1943 and went into a second impression two years later, and received enough attention to arouse the indignation of Bland, Backhouse's collaborator in writing the first "authoritative" biography of the Empress Dowager, *China under the Empress Dowager* (1910). He wrote an acerbic review, reviling Collis for his distortion of the Dowager's image.

The monstrously evil but nevertheless heroic image into which Collis cast Tz'u-hsi was taken yet further by Pearl Buck who made her into a heroic and very human figure. Her foreword, quoted below, to her novel about Tz'u-hsi, *Imperial Woman* first published by Methuen in 1956, is strangely reactionary. She puts herself squarely against revolution and change, on the side of the Old Buddha herself:

> Tzu Hsi, the last Empress of China, was a woman so diverse in her gifts, so contradictory in her behaviour, so rich in the many aspects of her personality, that it is difficult to comprehend and convey her whole self. She lived in a crucial period of history, when China was struggling against encroachment while at the same time the need for modern reform was obvious. In this period Tzu Hsi was conservative and independent. She was ruthless when necessary. Those who opposed her feared and hated her and they were more articulate than those who loved her. Western writers, with few exceptions, described her unfavourably and even vindictively.

I have tried in this book to portray Tzu Hsi as accurately as possible from available resources and my own memories of how the Chinese whom I knew in my childhood felt about her. To them she was the imperial woman. Good and evil mingled in her, but always in heroic dimension. She resisted modern change as long as she could, for she believed that the old was better than the new. When she saw change was inevitable, she accepted it with grace but an unchanged heart.

Her people loved her—not all her people, for the revolutionary, the impatient, hated her heartily and she hated them. But the peasants and the small-town people revered her. Decades after she was dead I came upon villages in the inlands of China where the people thought she still lived and were frightened when they heard she was dead. 'Who will care for us now?' they cried.

In Pearl Buck's hands the history of Tz'u-hsi's rise to power is dominated by a rather hackneyed "theme": the conflict between love and ambition. The young Tz'u-hsi, known by the Manchu name Yehonala and the pet name Orchid emerges from the hands of her author-creator (I have deliberately avoided "biographer") as a soppy little piece from a soap opera, who gives up her childhood love to enter the palace. Rather elementary use of stream-of-consciousness can be found—for example: "To be Jung Lu's image, the mother of his children—many children there would be, for they were passionate, he and she—or to be an imperial concubine? But he loved her only as she loved him and something more. What more? On the day of the imperial summons she would know." (p.14) The extract I have quoted below gives some idea of the standard of the work. Imagine the Jung-lu of the Chinese documents and of the diary of Ching-shan spewing this gibberish ludicrous even by B film standards, and the legendary Dragon Empress responding in the same vein in a supposedly torrid love scene, the result of which, the author clearly suggests, is the conception of the Emperor Tung Chih.

Her heart leaped in her breast, a thing alive and separate from her, and tears welled to her eyes and her mouth began to quiver.

Whatever she could do, this that she did shook all his will. He had seen her weep in pain and he had heard her sob with rage, but he had never seen her sit motionless and weep without a sound, helplessly, as though her very life were broken.

He gave a great groan and his arms went out to her and he strode across the floor. And she, seeing only those outstretched arms, rose blindly from her chair and ran to him and felt them enclose her fast. Thus locked together, in silence and in fearful ecstasy they stood, how long neither knew. Cheek to cheek they stood, until their lips met by instinct. Then he tore his mouth away.

'You know you cannot leave this place,' he groaned. 'You must find your freedom here within these walls, for there is no other freedom for you now.'

She listened, hearing his voice from afar, knowing only that within his arms she held him.

'The higher you rise,' he told her, 'the greater will your freedom be. Rise high, my love—the power is yours. Only an Empress can command.'

'But will you love me?' she asked, her voice stifling in her throat.

'How can I not love you?' Thus he replied. 'To love you is my only life. I draw my breath, my every breath, to love you.'

'Then—seal me your love!'

These were the bold words she spoke but in so soft a whisper that he might not have heard them, except she knew he did. She felt his shoulders shiver and his muscles loosen and his bones yield.

'If once I am made yours,' she said bravely, 'even here I can live.'

No answer yet! he could not speak. His soul was still not yielded.

She lifted her head and looked into his face. 'What does it matter where I live if I am yours? I know you speak the truth. There is no escape for me except by death. Well, I can choose death. It is easy in a palace—opium to swallow, my gold ear-rings, a little knife to open my veins—can I be watched day and night? I swear I will die unless you make me yours! If I am yours, I will do what you say—forever and my whole life long. I will be Empress.'

Her voice was magic, lovely with pleading, deep and soft and gentle, warm and sweet as honey in the summer sun. Was he not a man? He was young and fervent, still virgin because he had loved no one but her whom he now held within his arms. They were prisoners, trapped by old ways of life, jailed within the imperial palace. He was no more free than she was. Yet only she could do what she would. If she said she would be Empress, then none could hold her back. And if she chose death, then she would die. He knew her nature. And would he not devote his life to help her live? And had not Sakota herself imagined some such scene as this when she had bade him come here? At the last moment the Consort had laid her hand on his arm and she bade him do all he could—'whatever Yehonala asks' —those were Sakota's very words.

His soul's voice was stilled, he felt his conscience die and he lifted the beautiful girl in his arms and carried her to the bed.

...The drums of curfew beat through the courtyards and the corridors of the city of the Son of Heaven. It was the hour of sunset when every man must be gone from within the walls. The ancient command fell upon the ears of lovers hidden deep within the secret rooms and in Yehonala's bedchamber Jung Lu rose and drew his garments about him while she lay half asleep and smiling. (*Imperial Woman*, London, 1971, pp.54-55)

All pretty banal and unsophisticated stuff, down to the rather coy "..." and then the shift to drum beats in lieu of the scene in bed.

The characterization of Tz'u-hsi as a young girl and as a young mother seems to draw heavily on the author's imagination. Beautiful and passionate, a good mother, she gradually grows in stature, in cruelty and also dignity. Her atrocities are always dictated by a strong sense of her destiny and her duty to the Dynasty. She truly undergoes a sort of apotheosis, giving reality to her name "The Old Buddha". Pearl Buck wrote this novel long after Chinese Imperial rule was over. She was clearly nostalgic for the China of Wang Lung and *The Mother*. Hence she idealized and virtually deified the Empress Dowager, "who resisted modern change as long as she could, for she believed that the old was better than the new" (ibid., *Foreword*). This hearkens back to the old condescendingly benevolent attitudes of writers like Bland and Backhouse. Charlotte Haldane, in *The Last Great Empress of China* quotes from Bland and Backhouse a "charming" (Haldane's word; notes, p.291) description of Old Buddha by the country folk. A patronizing and condescending mentality might find the simplicity and ignorance of the country folk charming. To the more sensitive their very naïvety bespeaks deprivation and injustice.

> One of the writers had the good fortune once to see the Empress when proceeding in her palanquin to the Eastern tombs ... As her chair passed along a line of kneeling peasantry, the curtains were open and it was seen that the Old Buddha was asleep. The good country people were delighted. 'Look,' they cried, 'the old Buddha is sleeping. Really, she has far too much work to do! A rare woman—what a pleasure to see her thus!'

And yet there is no doubt, whatever image is projected of her, she is a "rare" woman indeed, one who captured the imaginations of all who came to know of her. The fact she was a woman has a great deal to do with her fascination. The famous dying words attributed to her are of interest in this connection.

> Never again allow any woman to hold the supreme power in the State. It is against the house-law of our Dynasty, and should be strictly forbidden...

Lest we take her too seriously, we may wish to remember that only a few hours previously she had decreed that her niece, Lung-yu, now the reigning Empress Dowager, should in an emergency have the last word in matters of policy. (Charlotte Haldane, ibid., p.259) Maurice Collis tries to sum up (*The Motherly and Auspicious, Introduction*, p.26), the mystique of Tz'u-hsi, this "extraordinary being". He makes out the case that though she knew how to rule men she was not like a man. "One feels indeed, that, dissimilar to most eminent European women, she had no masculine traits, but was the quintessence of the feminine, and that was the final secret of her power." He suggests that the image she projected, in its varied forms was essentially a feminine one, and that in the Western mind the extreme feminine is supposed to be allied with softness and surrender. One difficulty of the English-speaking world in trying to understand a person like Tz'u-hsi—and indeed, an Empress Wu or a Jiang Qing—is the absence of their like in their history. Queen Elizabeth I and Queen Victoria have some resemblance to her, but they do not have her overwhelming force. Collis calls it "the force of the female when fully concentrated".

By the middle of the century the Empress Dowager as a historical figure had receded from popular memory at least in the Western World. "Chinese Gordon", "the siege of the legations" and the Boxers had more or less passed into legend and only the very well-informed would know of these historical events. An occasional book would appear, to reach the status of a popular work, and jolt the memory of readers of such books. *The Dragon Empress* (1972) is read not so much by the specialist as the general reader, more as historical fiction perhaps than well-documented history. Hugh Trevor-Roper's excellently written and scholarly *Hermit of Peking* (1976) concentrates on the frauds of Edmund Backhouse, but incidentally revives interest in the Empress Dowager. Still, works like *The Dragon Empress* and *Hermit of Peking* have a relatively limited circulation and are not aimed at the great masses of readers who buy in bulk best-selling novels. Robert Elegant, a student of Chinese history and attitudes, started off as a journalist, and after writing six non-fiction works on China he embarked on bestselling novels—also about China. Into his fictional narrative he weaves historical fact and among his fictional characters are well-known figures from Chinese history. In *Manchu*, for example, the first Catholic convert, Hsu Kwang-chi, Mandarin of the First Grade during the Ming Dynasty, moves among fictitious creations such as the English soldier-of-fortune, Francis Arrowsmith, in a manner not a little disconcerting for someone like me whose acquaintance with him is limited to the cut-and-dry facts given in Chinese history books. He goes about as "Dr Paul", a roly-poly character who seems hardly dignified enough to be The Minister of Rites, a pragmatist and a schemer. Elegant's novels, *Manchu* and the earlier *Dynasty* (about Hong Kong) are clearly money-spinners. He uses again the same ingredients, the same devices in *Mandarin* (1983) which records the events of twenty-five years of Manchu rule in the mid-nineteenth century, coinciding with the rise of Tz'u-hsi to power. By 1983 the facts and fantasies of Tz'u-hsi's life had pretty much receded into the background—if they existed at all—of Western minds. She was totally unknown to the majority and only vaguely remembered by some; thus Elegant was free to take liberties with her character, personality and personal history, as opposed to the role she played in political history. She becomes, for all intents and purposes, very much a fictional character. Indeed the advertisement on the cover of the paperback edition (Sphere Book Ltd., 1984) reads:

> *Mandarin* unfolds an epic tale of love, war and ambition, peopled by characters who will haunt every reader's memory: the merchant Saul Haleevie, bidding for power alongside the great European trading houses... his daughter Fronah, torn between love and virtue... above all, the 'Virtuous Concubine', Yehenala, whose destiny would one day be inextricably linked with that of China itself...

Yehenala or "nala", as she is familiarly called in the novel, becomes an intensely human, intensely passionate and intelligent woman, and at least when young, a creature of extreme sensitivity. Elegant manages to do what Backhouse tried, as yet without success, to do, in his obviously spurious memoirs of his erotic experiences with the Empress Dowager. Elegant presents the young Tz'u-hsi in the sort of steamy, explicit near-pornographic love scenes which no contemporary best-seller seems to be able to do without. The fact that the parties are persons of such historical significance makes the scene so much more titillating. And the consciousness of the future Empress Dowager of the dynastic significance of their copulation—recorded by the narrator—heightens this type of effect. History, fantasy, fiction give us many versions of how Tz'u-hsi came to be the mother of the Tung-chih emperor. But according to Elegant, Tung-chih is the result of the coupling described in the extract quoted.

CHAPTER SEVENTEEN
August 8, 1855   The Forbidden City   Peking

... 'Your Majesty's cares are heavy.'

She consoled herself that he was only a man to be cajoled blatantly and guided discreetly. Actually not much of a man in the nuptial bed.

'*Kua*...' As always when dispirited, he used the self-pitying term reserved for the Emperor, who was always fatherless.

'This Orphan must produce an heir.'

'Your Majesty,' Yehenala soothed, 'is the father of us all.'

'One princess of Our getting... just one small female child from all these women.' He slumped against the scarlet bolster. 'These chattering, useless, barren women. Heaven knows We've tried. But they... their wombs are dry, I know it.'

'My Lord is potent... powerful and thrilling,' she murmured, still crouching at the foot of the bed so that her touch would not contaminate his sacred person until he signalled that he wanted her.

'The Court Astronomers have been busy with their horoscopes and their wands. They say this night your fate and Ours cross. Tonight, from our coupling perhaps, an heir...'

'I am honoured, Majesty, inestimably honoured that, for this instant, this slave's destiny and My Lord's join.'

Despite much practice, Yehenala strained to sustain the extravagant speech prescribed by Court Etiquette without falling into parody that could sound ludicrous even to his insensitive ears. 'I am no more than a she-turtle in the mud, a mud-turtle gazing upward at a brilliant comet... my Lord's flashing course across the heavens.'

'It will be well.' The Emperor slipped off his green-silk bed-gown and extended his long-nailed hand. 'This Orphan will get an heir upon you this night, We know it...'

Was there, Yehenala wondered, truly a spark of love? Of course there was. Besides, it was her duty to serve him and to love him...

She knew exactly how she would use that power to crush the rebels, banish the oceanic barbarians, and make the Dynasty all powerful again. Her devoted attention to state papers had already given her the knowledge to carry out those great tasks. The power she would wield as the mother of the heir was great. The power she might later wield as the mother of the Emperor would be immense, virtually illimitable.

This Emperor, who finally stirred under the caresses of her breasts, her hands, and her mouth, how long, she wondered, would he live? He was not robust, and his debauchery enfeebled him. To be the mother of the Emperor, that was certainly the purpose for which heaven had fashioned her. Why else was she endowed with intelligence, knowledge, and resolution surpassing any other woman—or any man—she knew?...

To lie quietly entwined with the Emperor, like any ordinary woman with any ordinary man once passion was spent, was even more joyous than to rouse his ardour or even to receive his seed. At this moment, they were one soul and one flesh. A free-spirited Manchu lady lay beside her man in equal communion as their ancestors had when male and female were equally esteemed because each contributed equally to the survival of the nomadic clan. Such equality no mean-spirited Chinese woman could know with any man, for those simpering females always remained inferiors. No Chinese female could, of course, ever aspire to such communion with the Son of Heaven. Sacred Dynastic Law permitted only ladies of pure Manchu blood to enter the Forbidden City and bear Imperial Princes.

Perhaps the Lord of Ten Thousand Years sensed the love that exalted her. Perhaps his blood responded to the unfeigned raptures that overwhelmed her for the first time with him. Conceived in their overflowing joy, a boy-child would assuredly grow in her womb. (Elegant, ibid., pp. 127-132)

Mandarin takes the story of Yehenala only up to 1875, when she is still a young woman, and throughout the novel we are confronted by descriptions of her flawless beauty. The image of perfect physical beauty in Oriental womanhood—myth, fantasy of many Western man, if you like, is perpetuated by Elegant. And the petite delicate shape and her femininity are contrasted with her "masculine" authority. And yet why should authority be masculine? We are reminded once more of the two components that persistently go towards the formation of the image in the Western mind of the Chinese woman—delicacy, beauty, fragility coupled with fierce determination and ambition.

> The kidskin-covered platforms of Yehenala's satin shoes rested on a high footstool set before the yellow-cushioned throne. She was so petite she would have appeared insignificant without those Manchu demi-stilts. The foot-stool kept her feet from dangling ludicrously, while the raised dais of the throne ensured that her eyes were level with the subordinates who stood before her...
> (Elegant, ibid., p.449)

Just a digression—but possibly an interesting one—Elegant insists on her petite size. This, of course, is said to be one of the charms of Oriental woman. Elegant also emphasizes it because he wants to show more forcefully the contrast between her power and her delicacy. Pearl Buck, in *Imperial Woman*, using her own aesthetic standards, describes her as "tall" by Manchu standards. Each writer takes the artist's liberties with fact; each is trying to create the "image" of a great beauty. But even so, the physical images differ. And the person, personality, life and times of Tz'u-hsi are the very stuff of which images are made. One historical incident, borne witness to by many, gives evidence of Tz'u-hsi's great showmanship. Peter Fleming's *Siege at Peking* (first published by Rupert Hart-Davis, 1959) gives an account of the fifty-five day siege of the Legations by the Boxers with the equivocal support of the Empress Dowager. When everything was over and the peace treaty signed, the Empress Dowager and the Kuang-hsu Emperor made the journey back to Peking with great ceremony.

> When they reached the enclosure between the wall and the outer lunette, the chairs halted and the Emperor and Empress Dowager stepped down to carry out the ceremonies prescribed by the Book of Rites for a homecoming, that is to say, to burn incense and recite prayers in the tiny temple built up against the side of the wall. In that temple there is a shrine to the tutelary god of the Manchus.

As she got out of her chair, the Empress Dowager looked up at the smoke-blackened walls and saw us: a row of foreigners, watching her arrival from behind the ramparts. The eunuchs seemed to be trying to get her to move on, as it was not seemly that she should remain there in full view of everybody. But the Empress was not to be hurried, and continued to stand between two of her ladies who held her up under the arms on either side, not because she needed any support but because such is the custom in China. At last she condescended to move, but before entering the temple where the priests were all ready to begin the ceremony, she stopped once more and, looking up at us, lifted her closed hands under her chin and made a series of little bows.

The effect of this gesture was astonishing. We had all gone up on the wall in the hope of catching a glimpse of the terrible Empress, whom the West considered almost an enemy of the human race. But we had been impressed by the magnificence of the swiftly moving pageant and by the beauty of the picturesque group, by the palanquins of yellow satin flashing with gold. Something told us that the return of the Court of Peking was a turning-point in history, and in our breathless interest we forgot our resentment against the woman who was responsible for so much evil.

That little bow, and the graceful gesture of the closed hands, took us by surprise. From all along the wall there came, in answer, a spontaneous burst of applause. The Empress Dowager appeared pleased. She remained there a few moments longer, looking up and smiling.

Above her, against the winter sky, the ruins of a once noble pagoda stood out black and jagged. It had been burnt through her folly. From emplacements in its gutted base Jung Lu's cannon, on her orders, had thrown shrapnel and roundshot at some of those who now, putting down their binoculars, clapped their fur-gloved hands, waved to her, and smirked.

She stood below them like a great actress taking her curtain call with all the hazards of an awkward first night behind her: bowing to everyone and to no one, smiling a secret smile, masking her pride behind a show of humility, savouring the moment.

And there, in the centre of the stage, we must leave her, and allow the curtain to fall.

In Western writing at least the Empress Dowager has, like a great actress, assumed many guises, taken on many roles.

Chapter II

Wives and Concubines:
Pearl Buck's Fusion of Type and Individual

Pearl Buck's first book *East Wind: West Wind*, published in 1930, received critical recognition but did not create any real impact. But the publication of *The Good Earth* in 1931 caused a sensation. It won the Pulitzer Prize and in 1937 appeared as a very powerful and successful film, which in the ensuing years was seen by some 23,000,000 Americans and by an estimated 42,000,000 other people all over the world (Harold Isaacs, *Scratches on our Minds: American Images of China and India*, New York, 1958, p.158). The novel, about Chinese peasants, gave its author the Howells Medal of the American Academy of Arts and Letters and with her subsequent work led to her winning the Nobel Prize for Literature in 1938. Although Pearl Buck, a most prolific writer who wrote more than fifty books, has published works dealing with American life, she is best known for her work as an "interpreter" of the Chinese people, a role for which her background and upbringing peculiarly fitted her. As the daughter of missionary parents she grew up in China and continued to live there after her first marriage until she returned to the United States in 1935. She knew Chinese and had been taught Chinese literature and history; she translated the Chinese classic *Shia Hu Chuan* under the title *All Men Are Brothers*, a task that took her four years to complete. Though her Chinese works, especially *The Good Earth*, brought her international recognition, Pearl Buck is generally not acclaimed as a great novelist. She was severely criticized by important writers and critics at the time it was announced that she had won the Nobel Prize, just as there had been an outcry when *The Good Earth* was awarded the Pulitzer Prize. My task in this essay is not to determine Pearl Buck's place among the great or less great writers of Western literature but to focus on her presentation to Western readers of images of Chinese women. It follows, of course, that her literary techniques are of direct relevance to the success with which she conveys these images.

Pearl Buck has an explanation for her virtual neglect by American critics: "They do not know what to do with me. I don't mind. I think they are not quite sure I should be included in the field of American literature and writers. Perhaps they are right. The Asians certainly think I belong to them. Perhaps they are right, too." (Quoted by American film director Jason Lindsey in a course of lectures on the six United States winners of the Nobel prize for Literature at Kursverksamheten of Stockholm University 1964-1966.) But the irony is that Chinese people are not generally drawn to her work. Leaving aside the questions relating to ideology, there are the basic problems intrinsic to the "interpretation" of a nation and a culture by one, who, in spite of long experience and intimate knowledge, is an "alien". Such an "interpreter" too often gives in to the fashion of patronizing his/her material by investing it with a deliberate quaintness or exoticism. Fellow Americans Helen Foster Snow (Mrs Edgar Snow) and Agnes Smedley, admired her work. In the Preface to her book, *Women in Modem China*, The Hague and Paris, 1967), Helen Snow writes, "I... take this opportunity to express appreciation to Pearl S. Buck. Her writing on China has been of historic importance in helping our benighted relations with that much misunderstood nation." (p.ix)

Agnes Smedley defended Pearl Buck against "hateful people" who disliked her because of her personal life and who were disappointed that her work did not deteriorate. She writes, "Many Chinese disliked Pearl Buck's books because she did not always show her characters dressed in their Sunday best." (Agnes Smedley, *China Correspondent*, [first published as *Battle Hymn of China* in 1943], London,1984, p.165) There is a some truth in this. Those Chinese who know Pearl Buck's work would be fairly intellectual, with a knowledge of the West. Understandably they would resent the repeated presentation of the most feudal aspects of their society, their most decadent practices, women at their most abject or empty-headed; it is tantamount to having the family's dirty linen washed in public, *and* by a foreigner. Many saw, and see, this as an exploitation, and the stilted language, especially dialogue, she had adapted to suggest our alien tongue tends to add to the irritation. Pearl Buck herself realized the possible hostility from the people she was trying to depict. In her letter dated October 14, 1931 to the publisher of John Day Co., Richard Walsh, the man who was to become her second husband, she wrote,

> I have been pleased that even the most chauvinistic—and how chauvinistic we have them—have granted my sympathy with my Chinese characters. It has been a relief to me, for so many of our ardent young patriots feel that to show China as less than a heaven upon earth and a perfect state is to show dislike and unfriendliness. Well, I have been very lucky. (Quoted in Theodore F. Harris, *Pearl S. Buck, A Biography*, London, 1970, p.140)

But she was not always to be lucky in this respect. Yet, in spite of very understandable adverse criticism to her writing from the Chinese, it seems fairly safe to say that, in the work of conveying images of Chinese women—and indeed of the Chinese people, especially rural people in the early decades of the century—to the West through literature, she still has no equal. She wrote fiction, and a great deal of it, which reached a wide readership. Compared to her, other apologists for the Chinese people of her day, like Smedley, Emily Hahn, Anna Louise Strong, Helen Snow (Nym Wales), even Edgar Snow, had a much smaller readership. It must be remembered that when Pearl Buck was writing her books about China, her readership had no real image of the Chinese beyond the "Chinamen" who ran hand laundries or the gangsters involved in Mafia-style "tong" wars. The stereotypical Chinese woman was the sultry Oriental siren popularized by the media. In this connection it is instructive to read Harold Isaacs's work *Scratches on Our Minds: American Images of China and India* (Isaacs, ibid.) in which he records the impressions of American people of the Chinese. The work of writers like Bret Harte and Mark Twain contributed towards unflattering images of ludicrous or sinister "Chinks". O-lan of Pearl Buck's *The Good Earth* and her husband Wang Lung can probably be said to be the first individual Chinese characters, with whom millions of Americans—and other Westerners—were able to identify and sympathize. Yet Isaacs comments that for all her success in humanizing the Chinese peasant Pearl Buck did not create Chinese *individuals*. Reading Pearl Buck's work, one tends to have a sense of "the Chinese" in general rather than of any individual character. This is not an entirely fair assessment but has some validity for Western readers who have read—as readers of novels will—cursorily one or more of her many works on China and the Chinese with the same centres of focus. They are confronted by a whole new civilization and milieu, a whole range of alien ideas. Not surprisingly the overall picture comes as a quaint whole, peopled by beings who gradually become familiar as "types" as more novels are read. When Pearl Buck is criticized for not dealing with individuals we should perhaps remember that some images which have been fixed in the minds of Western readers as Chinese stereotypes—the suffering wife, the greedy concubine, the weak young lord, the aspiring intellectual, the grasping servant, the loyal peasant—have been translated and interpreted to a large extent by Pearl Buck herself. To Chinese readers perhaps a legitimate cause of complaint would be that the emphasis is on reactionary elements and aspects of Chinese culture. Even as she was writing her earliest novels, China was on the brink of a whole new society, but she chooses to stay mainly in the rural backwaters, with the landed gentry and the peasants in her novels. I have mentioned in the previous chapter that she tries, in an ambitious project, *Imperial Woman* (1956), to humanize the Empress Dowager, but she does not cover the whole gamut of the society of her time, at least not in the form of detailed portraiture. But within the limits of the range of types she sets herself, it would not be totally untrue to say that the "types" are recognizable as familiar by Chinese people who are already part of the heritage and culture and race of which Pearl Buck is writing. The types are to varying extents individualized.

Feminist criticism centres on "*textual* analysis necessary to determine which works are novelistically successful, and the *contextual* analyses which considers the relevance of a group of works, even if artistically flawed, as a reflection of the situation of women." (Annis Pratt, "The New Feminist Criticism*", Essay in Feminist Criticism*, Amherst, University of Massachusetts Press, 1977, p.12) From the viewpoint of the latter there is no doubt that as a whole Pearl Buck's novels on China reflect the situation of a notably large group of women at a given period of time. In this study I shall consider the accuracy with which she reflects the situation of Chinese women in the early decades of the twentieth century and the success which she attains as a creator of novelistic images through the analysis of the wives and concubines portrayed in two of her novels, *The Good Earth* and *The Pavilion of Women*.

The Good Earth was the second of Pearl Buck's novels about China (1931), just following *East Wind, West Wind*. In these early works Pearl Buck was concerned chiefly with the lives of the poor peasantry and the rich Chinese gentry, with what has been described as "China at home". (See Peter Venne, "Pearl Buck's Literary Portrait of China and the Chinese", *Fu Jen Studies*, 1968, p.72) In *The Pavilion of Women* (1946) she returns to this first theme and tells of a large old-style family of the rich gentry. But in the characterization of the central woman character Pearl Buck has certainly moved towards much more complex novelistic techniques in the portrayal of one of her most complex characters, namely Madame Wu. In each novel, as in all of Pearl Buck's Chinese novels, there occurs marriage, the begetting of children, (and usually grandchildren) and death, with in each case the correct external rituals, according to the level the characters occupy in society. Even rebellious youths, fighting against the rigorous bonds of the old order, like Wang the Tiger or the husband and brother in *East Wind: West Wind*, are still tied emotionally, if reluctantly, to the old rites and rituals which have so shaped the lives of their forebears and, indeed, their own lives. Madame Wu, in so many ways, a precursor of the emancipated woman, is, paradoxically, inexorably imprisoned by tradition, however freely her spirit and mind soar above the confines of her limited existence.

When *The Good Earth* begins, Wang Lung is among the lowest levels of society, a poor farmer dependent on the fickleness of nature for subsistence. The sense of continuity of life is reflected in the existence of his old, helpless father dependent entirely on the labours of the son. In accordance with the cycle of regeneration Wang Lung aspires to marriage and heirs. Being so very poor, he can only look as high as the slave girl of a great household. But she is to be "his woman". And even when this apparently passive, stolid woman seems to have outlived her usefulness after bearing three sons and after Wang Lung has grown rich enough to no longer need to till the fields with her working by his side, O-lan remains central to the lives of her family, and indeed to the novel. Madame Wu of *The Pavilion of Women* is drawn in the sharpest possible contrast to O-lan. Beautiful, refined, educated and cultured, from first to last there is no doubt of her complete domination of her household. She came to the lavish courts of the Wu family as a bride at the age of sixteen, and at the age of forty, still exquisite and desirable, unilaterally makes up her mind to acquire a concubine for her husband and hence freedom for herself. Throughout the novel she holds her husband, sons and daughters-in-law, servants and slaves in awe of her beauty and intelligence.

In both novels, Pearl Buck introduces one concubine in the form of a seductive self-seeking woman: the much more detailed Lotus in *The Good Earth* and the perhaps even more sharply, though sketchily, etched Jasmine in *The Pavilion of Women*. In each there is also a third figure—an unhappy concubine, timid and afraid, caught up in a feudal society in which poverty-stricken but thinking and self-respecting women have virtually no chance of ever finding self-fulfilment. In *The Good Earth* Pear Blossom, the girl slave, sold into the family in a year of famine, learns to love Wang Lung, old enough to be her grandfather, with utter and absolute devotion because he has given her the only kindness she has ever known. She at last finds peace in a nunnery. In *The Pavilion of Women* Madame Wu, wanting to make certain of her precedence, chooses as concubine a young woman—like O-lan, like Pear Blossom—sold by her family because of dire financial need and desperate for protection and shelter. And this concubine, named Ch'iu Ming by Madame Wu, is so unhappy she tries to kill herself. The pattern of repetition becomes quite clear. In the First, Second and Third Ladies of the two novels is incorporated virtually every image of Chinese woman, historical and actual, however sketchily or sharply. Traditional Chinese thought in terms of the Confucian "five relationships" (with its many subdivisions), a system of order which is responsible for political and social stability. Each person has his or her duty prescribed within this order. O-lan and Madame Wu play out their roles as daughter, wife, daughter-in-law, mother, mother-in-law, grandmother, "older sister" to concubines. O-lan is a slave in a great household when the novel opens; Madam Wu is mistress of many servants and slaves in a great household. In Lotus and Jasmine we have images of the *femme fatale*, at once the sex object and the predator, survivors in an essentially hostile world. Each relies on her instincts and wiles for her survival. Lotus, in her sensuality and crude selfishness, seems to derive some of her characteristics from the infamous Chinese beauties of Chinese history and legend. Pear Blossom and Ch'iu Ming present images of hapless young women born to be passive victims of circumstances. Sold into slavery, as so many Chinese girls were in hard times, each becomes concubine to an older man, a fate by no means uncommon in real life.

O-lan and Madam Wu, Lotus and Jasmine, Pear Blossom and Ch'iu Ming occupy parallel roles in their respective novels, as the author employs the technique of repetition. And the first, second, third ladies of *East Wind: West Wind* provide a similar pattern. And yet each in the pair is carefully delineated to different degrees, illustrating the technique of individualizing of type.

A consideration of their names may be instructive. Madame Wu is called Ai-lien; the reader is not told what the transliteration means, nor is he told the literal translation of O-lan. The suffering concubine of *The Pavilion of Women*, so poor before she came to the Wu household that she had no name, known only as "Little Orphan" when little and "Big Orphan" when older, is given a meaningful name by Madame Wu, namely Ch'iu Ming. Pearl Buck uses the transliterated form, but through Madam Wu the meaning is brought out. "I will name you Ch'iu Ming. It means Bright Autumn. In this name I set your duty clear. His is the autumn, yours the brightness." (p.73-74) But she is not known by Bright Autumn in the novel. Thus of the six women, three go by transliterated names and three by the direct translations one associates with parody and lampoon, the music hall Chinese girl: Lotus, Jasmine and Pear Blossom. Lotus and Jasmine, especially Lotus, seem indeed to be based almost entirely on caricature and over simplification. But Pear Blossom is different. She is drawn with considerable subtlety as a woman of depth and compassion and suffering. She is an exception, but it would appear that Pearl Buck's "serious" women characters are not called Precious Stream or Translucent Jade. The three daughters of Madame Liang in the novel of that name (1968) are given the names Grace, Mercy and Joy, at once Western enough and Eastern enough to suggest the fusion of the two cultures in each, not obviously literal translation enough to make them comic opera personages. And in the Western context, the Christian overtones are clear.

The Chinese regard human existence as being essentially divided into four basic aspects, namely clothing, food, shelter or accommodation and transport. The six women I am analysing are to a great extent characterized by their associations with these four basic aspects of existence. O-lan is elemental, like the good earth. In the Guangzhou dialect is a nursery rhyme that goes,

Slap your lap
and sing a mountain song
Everybody says I have no wife,
Must bestir myself and marry one;
If I have money I'll marry a delicate maid
If I have none I'll marry a pock-marked hag.

The translation is my own. We can see that wives were blatantly like chattel. Only the rich could afford the luxury of beauty. When Wang Lung requests a pretty wife, his father retorts, "What will we do with a pretty woman? We must have a woman who will tend the house and bear children as she works in the fields, and will a pretty woman do these things? She will be forever thinking about clothes to go with her face!" (p.10) The reader shares Wang Lung's first glimpse of O-lan. "The woman's hair was neat and smooth and her coat clean. He saw with an instant's disappointment that her feet were not bound." (p.18) The large feet, shod in loose cotton cloth shoes, become a source of intense irritation and reproach years later. The Western image of Oriental women, as we have seen, dating from Marco Polo's time, is one of physical attractiveness, elegance and daintiness. In 1826 Thomas Hood wrote an essay called "Fancies on a Tea-cup" which parodies Lamb's "Old China". Lamb's beloved Hyson tea is used as the name of a dainty Chinese lady. In this he refers to Hyson's "almost invisible feet".

We can see, then, that the small bound feet had by Hood's time become part of the Western image of Oriental womanhood. The barbaric practice of binding feet dates from the T'ang Dynasty. It started as a fashion copied from the T'ang Dynasty court dancers who used to perform like ballerinas on carved lotus leaves. (See H.S. Levy, *Chinese Footbinding*, New York, 1967) The practice continued especially in rural areas even after its official abolition following the 1911 Revolution. And, as seen in Pearl Buck's narration, bound feet were still admired by reactionary country folk. This attitude is also borne out by Florence Ayscough, who gives an account of her conservative maid servant, her "Amah's" lament over the disappearance of dainty bound feet. According to Amah, unbound feet are "No handsome". And she proceeded to "stamp about the room in a ridiculous way initiating the stride of a modern young woman". (*Chinese Women Yesterday and Today*, London, 1938, p.30)

O-lan is a far cry from such an image. Physically she presents a counter-image to the slender, willowy Oriental woman. In her we find the image of the passive, stolid Chinese peasant woman, inured to pain and taught by the harshness of circumstances to survive at the most elemental level. Thus she combines the images of the oppressed wife/mother/slave with that of the strong, powerful, resourceful survivor, for it is O-lan who bullies her family into survival during the terrible famine which leaves them with nothing and brings them south as refugees. The oppressed peasant woman figure is given historical treatment by Jonathan Spence in his account of a 17th Century case involving Woman Wang in *The Death of Woman Wang*. (London, 1978) The traditional roles of the Chinese wife in a peasant household are brought out when Pearl Buck writes that Wang Lung sees her as "his woman of work and the mother of his sons and who kept his house and fed him and his father and his children". (p.189) Images drawn from the land, "the good earth" from which she and her family derive sustenance are used in her descriptions.

The colours associated with her are earthen colours. "She had a square, honest face, a short, broad nose with large *black* nostrils; and her mouth was wide as a gash in her face. Her eyes were small and of a dull *black* colour… It was a face that seemed habitually silent and unspeaking as though it could not speak if it would… He saw that it was true there was not beauty of any kind in her face—a *brown*, common, patient face. But there were no pock-marks on her *dark* skin, nor was her lip split." (p.19) She bears her children much as the beasts of the field bear their young, alone and with no fuss. She continues working in the fields until Wang Lung grows too rich for such work to be seemly. "The woman and her child were as *brown* as the soil and they sat there like figures made of earth. There was the dust of the fields upon the woman's hair and upon the child's soft *black* head." (p.38) "She had always been a *dark* woman, her skin ruddy and *brown* when she worked in the fields." (p.222) And when she grows ill and is on the verge of dying "her skin was sere and *yellow*". (p.222)

In many ways she exists on the level of a beast of burden, of work, and the many animal images bring out this aspect. As a girl slave in a great house she was beaten every day "with a leather thong which had been a halter for one of the mules". (p.118) Wang Lung "was ashamed that he reproached this creature who through all these years had followed him faithfully as a dog". (p.150) When it becomes obvious to O-lan that Wang Lung is bringing a concubine into the house, O-lan becomes more unkempt than ever, and Wang Lung shouts, "Cannot I say comb out your horse's tail of hair without this trouble over it?" (p.173) She develops a "fire in her entrails", clearly a malignant growth and in all the feudal superstition and ignorance of the China of that time, sees it as something inevitable. "Her belly was a great as though with child these three years, only there was no birth. But she rose at dawn and did her work and Wang Lung saw her only as he saw the table or his chair or a tree in the court, never even so keenly as he might see one of the oxen drooping its head or a pig that would not eat." (p.211) Years later in prosperity, with four children and time on his hands Wang Lung grows restless and weary of his stolid peasant wife. In this section of the novel, when she is tracing the stages by which Wang Lung comes to take a young concubine into the house, Pearl Buck uses a technique which comes near to stream-of-consciousness. She has been describing Wang Lung's increasing distaste for his physically totally unattractive wife, this "dull and common creature, who plodded in silence without thought of how she appeared to others... He saw for the first time that her hair was rough and brown and unoiled and her face was large and flat and coarse-skinned, and her features too large altogether..." As he gazes at her in disgust she sits on a bench working on a shoe sole. Her mouth gaps open and shows "her blackened teeth" when she realizes she is being looked at. (p.149) He gazes at her with revulsion, and yet revulsion mixed with some self-reproach and guilt. He says gruffly, "I mean, cannot you buy a little oil for your hair as other women do and make yourself a new coat of black cloth? And those shoes you wear are not fit for a land proprietor's wife, such as you now are." She does not answer but only looks at him humbly, trying poignantly to hide her feet one over the other under the bench on which she sat. "It seemed to him that she was altogether hideous, but the most hideous of all were her big feet in their loose cotton cloth shoes, and she looked at them with anger so that she thrust them yet farther under the bench." (p.150) For all her stolid passivity, O-lan is given certain human—indeed feminine—feelings. She feels aggrieved when a second lady is to be brought into her house. Unlettered and deprived she is yet conscious of having fulfilled the primary duty of a feudal Chinese wife, that is, to ensure the continuance of the family line by begetting male descendents. Those who were barren or unable to give birth to a son could be legally divorced by their husbands. But, as O-lan asserts, she has done her duty. "I have borne you sons—I have borne you sons." (p.173)

The portrayal of her as a victim of oppression is perhaps nowhere as clear as in the scene of the confrontation between her and Wang Lung over the question of having her old tormentor from "the big house", Cuckoo, come to live in her own house as servant to Wang Lung's concubine, Lotus. O-lan, usually so silent and repressed, is moved to impassioned pleading. She fails to win her husband over. The description of her response reminds the reader of a tortured and anguished, yet powerless, beast.

> Then O-lan waited and when he did not speak, the hot, scanty tears welled slowly into her eyes, and she winked them to hold back the tears, and at last she took this corner of her blue apron and wiped her eyes and she said at last, 'It is a bitter thing in my own house, and I have no mother's house to go back to anywhere.' And when Wang Lung was still silent and answered nothing at all, but he sat down to his pipe and lit it, she looked at him piteously and sadly out of her strange dumb eyes that were like a beast's eyes that cannot speak, and then she went away, creeping and feeling for the door because of her tears that blinded her. (p.180)

One would hardly associate O-lan with jewels and ornaments; yet in descriptions of Chinese beauties in Chinese literature references to jewels and precious stone tend to abound. And the tendency in the Western mind is to associate jewelled splendour with the East in general since the fabulous tales of the court of the Khans. Witness the opening of Book II of Milton's *Paradise Lost*:

> High on a Throne of Royal State, which far
> Outshon the wealth of *Ormus* and of *Ind*,
> Or where the gorgeous East with richest hand

shows on her Kings Barbaric Pearl & Gold...

At the time Pearl Buck was writing translations of T'ang poetry which were gaining popularity—limited, of course, in terms of the total Western public—through the work published throughout the 1920s of Ezra Pound, Arthur Waley, Amy Lowell, Florence Ayscough and Witter Bynner. Palace ladies were associated in these poems with jewels and ornaments. In the previous chapter I have noted that in historical accounts of the Empress Dowager, for example, Princess Der-Ling's *Two Years in the Forbidden City* (London, 1912), Pearl Buck's own *Imperial Woman* (London, 1956), and, much later, Marina Warner's *The Dragon Empress*, (London, 1972), the reader is regaled by lavish descriptions of exquisite ornaments: hairpins, brooches, ear-rings of jade and pearl, turquoise and all manner of rich materials. This world of jewelled splendour and silken robes is totally alien to O-lan. Yet jewels play a part in the completion of the image of deprivation. O-lan is given a pair of gold-washed ear-rings on her wedding day by her husband. It is her only item of jewellery. The bleakness of her existence in the early years of struggles on the land makes all luxury unimaginable. But it is O-lan who makes Wang Lung's later wealth and—indirectly—dissipation possible by coming upon and seizing a store of precious stones in the confusion of looting a rich man's house. Consider Pearl Buck's description of the stones when they are taken from the peasant woman's sooty bosom and laid out in all their glory:

> There were such a heap of jewels as one had never dreamed could be together, jewels red as the inner flesh of water-melons, golden as wheat, green as young leaves in spring, clear as water trickling out of the earth... (p.129)

They are gems described through the consciousness of the peasant couple, who, not knowing their names, compare them to the earthy objects with which they are familiar. What would be incongruous in juxtaposition with the dour woman who has got hold of them, becomes part of her world through the comparisons. One incident is used by Pearl Buck to reinforce the image of oppressed and injured femininity. O-lan is allowed to keep two small white pearls, after poignant entreaty.

> I would keep them—I would not wear them... only keep them... I could hold them in my hand sometimes. (p.130)

Pearl Buck here does not rely on implication or suggestion. The deprivation and pathos of this suffering woman is explicitly stated. Hers is the yearning of a "dull and faithful creature, who had laboured all her life at some task at which she won no reward and who in the great house had seen others wearing jewels which she never even felt in her hand once". (p.130) O-lan treasures the pearls, wrapped and hidden between her breasts, until they are wrested from her by Wang Lung who wants them to placate his demanding mistress, soon to be concubine, Lotus. He argues his daughter should not have the pearls. "Why should that one wear pearls with her skin as black as earth? Pearls are for fair women!" (p.165)

As poignant and moving as any revolutionary plea for women's liberation is the image of the defeated O-lan, defeated without a real fight:

> But O-lan returned to the beating of his clothes and when tears dropped slowly and heavily from her eyes she did not put up her hand to wipe them away; only she beat the more steadily with her wooden stick upon the clothes spread over the stone. (p.166)

A very different set of images emerge in the portrait of the First Lady of *The Pavilion of Women*, which was written some fifteen years after *The Good Earth*, when Pearl Buck no longer lived in China. Madame Wu is a much more complex personality than O-lan. Peter Venne gives a brief description of Pearl Buck's achievement in characterizing Madame Wu:

> The central character of the novel, Madame Wu, might well be considered the embodiment of the author's innermost thought and wish. In delineating the physical and mental picture of this woman Pearl Buck reveals her high art of characterization; stroke by stroke the contours and colours of the portrait become complete; tactfully yet realistically the description penetrates into the subconscious depths of the heart. But the Chinese features

of the heroine which are at first clear and distinct become more and more blurred and broadly human as the story progresses and, in the end, Madame Wu becomes a mouthpiece for the philosophical reflections which obviously do not belong to her but to the author. (P. Venne, *Fu Jen Studies*, No.1, 1968, p.77)

The portrait of Madame Wu is essentially the portrait of a strong, individualistic woman who longs for freedom to pursue her own interests while tied irrevocably by the duties of wife and mother. The predicament of Madame Wu is essentially a universal, rather than a narrowly Chinese, one. But the Chinese colouring, especially in the initial stages of the portrayal, is very strong, and into the Chinese aspects of the portrait Pearl Buck has fused a number of physical images of Chinese women, all different from, indeed diametrically opposed to, the physical image presented by O-lan.

Four great Chinese beauties have established themselves from historical times. They are Hsi Shih (西施), Tiao Chan (貂蟬), Chao Chun (王昭君) and Yang Kuei-fei (楊貴妃). As I have indicated in my Chapter I, the story of Yang Kuei-fei is well-known to the main body of Chinese. And the lady Yang is possibly the best-known, relatively speaking (since the cognoscenti would be few), of the four beauties to the Western reader because of translations of the very popular T'ang poem, Po Chu-i's "Song of Everlasting Sorrow", relating as it does the story of the lady's triumphs and her tragedy. Details of her physical attributes and dress can be regarded as representative of the traditional ideal of Chinese feminine pulchritude, though contemporary Chinese ladies may regard her as being too plump. The narrator-heroine of Pearl Buck's earliest novel about China, *East Wind: West Wind*, takes pride in her traditional beauty and claims lineage from Kuei-fei. The snow white skin, white as mutton-fat jade or nephrite, is traditionally prized by the Chinese, the moth eye-brows, the gleaming jet black hair, the perfect oval face, the delicate figure traditionally regarded as indispensable to beauty are all dwelt upon by Pearl Buck in her descriptions of the apparently flawless Oriental beauty of Madame Wu. In her earlier novel, *East Wind: West Wind,* Pearl Buck seems not yet to have come to terms with the aesthetic standards of the Chinese. Her Chinese narrator is shocked by the objectivity of the aesthetic judgments of her Westernized husband, and the reader, who has been led to share her vision of herself as truly beautiful is shocked along with her into a consciousness of conflicting standards—the scented hair, the heavy powder and rouge, the heavy ornaments and the ungainly wobble of bound feet are seen through a Westernized perspective. In the more mature work, *The Pavilion of Women,* Pearl Buck assumes the standards of Chinese beauty and in the case of Madame Wu makes the reader accept these norms as universal ones: Madame Wu is exquisite. That beautiful Oriental women have found the secret of eternal youth is a myth which does have some foundation in fact. In Madam Wu we find an exemplification. At forty she looks as she did at sixteen.

The novel opens with the elaborate rituals of washing and combing and soaking with perfume and oils and the donning of exquisite garments and jewels which take place in Madame Wu's boudoir on the morning of her fortieth birthday. Nothing could be further from the drab colourless world of O-lan. "[Madame Wu] did not fear age, for age had its honours for her. She would with each year gain in dignity and in the respect of her family and friends. Nor was she afraid of losing her beauty, for she had allowed it to change with the years so subtly that it was still more apparent than her years. She no longer wore the flowering colours of her youth, but the delicacy of her face and skin were as clear now as ever against the soft silver blue and grey greens of her costumes." (p.6)

As O-lan's big feet shod in shapeless cotton shoes are objects of comment so Madame Wu's delicate narrow feet are objects of praise. In line with her zeal for "interpreting" the Chinese and their customs to her readers Pearl Buck makes the description of Madame Wu's delicate narrow feet the starting point for a discourse on the sufferings incurred by misguided ideas of feminine beauty and on attitudes, feudal and liberal, towards bound and unbound feet.

Madame Wu's feet were a little narrower than they might have been by nature.

Her mother had started to bind them when she was five, but her father, influenced by Western ideas, had unbound them on his return from travels in foreign parts. Madame Wu had been fortunate in finding a liberal family who were pleased her feet were unbound. Possibly because the custom is so alien and barbaric to the West, the bound/unbound feet motif takes on considerable significance in Pearl Buck's work, as can already be seen in Wang Lung's disgust at O-lan's big feet. The delicate embroidered slippers of Madame Wu contrast sharply with the shapeless cotton shoes of O-lan, and the bound and unbound feet of the city wife and country wife, the two daughters-in-law of O-lan in *Sons*, the second of the trilogy, *House of Earth*, (of which *The Good Earth* is the first) play a part in their characterization. We have seen the sense of oppression and deprivation brought out by the association of O-lan with jewels. *The Pavilion of Women* contains many detailed descriptions of jewelled ornaments, and the association of jewels with Madame Wu enhances her beauty, desirability and position in her household. As O-lan is seen by Wang Lung as a faithful dog, Mr Wu says to his wife, "You, pearls and jade, sandalwood and incense." Even after she has taken her decision to present him with a concubine, Mr Wu for some time still seeks her favours and remains worshipful and, in his shallow way, faithful to her. He bears her gifts in an effort to persuade her to change her mind. "I have brought you a present—flowers of jade and seed pearls and gold. I saw these yesterday, and they made me think of you." (p.120)

While O-lan is associated with the earth and the creatures of the fields and domestic hearth, apart from jewels Madame Wu is associated with flowers. Her cool elegance is symbolized throughout the book by the silver orchid. The peony is too garish for Madame Wu's liking. Through gentle manipulation she had early in her marriage inveigled her mother-in-law into replacing the peonies in the garden with orchids. "She had the finest orchid garden in the city. She spent a great deal of time in it." Pearl Buck focusses on their silver grey colour and their scentlessness, to bring out Madame Wu's own cool elegance; Pearl Buck is emphatic about the association:

> The orchid she had plucked an hour ago lay on her knee, still fresh. So quiet was she that in her presence flowers lived many hours without fading. (p.10)

> Madame Wu did not care for lotus. The flowers were too coarse and the scent was heavy. (p.7)

A great deal that is Chinese has gone into the physical delineation of Madame Wu. But, as I have indicated, Madame Wu is very much a creature of the spirit as well. What of the mental picture? Strong willed and the clear intellectual superior of her husband, Madame Wu embodies other traditional concepts and counter concepts of Chinese womanhood. Until recent times education was considered the monopoly of men. The Confucian saying "A woman without learning is virtuous" reinforced the idea that women would keep their subservient positions only if deprived of education. Attitudes and conditions were already beginning to change by the time Pearl Buck was writing. Indeed the year 1912 was a turning point. Popular interest in young women's education grew; middle schools for their use were opened by private individuals as well as by the government. In the conservative worlds of peasants and rural gentry which form the background of *The Good Earth* and *The Pavilion of Women* we do find peripheral images of educated "emancipated" women, for example Madame Wu's daughter-in-law, Ru-lan and American-returned teachers. As for Madame Wu herself, she has learned to read and write because of her liberal Westernized father. After meeting Brother Andre, the Italian renegade priest, her intellectual curiosity is awakened and her desire to broaden her horizons intensifies. It would be an exaggeration to suggest that in drawing her mental portrait Pearl Buck has drawn on the traditional Chinese image of "the woman of talent" usually in literature and/or the arts. Florence Ayscough gives a listing of such "artists" and includes the poet Li Ching-chao, the calligraphist, Wei

Fu-jen and the painter, Ma Ch'uan. But throughout the novel Pearl Buck does place a great deal of emphasis on the great intelligence of Madame Wu and her receptivity to all forms of knowledge. There does seem to be a touch of "the woman of talent" in her composition.

Madame Wu's husband speaks teasingly when he calls her "You plotter and planner of men's lives". But his remarks contains more than a grain of truth. Madame Wu constantly plots and plans, that she may order the lives of those it is her duty to take care of, so that she may ultimately achieve the freedom of spirit she longs for by being able to doff the impossible burdens of duty and responsibility which constantly weigh her down in her many roles. She is in complete control of the household and ancestral lands. Her supremacy in the household gives her a role quite opposed to that of O-lan. She presents a counter-image to the traditional one of subservience of wife to husband. And yet this counter-image of women is almost equally familiar in Chinese literature and history: what is presented is a benevolent, humanized version of the historical Empress Wu or the Empress Dowager Tz'u-hsi. The paradox is that a society which for so long held women in inferior positions has a preponderance of premier historical villains who are female. Madame Wu marries into a wealthy family and wins the esteem of her father-in-law, the Old Gentleman, and through a combination of charm and craft, gets her way. Mr Wu is generous but weak and seems patterned on the emperors whose weakness and sensuality their consorts or mothers took advantage of. Madame Wu does not lust for the sort of power that the Empress Wu or Tz'u-hsi craved. She wants power over her own body, power to order her own existence and fulfil her own potential. Seen from the eyes of traditional and indeed less traditional Chinese, Madame Wu is selfish and unamiable. Against the wishes of her entire family she jeopardizes the harmony of the household by insisting on bringing a second lady into the house. Herself so full of sensibility, she underestimates the sensibility of the second lady, Ch'iu Ming, with almost fatal consequences. Her old friend Madame Kang reproaches her for her inability to love anyone.

Pearl Buck's biographer, Theodore F. Harris, writes of *The Pavilion of Women*: "There is much autobiographical material in that book, for it is the search that a brilliant and intelligent woman makes to find her complement in a man." (Harris, ibid., p.250) Whatever Pearl Buck's attitudes and intentions with regard to her own creation, the fact remains that the reader's response to her is likely to be ambivalent and I suspect Pearl Buck did not mean Madame Wu to be unequivocally attractive as a human being. She is a complex of many diverse images of Chinese women at least on a superficial level: the willowy, delicate flower-like beauty; the woman of talent; the selfish manipulator and plotter. In the book there is the fusion of traditional Buddhist and Christian philosophies. Madame Wu takes over Brother Andre's role and becomes philanthropic patroness to a group of foundling girls. She lodges them in the family temple on the Wu estate and moves serenely among them in her pale silken robes, giving an image of the Chinese goddess of Mercy, Kuan-yin. Kuan-yin has traditionally been a favourite subject for Chinese artists and craftsmen. Westerners may well have seen the figure, with folded arms, sitting on a lotus, without knowing her identity. Pearl Buck makes a specific connection between Madame Wu and the Kuan-yin image when she describes Mr Wu's feelings about his wife. "Ch'iu Ming he did not understand. She was not as wise as Madame Wu, whom he steadfastly adored as a priest might adore the Kwanyin whom he daily served." (p.193)

By the time Pearl Buck was writing her novels about China, the Soong sisters, especially Ching-ling, wife and then young widow to the hero of the 1911 Revolution against the Manchus, Dr Sun Yat-sen, and Mei-ling, wife of the Nationalist leader, Chiang Kai-shek, had taken hold of the imagination not only of the Chinese but of Western writers in China, and indeed to some extent, the Western world. It would appear that the elegance and poise of Madame Wu owe something to the Western impression of the famous sisters. The American interest in the Soong sisters has always been particularly great because of the American links of the Soong family, from the father Charlie Soong through the sons and daughters, all of whom were educated in the United States. The interest in Mei-ling particularly during the war years, when China was an ally, was especially great. Emily Hahn was completely disarmed by their charm and became their zealous and enthusiastic chronicler. (*The Soong Sisters*, London, 1942) History has passed many differing judgments on the Soongs, from the guileless admiration of Florence Ayscough (*Chinese Women Yesterday and Today*, London, 1938, pp.113-121) to the cynical sarcasm of "Vinegar Joe" Stilwell in *The Stilwell Papers* (arranged and edited by Theodore H. White, New York, 1949) to the scathing attacks on Madame Chiang and Madame Kung in Sterling Seagrave's *The Soong Dynasty* (New York, 1985), banned in Taiwan. But the outward elegance and charm of Mei-ling and the much more unequivocally admired Ching-ling are never really in dispute. The image of poise, intelligence, grooming and social grace remains intact. Agnes Smedley writes:

> Madame Chiang Kai-shek came to town for treatment of an old back injury, and I met her for the first time in the home of one of her sisters, Madame H.H. Kung. A few foreigners had once tried to arrange a meeting between Madame Chiang and myself, but I had been unwilling to run the gauntlet which her followers had arranged for my benefit. Once her devotees were out of the way, I met her, and found her cultivated, tremendously clever, and possessed of charm and exquisite taste. She was groomed as only wealthy Chinese women can be groomed, with an elegant simplicity which, I suspect, must require a pile of money to sustain. Next to her I felt a little like one of Thurber's melancholy hounds. She was articulate, integrated, confident. As the years had made her other sister, Madame Sun Yat-sen, older and sadder, so had they increased Madame Chiang's assurance and power. (Agnes Smedley, *China Correspondent*, London, 1984, p.361)

Pearl Buck herself had occasion to meet the Chiangs and was unimpressed. She wrote to Mrs Roosevelt warning the

United States against the Kuomintang leader and the Soong clique. (B.W. Tuckman, *Stilwell and the American Experience in China, 1911-1945*, New York, 1970, p.354) But one can see how the celebrated image of Mei-ling the charmer may have contributed to her delineation of the outwardly possessed, and assured and articulate Madame Wu. Agnes Smedley's feelings of ungainliness in the presence of the delicate lady can be seen reflected in the feelings of inferiority and awkward embarrassment felt by the poor English missionary woman, Little Sister Hsia, in the presence of the ever-youthful and elegant Madame Wu.

> [Little Sister Hsia] had never, in spite of many years of living in the city, learned to be wholly at ease with the ladies. She laughed incessantly while she talked…
>
> There was something unapproachable in Madame Wu's dignity as she said this that Little Sister Hsia began to read nervously… (pp.11 & 13)

Edgar Snow's wife first met Soong Ching-ling in 1932 when she was in self-imposed exile in the French Concession in Shanghai, "holding a torch for civil liberties in total darkness". This is an extract from Helen Snow's description of the woman she describes as "the nearest to a saint that any nation has produced since Joan of Arc" at that first meeting, when she had been seven years a widow:

> And there was helplessness in her thin, nervous figure, a quality which has turned many men into Galahads for her. She was pale and delicate… but still retained much of the flower-like beauty of her youth, when she had been considered the beauty of all China. Her features were fine and perfectly formed, a very Chinese type of beauty. (Helen Foster Snow, *Women in Modem China*, The Hague, 1967, pp.117-8)

Harold Isaacs in *Re-encounters in China* (New York & Hong Kong, 1985) unashamedly admits his lifelong devotion to, and admiration of, the lady.

We can see that Pearl Buck has moved from the essentially one-dimensional characterisation of the faithful O-lan to the much more complex Madame Wu. The Chinese elements, embodied in a number of archetypes as well as a few individuals are fused with the universal. Pearl Buck translated the Chinese classic *Shui Hu Chuan* and called it *All Men Are Brothers*. May it not be that in showing a Chinese woman manifesting an educated, liberated feminine sensibility she is furthering her task of showing that in the four seas all men are brothers and all women are sisters under the skin? Outwardly self-possessed and in control of the situation, Madame Wu is not altogether unlike Jane Austen's Emma in her contradictions. The irony of Jane Austen is not in evidence in the author's narration—not on the surface level. But Madame Wu's judgment is seen to err again and again. She assumes that she is the best custodian of her family's interests once she decides to free herself from her husband's bed. She chooses a concubine. This is in line with traditional practice. "The wife always tries to insist upon the ancient right to choose her husband's concubines as well as her sons' wives. It is embedded in Chinese ethics that, if an individual places you in a position, you are eternally obligated." (Snow, ibid., p.38) Madame Wu chooses for her youngest son the daughter of her best friend, using her best subterfuge to make the match seem spontaneous. The partners turn out to be mismatched and in the end it is the young people themselves who work out a tolerable, but not ideal, solution. Madame Wu also chooses a person she assumes will be an ideal concubine: a slave girl bought by herself, docile, without a family. She assumes in her self-confidence that she knows the ways of country girls. They do not mind the sexual act with a relative stranger, as long as they have security and a place in a great household. She sadly miscalculates and Ch'iu Ming wastes away in deep unhappiness, finally attempting to take her own life in desperation. Cool and elegant and impeccably groomed and organized, Madame Wu shows fond tolerance—but her actions show a degree of condescension—for her fat, ungainly and disorganized friend Madame Kang. While Madame Wu has made up her mind to give up entirely her sexual life with her own handsome husband, Madame Kang is pregnant at over forty.

This state is considered deeply disgraceful to old fashioned Chinese. Madame Wu assumes the entire blame rests with Mr Kang, a pudgy and sloppy man. In her fastidiousness and adherence to "appearances" she also assumes her friend to be in deep unhappiness. To her surprise Madame Kang is secretly delighted with the thought of another life within her. When Madame Kang nearly dies in childbirth and is saved only by the calm skill of Madame Wu, Madame Wu is astounded to find a deep and genuine love between the unprepossessing couple, a love she would assume most incongruous, and out of keeping with their appearances and actions in general. In the outwardly slatternly Mrs Kang, Pearl Buck shows a figure capable of warmth and affection and spontaneity. And she can be seen as a foil to her cool and detached friend. Madame Wu thinks she has left behind love and passion only to find she has fallen in love with, and loves still, deeply and with great commitment—a most unlikely object, namely the dead foreign priest. While she is going through all this internal turmoil, her family and retainers ironically still look up to her as a figure of wisdom, able to deal with all the new problems and vexations in the household. Ru-lan, her second daughter-in-law, an emancipated young woman, educated and of strong opinions, cannot get along with her husband even though theirs has been a love match. Madame Wu thinks she sees the root of the problem. Ru-lan must become feminine and make herself attractive to her husband as a woman, not just as an intellectual equal. Her own maid is sent to dress Ru-lan, who is also given Madame Wu's own scented oils to use on the day appointed for her long absent husband's short visit. Madame Wu is proven right. The two are reconciled; the marriage will last—but true to the Chinese saying "Man's wishes are not equal to those of the heavens", the young husband dies almost immediately after the reconciliation in a plane crash, in the sight of his family. Thus Madame Wu's many schemes come to the same end as many of the best "schemes laid by mice and men". There is a touch of *peripetaeia*, of tragic reversal, in Madame Wu's plight, and yet Madame Wu does not emerge as a tragic figure. Pearl Buck has prevented this by putting in strongly the motifs of "learning through suffering" and growing through the power of love. The younger generation, with her support, work in the country, bringing knowledge and education to the underprivileged children and helping towards the modernization of a country then undergoing all the traumas of transition from a feudal to a modern society.

From O-lan and Madame Wu I shall move on to the self-seeking concubines of the two novels. Lotus is the "second lady" of *The Good Earth*. She is drawn almost as a caricature. Her name, Lotus, is almost archetypical for the Chinese *femme fatale* of the Western popular novel or stage presentation. We have seen that the lotus flower, at least for Madame Wu, has connotations of ostentation and lack of subtlety. Pearl Buck interpolates Madame Wu's sentiments into her narration of the events preceding Madame Wu's birthday party.

> A small oval pool lay at their feet. At its bottom a clump of water lilies was rooted. Two blue lilies floated on the surface. Madame Wu did not care for lotus. The flowers were too coarse and the scent was heavy. (p.7)

Like the flower for which she is named, Lotus is coarse and her sensuous appeal all too gross. She is working in a tea house when the newly rich and idle Wang Lung comes to while his time away. Well into middle age he can, for the first time, afford the luxury of a beautiful woman. He responds to the obvious allure of Lotus like an adolescent. The reader's first impression of Lotus is through the consciousness of Wang Lung, besotted by the sight of a woman whose beauty and delicacy he thought existed only in dreams. The picture is deliberately filled with exotic evocations of things and associations Chinese (italics my own):

> He looked at her and he saw the figure *slender as bamboo* in its tight short upper coat; he saw the small pointed face set in its painted prettiness above *the high collar* lined with white fur; he saw the round eyes, the shape of apricots, so that now at last he understood *what the story tellers meant when they sang of the apricot eyes of the beauties of old*. And for him she was not flesh and blood but the painted picture of a woman. Then she lifted that small

curling hand and put it upon his shoulder and she passed it slowly down the length of his arm, very slowly…

Then he heard laughter, light, *quick tinkling as the silver bell upon a pagoda shaking in the wind*, and a little voice like laughter said, 'Oh, and how ignorant you are, you great fellow! Shall we sit here the night through while you stare?'

And at that he seized her hand between both of his, but carefully, because it was like a fragile dry leaf, hot and dry, and he said to her imploringly and not knowing what he said, 'I do not know anything—teach me!' And she taught him. (p.160)

We have here a contrast between her apparent delicacy and fragility on the one hand and her knowing coquetry on the other. Lotus has all the characteristics of the stereotypical Chinese beauty, but Pearl Buck has added a touch which shows her personal observation of Chinese women: some do indeed have round, not narrow slanted, eyes. The foot motif, with reference to the presentation of Chinese women appears also in the portrayal of Lotus. The incredible smallness of her hands and feet hold Wang Lung enthralled.

If one had told him there were small hands like these he would not have believed it, hands so small and bones so fine and fingers so pointed with long nails stained the colour of lotus buds, deep and rosy. And if one had told him that there could be feet like these, little feet thrust into pink satin shoes no longer than a man's middle finger, and swinging childishly over the bed's edge—if anyone had told him he would not have believed it. (p.159)

Lotus in many ways is like a self-centred child, ready to throw tantrums to get her own way. The language associated with her brings this out. Her tiny feet are seen "swinging childishly" (159); her speech runs continuously, light and interspersed "with laughter like a child's". (p.161) We have seen with what difficulty and agony of the spirit O-lan is reduced to tears. But Lotus can call upon her tears at will, or throw a tantrum—like a child—to get her way, "pouting her lips" and "hanging her head away" from Wang Lung. (p.183) She is constantly nibbling on sweetmeats and other delicacies. Indeed in her portrayal Pearl Buck has included a very large number of references to, and descriptions of, material pleasures and yearnings. In particular, food is an important element of the portrait—"lichee nuts and dried honey dates and curious cakes of rice flour and nuts and red sugar, and horned fish from the sea and many other things" (p.182)—this emphasis on dainty foods providing a contrast to the simple fare provided by O-lan and concretizing Lotus's self-indulgent egotism. Legend has it that horsemen rode in relays to bring lychees fresh from the trees of the South to satisfy Yang Kuei-fei's craving for the fruit. The use of food metaphors to suggest sexual appetite is a familiar device in Western literature. Pearl Buck sinicizes the metaphor in one passage relating to what gastronomic delight Lotus will give to Wang Lung after his years of very plain fare.

> I have never seen another more beautiful and it will be as sweet as the eight-jeweled rice at a feast after your years with the thick-boned slave from the House of Hwang.

Apart from food images there are also many descriptions of Lotus's splendid silk garments, her dainty embroidered slippers and her jewels. In Pearl Buck's novels the contrast of silk and coarse cotton garments is made effective use of in the presentation of women in feudal households. When she first comes to the Wang household, she is already no longer as young as the inexperienced and besotted Wang Lung supposes. Wang's sly and worldly-wise Aunt comments,

> She is not so young as she looks, my nephew! I will dare to say this, that if she had not been on the edge of an age when men will cease soon to look at her, it is doubtful whether jade in her ears and gold in her fingers and even silk and satin would have tempted her to the house of a farmer.

Lotus has many qualities of "the other woman" in Chinese— or indeed Western—melodrama of yesterday and today. She is not given a single redeeming quality. A familiar motif in Chinese history, as we have seen, is the woman as "subverter of kingdom", one who uses her beauty as a political tool. The weak monarch would neglect affairs of state because of gross infatuation, and the lady's relatives would grow rich, powerful and corrupt. Such are the stories of Yang Kuei-fei and of the Empress Wu. But Lotus is cast in a much meaner mould. She has nothing of the subtlety or grandeur of the historical Chinese *femme fatale*. She loses her hold over even the unlettered farmer, Wang Lung, not long after becoming his concubine. The conception of her as a self-indulgent child continues into the second book of the trilogy when in her old age she has grown into a mountain of flesh but is still as greedy as ever, spending her days in gossip, gambling and, of course, eating.

The image of the grossly overweight Chinese lady is an image that occurs in Chinese literature and history. Katherine Carl (*With the Empress Dowager of China*, London, 1906) and Der-ling (*Two Years in the Forbidden City*, London, 1912) describe the tremendous amount of weight the Empress had put on and what a great to-do it was in her last years to have her carried about in a sedan chair. Lotus presents an image of a gross, self-indulgent mountain of fat in her old age. Pearl Buck also gives a comic account of the difficulties relating to getting her on to a sedan chair for Wang Lung's funeral procession. As a Manchu the Empress Dowager did not have bound feet, and for Chinese ladies like Lotus who did, their feet contributed towards their obesity as well as their clumsiness, once obese.

Chinese readers of *The Good Earth* and *Sons* may well have been displeased by the caricature of a Chinese woman presented by one hailed by their own compatriots as "an interpreter" of the Chinese people to the West. Is Pearl Buck motivated only by the desire to exploit the already established stereotypical image and—to Westerners—the "quaint" institution of concubinage which existed especially in rural areas well after its official abolition? The problem of the concubine is fundamental to the status of women, in spite of the justifications put forth by the American translator and sinophile, Florence Ayscough, echoing no doubt the sentiments of "Amah," her illiterate Chinese servant (Ayscough, ibid.), "There was not much economic justification for this institution because the monopoly of several women by the wealthy left the poor without wives, as no surplus of available wives exists." (See Helen Foster Snow, ibid., pp.51-4) In theory the First Lady had precedence over the concubine, but in practice the situation varied and too often the First lady is relegated into a position of subservience and neglect. Pearl Buck deals with the deep unhappiness of "the first wife" in a short story of that name. (*The First Wife and Other Stories*, New York, 1933) In the two novels under discussion Pearl Buck presents almost all the permutations of the "lawful wife"—concubine(s) relationships in the relationships of the six women. Lotus is totally shallow and exploitative, without any of the Confucian virtues of respect. In his biography of Pearl Buck Theodore F. Harris claims that she is interested in people, not situations: "Her people! She knew them all. They were there in her inner being, ready for her to bring them to life." (Harris, ibid., pp.136-7) Lotus is seen, then, as a type who responds to the low conditions imposed by her birth and sex in a hostile feudal society in the instinctive way of an animal seeking survival. Very much a victim of society, she learns to make use of her short-lived beauty to victimize others.

But within the framework of Confucian ethics, in death O-lan regains the precedence due to her as First Lady, and Lotus, for all her scheming, merely brings out the lack of dignity and pathos of woman's lot in those bad times: she depends on the good will of men all her life. The old Chinese saying goes: A woman must depend on a man all her life, her father, then her husband, then her son. Lotus has no son—the ultimate deprivation for the feudal Chinese woman, and lives on in the Wang household through the sufferance of O-lan's sons.

At the banquet following the presentation of the Nobel Prize to Pearl Buck in 1938, Herr Lindblad, Professor of Astronomy, had this to say, "You have taught us by your works to see those qualities of thought and feelings which bind us all together as human beings on this Earth..." Underneath the exotic trappings and rituals Lotus can be seen as the archetypical self-seeking, exploitative, small-minded woman of any culture. Pearl Buck began to read the works of Charles Dickens at the age of four. "Dickens had more influence on her writing than anyone else, she says except her mother, who required her to write something each week." (Harris, ibid., p.86) The strong streak of caricature in Dickens' characterization may have influenced Pearl Buck in her delineation of Lotus. And yet we can well imagine the impact of the shrill coquette, growing from willowy slenderness to grotesque obesity, on the millions of American readers and subsequently film-goers, only a very few of whom had any but the vaguest notions of the Oriental *femme fatale*. Here the type is given flesh and blood and set in her own milieu. What is fairly stereotypical for the Chinese reader would strike the Western reader fresh to reading about the Chinese as individual. Having presented Lotus as the self-seeking exploitative second lady in her most elemental form, Pearl Buck does not throw away the mould, but presents a version with variation, more shade and subtlety. Let us consider Jasmine of the later novel, *The Pavilion of Women*.

Jasmine is another victim of a feudal system which gives women no opportunities. Like Lotus she uses the only weapon at her disposal—her sexuality—to gain survival. The daughter of an old mother who had been a "flower" girl in her youth she "had been taught to take care of herself". (p.195) Physically she is differentiated from Lotus in that she starts off by being younger, plumper, and more genuinely childlike than the coquettish Lotus. She smiles a great deal more than Lotus and, kitten-like, wants to please. In the young Lotus, Pearl Buck wants to present a total contrast to O-lan. A great deal of emphasis is placed on her willowy figure, her ethereal face and tiny hands and feet. In the case of Jasmine, the first lady, Madame Wu is everything—and much, much more—than Lotus is physically, and has cultivation and style as well. Thus, Jasmine is the more appropriate foil with her pudgy rustic appeal. Pearl Buck specifically points out that Madame Wu feels antipathy for the type represented by Jasmine.

> Thus Madame Wu looked up and saw Jasmine. She was at the same instant aware that this was the sort of woman whom she naturally most disliked, a robust and earthy creature, coarse and passionate. She averted her eyes and felt her soul stagger between yesterday and today. Her dainty flesh shivered. (p.22)

When Jasmine first confronts the formidable First Lady of the Wu household she is reduced to a snivelling child. We see her as a frightened victimized creature who has been taught to be suspicious of a society apparently designed to exploit poor and ignorant women like herself. The following exchange is indicative of the type of treatment which has induced a cynical, exploitative nature in Jasmine, who needs to protect herself against an unsympathetic world.

'...If you come for rice and shelter, I beg you to tell me. I will promise you these. You may have them freely without having to buy them here with your body.'

Jasmine looked shrewdly at Madame Wu. 'Who gives a woman something for nothing?' she asked. 'You have never had food or shelter freely,' she murmured. 'It is hard for you to believe me.'

'I believe nobody,' Jasmine said. (pp.221-222)

Pearl Buck has made a more careful attempt to create a character more sympathetic and human than Lotus. Of course a place as Third concubine in the prestigious Wu household is much more of a prize than the position of Second lady in a farmer's home, and Jasmine has to resort to all the pathetic tricks at her disposal. But Pearl Buck shows Jasmine actually capable of a gratitude allied to love for the middle-aged "old head", the term culled from the "jargon of the street" (p.222) with which Jasmine refers to Mr Wu. She loves him because he is the only man to have treated her with consideration and a degree of gentleness. Madame Wu recognizes this love and allows her to enter the household. The scene in which this exchange takes place gives a very poignant contrast between the two women. Madame Wu is regal and composed, having happily settled her foundling children in the family temple. Jasmine's childish awkwardness is emphasized by Pearl Buck's clothes motif. The silver-grey brocaded elegance of Madame Wu is set against the gaudy satin of the aspirant concubine. The abashed Jasmine "looked down at the stones under her feet. She wished she had put on her blue cotton jacket and trousers instead of her green satin ones." (p.221) In feudal times, while Chinese women were not placed behind veils or subject to purdah, a premium was placed on modesty. The lowered eyes, the sidelong glance, subdued laughter tend to be characteristics of the Western idea of Chinese women up to recent times. In the T'ang poet, Po Chu-i's poem, "The Song of the Pipa", rather prosaically rendered as "The Song of a Guitar" by Witter Bynner, the beautiful singer comes in with her face half-hidden by her pipa. And this is described in one of the best-known lines of T'ang poetry:

> Yet we called and urged a thousand times before she started toward us,
> Still hiding half her face from behind her guitar.
> (Translated by Bynner)

In Hong Kong society today some relatively old-fashioned or ill-educated women still tend, when confronted by unfamiliar social situations to hide their faces with their hands, lower their eyes in coyness or shyness which is either natural or assumed because it is considered the "proper" way. Pearl Buck's Jasmine has been forced by circumstances to be as bold as brass. But her creator adds a poignant little touch in the detail about her handkerchief.

> She pulled out a bright red silk handkerchief out of her bosom. One end of it was fastened to a button, but she twisted the other about her fingers. (p.222)

On their second meeting -

> Jasmine pursed her red mouth and looked hard at the corner of her brightly flowered silk kerchief. One corner of it was fastened to the glass button on her left shoulder, and it hung from this like a scarf. With the kerchief she concealed her face, or she played with it when she wished not to look at the one to whom she was talking.

The gaudy colours and the fidgeting focus on the difference between Jasmine and Madame Wu. In this more mature novel Pearl Buck has created a much more sympathetic flower-house girl than Lotus. The fault, as narrative comment and dialogue indicate, lies with society and its injustices, not with Jasmine, who is, in Madame Wu's mind, "this common rosy little street girl, this creature of ignorance and earthy innocence". (p.235)

Mr Wu explicitly comments, "What opportunity has she had, after all? The story of her life is a sad one, poor child!" The figure of the concubine has evolved from the stereotypical villainess figure to a sympathetic one. If not for Westerners at least for the Chinese, the wily concubine, plotting against the legitimate wife and her children by using first sexual enticements and then any sort of intrigue, is a figure familiar in popular story and media presentations. In delineating Jasmine, Pearl Buck almost too insistently uses authorial comment to "explain" the character.

In the cases of the four women I have discussed, they each find security in marriage. In the case of Madame Wu she finds absolute control over the household. Marion J. Levy, (*The Family Revolution in Modern China*, Cambridge, 1949, pp.148,149) takes sharp issue with Pearl Buck on the question of Chinese women and attacks the "loose talk and writing about the position of Chinese women in the West. One of the most erroneous ideas so promulgated has been the idea of great security inherent in the woman's position in China." He comments that individual case where a "woman dominated her husband or son" cannot invalidate the general argument that "in the family patterns of 'traditional' China the locus of power and responsibility was overwhelmingly in the hands of the males." And yet it seems unfair for Levy to take such sharp issue with Pearl Buck on the question of security inherent in the woman's position. It is true that she presents figures like Madame Wu, Madame Kang and Madame Liang in *The Three Daughters of Madame Liang* (1968) and the mother of the narrator in *East Wind: West Wind* (1930). These hold the position of matriarch in their respective households. But O-lan, while secure in her position as "woman of work and mother of sons", by no means dominates Wang Lung. Quite the contrary. And while the harassed and suffering peasant mother in *The Mother* (1934) is secure in the headship of the household, it is only because her feckless and irresponsible husband has chosen to walk out on her, on his mother and their children. And in the portrayal of the fearful but outwardly defiant Jasmine the motif of woman's insecurity is brought out quite clearly. And this motif is certainly foregrounded in the portraits of Ch'iu Ming, second lady in *The Pavilion of Women* and Pear Blossom, third lady in *The Good Earth*. Both girls were sold as slaves when very young at a time of famine. Because girls were regarded as liabilities this was a common custom. Slavery became illegal after the 1911 Revolution, but for years afterwards and indeed during the time when Pearl Buck was writing her best-known Chinese novels it was still prevalent, since it was extremely difficult, especially in rural areas, to enforce laws against this rooted custom. In time of famine, mouths were too many. Parents sold little girls to keep them alive. O-lan is sold in a famine year and, for the sake of survival, without sentimentality, is quite prepared to sell her own daughter.

Pear Blossom comes into the Wang household in the usual way of girl slaves. She is portrayed as quite the reverse of the brassy Lotus and the earthy Jasmine, both physically and emotionally. Her name is symbolic of her pale refined beauty. Wang Lung perceives that she is "pretty and pale as a pear blossom". The child-woman image dominates, as in the case of Jasmine, but whereas Pearl Buck emphasizes the childish coltishness and impudence of Jasmine, in the portrayal of Pear Blossom she focusses on childish defenselessness and need of protection. Wang Lung's bandit cousin takes over the household for a time, and, in the hope of dissipating his destructive energies, a plan is conceived to give him a slave for his pleasure. He insists on "the little pale one who sleeps on the bed of the Mistress" (ie. Lotus). Little, pale are to be key epithets in her physical portrayal. The narration continues:

> Now this *pale* slave was called Pear Blossom and the one Wang Lung had bought in a famine year when she was small and piteous and *half-starved*, and because she was delicate always they petted her and allowed her only to help Cuckoo and do the lesser things about Lotus... (pp.237-8 – italics my own)

In one way she epitomizes one ideal of traditional feminine beauty—the Dai-yu image from *The Dream of the Red Chamber*. The very pale complexion was held highly desirable, as was "a little soft, oval face, egg-shaped, exceedingly delicate and pale, and a little pale red mouth." The paleness, the smallness are underlined to bring out the hopeless pathos of her lot. The narrative tells us that men are attracted to her physically: the notorious cousin of Wang Lung, the brooding, intense number three son and the aged Wang Lung himself. O-lan, Lotus and Pear Blossom share much the same beginnings of the most desperate poverty and insecurity. But nature and circumstances and individual dispositions impose different fates. Pear Blossom is seen as a victim throughout. She is afraid of men. It is suggested in the narrative that she might have been fed horrifying stories or gone through harrowing experiences of sexual harassment. Her repeated cry to Wang Lung is,

"Young men are not kind—they are only fierce" and "I like old men—I like old men—they are so kind." (p.248)

The relationship between Pear Blossom and Wang Lung is clearly based on a sort of Electra complex: Wang Lung's short-lived passion becomes fatherly solicitude; he constantly addresses her as "child", and she, in turn, looks up to him and loves him as the father she's never known. And, until Wang Lung's death theirs is a peaceful existence in the inner courts, just the two of them and Wang Lung's imbecile daughter, "the fool". We are almost reminded of Lear's picture of a happy imprisonment, alone with Cordelia. This is a happy resolution of a situation not unfamiliar in the China of the bad old days. Within living memory are many cases of girls barely grown to womanhood, at fifteen or sixteen, forced to be concubines of septuagenarians, the tougher surviving, the more sensitive pining away. Pear Blossom's relationship to Lotus is clearly that of an inferior; not for her the role of the supplanting favourite.

Apart from making Pear Blossom convey the image of the frightened slave girl, the girl-woman who seeks security in a union with a surrogate father, Pearl Buck also uses her character to be a vehicle for yet another traditional Chinese image, that of the "person who leaves home" for a nunnery or monastery. Nuns, both Buddhist and Taoist, though especially the former, were plentiful in feudal China. By the early twentieth century at a rough estimate there were at least a hundred thousand scattered through the provinces. Women followed the way of religion for many reasons. Poverty forced parents to give away children of both sexes to temples. Illness too played a role; parents often dedicated a sick child to a celibate life in the hope of securing their recovery; rich widows became nuns. Young girls ran away from brothels and offered themselves to a nunnery, or worn out prostitutes sought peace within convents. (See Florence Ayscough, ibid., p.89) Pear Blossom has every motivation to retreat from life. She lavishes her devotion on creatures maimed as she has been maimed emotionally by life—Wang Lung's "fool" and the hunchback son of Wang the elder. When asked by Wang Lung to poison the fool as an act of mercy once Wang Lung himself dies, Pear Blossom evokes the Buddhist abhorrence of killing any living thing when she replies,

I can scarcely kill an insect and how could I take this life? (p.254)

Through narration, description, dialogue and authorial comment, Pearl Buck presents the quintessential opposite to Lotus, and indeed to O-lan. Pear Blossom's response to the slings and arrows of life is to withdraw from life. She has no greed and, whatever her feelings for Wang the Tiger, Wang Lung's third son, she keeps them entirely hidden, even from the reader. The image of the beautiful, enticing nun would certainly be familiar to Chinese who know the story of the Empress Wu, who had to go to a convent after her widowhood, but was reprieved by her late husband's son and reinstated as Imperial Concubine. Pear Blossom is a country girl who seems never to have known laughter, a melancholy, frightened self-sacrificing woman, who is herself a sacrifice to the barbarous times. In novelistic terms she is rather a flat character.

This is not the case of Ch'iu Ming, the "feeling" concubine of *The Pavilion of Women*—a foundling, reared by her foster mother in the hope that she will grow up to be the wife of her only son, and no expense involved. Her intended husband dies in adolescence, and Ch'iu Ming, with unbound feet and the fresh prettiness of the country girl, is sold by her stepmother to Madame Wu, who has chosen her to be Mr Wu's second lady. She is chosen, as an animal might be chosen at market, with every part of her inspected in a humiliating fashion. Ch'iu Ming starts off by being disarmingly innocent, eager to please, and extremely responsive to the detached kindness shown her by the great and elegant first lady. But, she cannot love Mr Wu and the sexual act is clearly an ordeal for her. She grows pale and melancholy, and seems unhappier still after becoming pregnant. Here Ch'iu Ming is given sensitivities beyond the usual image of the sturdy country wench, happy to have found security at last and soon to be irrevocably tied to the household by begetting offspring. This is Madame Wu's concept of the stereotype: "She had taken it for a matter of course that Ch'iu Ming was a common girl, country-bred, who would welcome as a beast does the signs of its own fertility. The cow does not think of the sire, but of the calf." (p.133) Ch'iu Ming tries to hang herself from the old pomegranate tree—the detail is a picturesque "Chinese touch". In real life and in stories, Chinese concubines, supplanted by others, or intolerably treated by wives, hanged themselves, jumped into wells or swallowed earrings. Life has been too much for Ch'iu Ming, and the prospect of bringing another girl—"a foundling"—as she calls it, like herself, into the remorseless and cruel world overwhelms her with despair. Pearl Buck contrives a happy ending for Ch'iu Ming, through an almost Dickensian chain of coincidence, which includes reunion with her now well-to-do family in the north and eventually marriage to an equal partner. But the portraits of Pear Blossom and of Ch'iu Ming give new facets to the image of the concubine. Once they are in their respective households as concubines, they do not suffer from overt and blatant acts of cruelty or violence common in legend and story. Yet both are sensitive enough to respond to delicate nuances of feeling, and have generalized beyond their lot to the sadness inherent in the human condition, especially the condition of women like themselves.

Pearl Buck uses the image of a beautiful moth, which is impaled for a transient moment of selfish human pleasure and then dies, in association with Ch'iu Ming. The symbolism may seem too heavy-handed, but the surrounding images evoke a sense of Chinese-ness and the symbolism is, in its way, effective in encapsulating the fate of hapless young Chinese women like Ch'iu Ming.

The court was lit with red-paper lanterns, and these drew the moths out of the darkness. Many of them were only small gray creatures, dusty wisps. But now and again a great moth would flutter with pale green-tailed wings, or wings of black and gold. Then all the women cried out and none could rest until it was imprisoned and impaled upon the door by a pin where all could exclaim at its beauty while they sat in comfort and ate their sweetmeats. Old Lady especially enjoyed this sport and clapped her hands with pleasure...

One such moth had just been caught when Ch'iu Ming came into the court Now, as they were all looking at the new moth, she, too, went to look at it. It was of a creamy yellow colour, like the yellow of the lemon called Buddha's hand, and it had long black antennae. These quivered as it felt itself impaled. The wide wings fluttered and dark spots upon them showed green and gold for a moment. Then the moth was still. 'How quickly they die!' Ch'iu Ming said suddenly.

They all turned at the sound of her voice, and as though she had surprised herself by speaking, she shrank back, smiling her half-painful, half-shy smile (p.131)

Chapter III

Reactionaries and Revolutionaries: Agnes Smedley's Use of the Individual to Depict the Generic

Writing at roughly the same time as Pearl Buck was the American journalist Agnes Smedley. To her we are indebted for many portraits of women who, if they are mentioned at all in the work of Pearl Buck, play rather peripheral roles. I have mentioned the progressive second daughter-in-law of Madame Wu, Ru-lan. She is from Shanghai and has short hair and ideas about equality and free choice in marriage, but in the end her creator makes her win her husband back—if only for a short time—by means of such old style feminine wiles as powder and perfume and silken garments. It is only at the end of the novel that, widowed, she shows the strength and competence and confidence of the "new" Chinese woman. By contrast Agnes Smedley focuses a great deal on the new woman fighting the good fight against the shackles of a feudal society. Both Agnes Smedley (1892-1950) and Pearl Buck wished to interpret the Chinese people to the West. But the backgrounds and personalities of the two women are very different and perhaps this difference contributed in some measure to their different outlooks and approaches to the subject of China in general and Chinese women in particular. Agnes Smedley was born in rural poverty in Missouri, passed an unorthodox childhood and became famous as a writer, a participant in revolutionary movements and a vigorous feminist. She exposed prison conditions in the United States; worked to establish birth control clinics in Germany, India and China; raised funds and helped organize the Indian revolutionary movement against the British; defended Chinese writers against persecution by Chiang Kai-shek; became a war correspondent of international stature (for the *Manchester Guardian* among other papers); raised funds for Chinese war relief; nursed wounded guerrillas for the Chinese Red army; and at the end of her life fought McCarthyism in the United States. Agnes Smedley worked in and wrote about China during the years of war and revolutionary turmoil from 1928 to 1941. Smedley's autobiographical and only novel, *Daughter of Earth*, was first published in 1929. It was republished by Virago in the United Kingdom and the Feminist Press in the United States in 1973. This rescued the work from its undeserved obscurity. *Daughter of Earth* is becoming an important text in American literature courses, as well as in the newer curricula of courses in autobiography and in women's studies generally. But for some time this novel and her biography of Chu Teh were the only works readily available to Western readers. With the resurgence of American interest in China, Agnes Smedley's works on China and the Chinese gained new attention. Her *Battle Hymn of China*, first published in 1943, was republished by Pandora Press in 1984 as *China Correspondent*. More significant, from the point of view of my study, is the appearance, in 1978 of *Portraits of Chinese Women in Revolution* (ed. by Jan and Steven MacKinnon, New York: Feminist Press, 1976) which brings together in one volume most of her writing about Chinese women.

Jan and Steven Mackinnon, who contributed the introduction to the volume, have written authoritatively about women in Chinese history and about Smedley's life, especially the period in China. (e.g. "Agnes Smedley: A Working Introduction", *Bulletin of Concerned Asian Scholars*, 7, No.1, Jan.–Mar., 1975, pp.6-11) From their introduction to *Portraits of Chinese Women* we get a sense of how much Chinese history and culture Agnes Smedley was able to capture in her stories and sketches. Unlike Pearl Buck, Agnes Smedley was not a sinologist; indeed she knew very little Chinese. The bulk of her work on China, indeed the bulk of her work, is far, far less than Pearl Buck's, and her methods as a writer are far more parsimonious. But this is not to say that Agnes Smedley has been less successful in giving the West very effective, powerfully moving images of Chinese women. Agnes Smedley wrote to her publisher from the Chinese battlefront in the late thirties with a desperate plea for help in editing her manuscript. As its conclusion she wrote: "So I beg of you to help me by editing my manuscript—yet do not make it 'literary'." (Agnes Smedley, *China Fights Back*, London: Victor Gollancz Ltd., 1938, Forward, p.14) The term "literary" is, of course, difficult to define. Agnes Smedley, with her identification with the ordinary people, probably disparaged an emphasis on "the literary" because of its associations with "style", which she saw as related to class privileges. What mattered to her principally was "content". But it would certainly be wrong to conclude that her work as a consequence had no "literary" merits. Agnes Smedley was a careful writer. Her writing about Chinese women suggests that she experimented with different forms and methods, and deepened her craft as a writer as well as her political convictions during her years in China.

It becomes clear even to the most undiscerning reader that Agnes Smedley was writing with a strong political purpose—to arouse sympathy for the Chinese cause. As she herself wrote on her return to the United States, "I was hoping to be able to tell Americans about the way Chinese lived and how they fought for freedom. I had become a part of the vast struggle of China." (*China Correspondent*, p.363) It may be suggested that her role as a partisan put her objectivity at risk. Her work reflects clearly what she was: a feminist of a working class background living in China during a decade of revolution. Her images of Chinese women are images of women caught between tradition and change. Harold Isaacs, who at one stage was a fellow traveller in her early days in China, has written of her,

> Agnes Smedley seemed to see people as poster-figures, nearly as cartoon caricatures, often puppets pulled by the strings of class forces, playing out a harsh morality play in which the 'good' were pitted against the 'wicked'. (*Re-encounters in China*, New York and Hong Kong, 1985, p.62)

While this is not an entirely fair appraisal, we can see something of this simplicity of vision reflected in her images of Chinese revolutionaries or Chinese reactionaries. After reading her work we may well be left with isolated images of Chinese women either blindly oblivious of changes and clinging to a feudal and outmoded way of life, or eager young revolutionaries courageously fighting and often sacrificing everything, including their lives, in a struggle to break away from tradition-bound existences. Her work contains many sharply-etched isolated vignettes of women at war or in states of desperation and heroism. She tells of these women through stories and reportage. Most were first published in newspapers and news magazines. Agnes Smedley arrived in China in time to become the close friend and admirer of the Chinese writer Lu Hsun during his last years. Lu Hsun is often called "The Father of Modern Chinese literature"; like Smedley he was a self-taught writer. By the time she came to know him he was a political activist and the author of three volumes of short stories, written mostly between 1919 and 1926. Smedley helped to translate his stories, lived for a time with his family and worked with him on several other literary projects. Like Lu Hsun, Smedley was "tortured always by... inequality". (*China Fights Back*, p.31) Lu Hsun's stories cover a broad range of Chinese people, but the focus is on the unfortunate, the helpless victim. There is little hope in his stories, only a sense of remarkable endurance, with few indications of a struggle for change though there are occasional glimpses of consciousness from a narrator or character. Agnes Smedley had a much more clearly active political movement about which to write and with which to identify. While Lu Hsun gives only glimmers of hope for a better future, Smedley focusses on the idea of courage and hope for a new society purged of the evil reactionary past. In "The Dedicated", the heroine, Chang Siao-hung at the conclusion of her monologue, asserts confidently,

> You wished to know the role I play in China. It is enough to say that I am a communist for that means I am fighting in the ranks for a new world. It means that I may one day cease to appear on this

stage of historical events—but it means also that all that I work for now will be carried to fruition by the revolution of which I am but a part. (*Chinese Destinies*, New York: the Vanguard Press, 1933,p.89)

Her vision of Chinese women remains that of the outsider, albeit a deeply sympathetic, indeed passionately committed and partisan, outsider. She writes in "Mining Families" (from *China Fights Back*) that she is not and can never be one of the miners and that she is "nothing but a writer, a mere onlooker". "What I write is not the essence of the Chinese struggle for liberation. It is the record of an observer", albeit one who suffered, sorrowed and struggled with the people whose cause she had adopted, especially the women who were struggling to free themselves from the Old China which bound their feet and killed their daughters.

Her first purpose was to tell the world, especially her own compatriots, "the truth about China". She concludes *Battle Hymn to China* thus:

I had vowed by everything that I believed not to forget [the] words [of a Chinese General]: 'Tell your countrymen… Tell your countrymen…' (*China Correspondent*, p-365)

In order to achieve this she has to use strokes which may first suggest a lack of subtlety. I have noted that she aroused scepticism as well as sympathy in Harold Isaacs because he felt that she saw her Chinese characters as puppets in a morality play. Smedley does indeed sometimes oversimplify "good" and "evil"; "good" is seen usually as anything relating to change and revolution, evil to the forces of reaction. It is the case with morality play figures that the more carefully drawn the character the less clear the moral message. Edmund Spenser's Una in the Elizabethan epic poem *The Faerie Queene*, for example, can be seen more clearly by readers as a symbol of Truth, or True Church than can, for example, Isabella in Shakespeare's *Measure for Measure*, with all her ambivalent, more "human" qualities, be seen as a symbol of Truth or Mercy or any other abstraction. Smedley sometimes operates on the level of stylizing and simplifying. In Pearl Buck we have seen the simplification of the stereotypical wicked, conniving and greedy concubine in the character of Lotus. There are a good number of one-dimensional figures in Smedley, some functioning as central figures in her sketches and stories, more occupying the background of her vision of Chinese humanity, caught in work which is a mixture of autobiography, travel narrative, war reporting and social observation. In the insistence on characters who are totally "good" and totally "bad" the reader is reminded of the stylizations of Peking opera, where make-up, costumes and gestures proclaim the moral status of characters. The same is true of traditional Cantonese opera, and indeed of Cantonese soap opera in the recent past. Characters were either "evil", "treacherous" or "loyal", "good". An outstanding example can be found in "The Story of Kwei-chu" in which the father is unspeakably cruel and unrelenting to both the hapless daughter-in-law and Kwei-chu. The inhuman cruelty of the old man gives Smedley the passionate feminist and fighter for liberty the opportunity to expose and dwell, for her Western readers, on the incomparably wretched lot of women, sent into alien, often hostile and ignorant families, into a lifetime of slavery and child-bearing. Liang Shiang, Kwei-chu's wife, is an extreme case of such victimization. The following quotation from the story will help to illustrate my point about the villainy of the father. It incidentally illustrates the effectiveness of Smedley's matter-of-fact style spiked with the ironical turn of phrase—"this honourable pursuit":

> He found his father in the shop filling boxes with little cakes. The old man would fill the bottom with small, bad, ugly cakes and then cover them all with a nice layer of big round fresh ones. The peasants were simple and honest folk and they would not know the difference until they got home. The old man paused in this honourable pursuit to listen to his son's request for a conversation. Kwei began in a respectful manner, saying that Lian Shiang was becoming thin and ill from overwork, insufficient food, and bad treatment. He asked that this cease. His father's only answer was to turn angrily and leave the shop without a word. That his son should appeal for his own wife filled him with disgust. (*Chinese Destinies*, p.148)

Dickensian in its almost caricature effects, the detailed portrayal of the father paradoxically sets into relief the shadowy image of the mother—generic, passive, suffering wife. She is not described except in the sketchiest possible way. Indeed specific reference to her occurs only on three occasions, each time in relation to either her husband or her son. Agnes Smedley brings out the passivity and helplessness of feudal women in arranged marriages in the midst of a physical description of the father:

> Despite his long nose that everybody said meant riches for a man and that had been the chief inducement when his wife's parents chose him as a son-in-law, he had not become rich (ibid., p.147)

She goes on to describe the avaricious, although unsuccessful, man's hopes that his son should become an astute businessman, then comments, "But Kwei was much like his gentle little mother". This "gentle little" woman remains in the background, presumably a passively acquiescing witness to the incredible treatment of her daughter-in-law. She is referred to once more only, when her son returns from Japan, and is beaten unconscious for lack of filial piety by his father. "When Kwei came to consciousness, the sad tearstained face of his gentle mother was bending over him." (ibid., p.153) *Gentle, little*—and helpless. The lack of light and shade, the deliberately matter-of-fact approach to story telling serves her purpose of "socializing reality" well. But it would be wrong to assume that Agnes Smedley limits herself to one method of telling her people about the Chinese. It is true that she was to a large extent concerned with the generic, of giving a sense of the effect of the pull between reaction and change on different types and classes of Chinese people. This clash of the old and the new in this historically very significant period of transition is the motif which ties together her portraits—and here I am interested in her portraits of Chinese women in particular.

Agnes Smedley was fascinated by the life of the peasant general Chu Teh. She worked on his biography even after she had left China, during the last period of her life in the United States. The biography was published posthumously.

Her avowed motive for writing about Chu Teh throws light on Smedley's interest in depicting the generic. Her interviews with Chu Teh took place at or near the front during the mid-thirties. She tells him that she wants to relate the story of his life because "you are a peasant. Eight out of every ten living Chinese are peasants. Not one has ever told his story to the world." (*The Great Road*, New York: Monthly Review Press, 1956, p.xi) Chu Teh, the individual, is interesting because he can represent the generic. In her stories written about Chinese women, indeed in all the stories written during her years in China, we can see the interplay of the individual and the generic. In some stories the individual is sacrificed and in others it is highlighted. I have chosen five stories from Smedley's *Chinese Destinies* to discuss Smedley's effort to work out a compromise between individualizing and generalizing. I have also chosen these stories because they collectively present a spectrum of images of many different classes and persuasions of Chinese women. The five are "Hsu Mei-Ling", "Shan-Fei, Communist", "The Dedicated", "The Martyr's Widow" and "Some Women of Mukden". Both in terms of content and treatment these five stories stand out in any collection of Agnes Smedley's work on Chinese women. "Hsu Mei-Ling", "Shan-Fei" and "The Martyr's Widow" show an emphasis on individualizing while "The Dedicated" and "Some Women of Mukden" focus on the generic. Indeed we can see "Hsu Mei-Ling" and "Some Women" as representing two poles in terms of presentation. In the former the heroine is totally, poignantly individualized while in the latter the women are not individualized at all but presented as samples of types. And yet, while Hsu Mei-ling is carefully depicted as an individual, Agnes Smedley does not lose her opportunities to use the individual suffering of women to bring out the "moral" of the story, the generic problems caused by the clash of the "old-fashioned" with the "modern". Characters like Hsu Mei-ling and Hwa-chuan, the "martyr's widow", are endowed with much more interest as individuals than the usual morality play figures.

I have noted that Smedley disdained "literary" methods and yet "Hsu Mei-Ling" exhibits the very conscious stylistic effects of the "literary" artist. She adopts the stance of the omniscient narrator who is also a participant in the action at crucial points of the story. In this particular story, while essentially maintaining the "spare" outline used by traditional Chinese story-tellers Smedley infuses a great deal of detail into the description of the heroine. The empty-headed husband, on the other hand, remains a cardboard figure, a target of mockery, effectively representing the blind and misguided worshipper of "modernity" and America, of whom there were so many in China of the thirties. Smedley deliberately opens the story with an unqualified generalization. "Hsu Mei-ling was an *old-fashioned* girl, with the faults and virtues of an *old-fashioned* girl. She was brought up in the *old-fashioned* way—taught reading, painting and embroidery on silk, household management, and how to write beautiful characters." (*Chinese Destinies*, p.9 – italics in this and following quotes my own) *Old-fashioned* is repeated three times in this short paragraph. It becomes one of two key words in the story. The other is *modern*. The two words are played against each other with increasing irony. The coming of Westernization to China had claimed many victims and called for a reassessment of terms like *modern* and *old-fashioned*.

[Mei-ling's] husband graduated from an American mission school and then a mission college. He is one of the worshippers of *modernity* which he confuses with Americanism. He knows American songs, history and literature, and he can write better English than Chinese. He speaks English through his nose... He is a clerk in a bank in Shanghai. For some insane reason he moved Mei-ling and the children also from the interior to Shanghai, and he set about to make them as *modern* as himself.

The old rambling Chinese houses with their coloured tiled roofs, their lovely filigree windows... he regarded as symbols of things to be destroyed. He is a *modern* man. So he rented a small, *modern* flat where the windows are very square and the walls very blank and white...

Mei-ling moves about this strange ugly flat like a ghost over some long-forgotten Chinese battlefield. She is *old-fashioned*, loving the old things of China. Her whole being breathes the reserve, the dignity and the composure of the *old-fashioned* girl…

Her husband talks *modernity* night and day. (ibid., pp.10-11)

Ironically it is her very old-fashioned attitude to the role of the wife that leads her to become "modern"—by listening to jazz records, going to the cinema, by finally trying to dress in the modern style and to dance on her poor bound feet in the Western fashion. The narrator interposes with the rhetorical question:

…and is it not a virtue for the wife always to bow to the will of the husband? (p.11)

The husband is so modern that he wants to "put away" Mei-Ling because she is "ignorant and old-fashioned" and he wants to replace her with a *"modern"* Russian girl. The narrator as participant counters with the terse but very telling remark,

"To put her away is *old-fashioned*." (p.12)

The husband is indeed a pasteboard figure "as modern and as empty as most clerks". The Russian "other woman" is not individualized either. "She is a doll-faced, curly-haired dancing girl in a Shanghai night cafe," an "empty-headed dancing girl for an empty-headed husband". But for all the stereotypical ingredients of the story, the figure of Hsu Mei-ling is so poignantly drawn that here we can see how, through individualizing, Smedley has no less generalized and written a tale with a clear "moral" but by no means clear solutions. The vision that is presented is not a simplistic one. Betterment is not repudiation of everything simply on the grounds that it is old. In Agnes Smedley's telling of the story of Hsu Mei-ling we have a refutation of Isaacs's charge that she sees people *only* as caricatures. Smedley's sympathies are clearly on the side of Mei-ling and certainly at least some old-fashioned virtues. Mei-ling's physical description is fairly stereotypical, embodying most of the qualities of the traditional Chinese beauty—the delicate fair skin, the glossy black hair, slender body and graceful demeanour. "Her whole being breathes the dignity and composure of the old-fashioned girl." And Smedley, like so many other Western writers about Chinese women, makes capital of Mei-ling's bound feet, imposed upon her by a decadent feudal society. This, and the arranged marriage and the clearly subservient role of the wife who can be "put away" at the convenience of the husband, are all part of the general plight of women living in that society. But that society is trembling on the verge of change, and this makes the plight of Mei-ling unique to her time and setting. "The Shanghai setting has come upon her like a disaster." Her background and upbringing, while imbuing her with dignity and composure, have also made her "ignorant, superstitious and suspicious, and [she] understands only one relationship between men and women".

The very "virtues" which have been inculcated in her make her unable to adapt to the superficial "Americanization" which her husband wants. In her description of Hsu Mei-ling's fastidiousness and revulsion at the frequent pictures in cinemas of "foreign women" in low-necked gowns embracing men and kissing them shamelessly, Smedley makes Western sexual mores the butt of her satire. Smedley's choice of adjectives in connection with people and objects considered by the husband to be "modern" contrast strongly with the adjectives used to describe much of what he considers old-fashioned.

Cheap furniture, *gaudily coloured* prints, *blank* walls; *empty-headed* dancing girl contrast with *delicate*, fair skin; *glossy* black hair; *sweet-smelling* blossoms; *slender* body; *lovely* filigree windows; *delicate* pines; *black and penetrating* eyes; *graceful* gown. Little details add to the poignancy of Mei-ling's plight. She is in the unusual position—for Chinese women of those days—of being all of five years older than her husband. Parents did often overlook age differences in arranging suitable marriages, but with all the feudal emphasis on a women's youth, Hsu Mei-ling's position is indeed much more difficult. Smedley brings this out directly.

'Hsu Mei-ling is jealous;' laughing knowingly. 'She is an old-fashioned girl. She is also old.' For in China people still think of a girl of thirty as old.

—"like old tea leaves," as the old saying goes. If what Hsu Mei-ling does makes her appear a fool—"a miserable woman trying to compete with an empty-headed dancing girl for an empty-headed husband"—Smedley's account of her attempt to mimic all that is alien and unattractive to her nature is a poignant and heart-rending appeal on behalf of all enslaved and dependent women. Agnes Smedley's technique depends a great deal on restraint. In "Hsu Mei-Ling" she is rather less parsimonious than usual. The last scene in the story when Mei-ling asks the narrator to teach her to dance is detailed and extremely moving; it concludes thus:

> But to dance there must be joy in the heart and the feet must be elastic, and light. And Mei-ling's heart was as heavy as lead and her feet had been crippled while she was still a child. After taking a few lame steps she stopped suddenly in the middle of the floor and wept like a little girl, holding the sleeve of her gown before her face. Two of the children stood in the doorway watching their mother. Their eyes were big with wonder. Behind us the phonograph yelped out:
>
> 'was in November and my heart was full of vodka
> Yup! Alay Yup! -
> That's when I'm thinking of you, Sonya!'

The portraits of the women in "Some Women of Mukden" are much more sparsely sketched. Apart from the first portrait, of the wife of Li Shing-jen, the other portraits are of women deliberately unnamed; their function as representative figures is thus underlined. In "Hsu Mei-Ling" the interest is focussed on the individual suffering woman and from her the readers' attention is broadened to suffering Chinese womanhood; in "Some Women" the canvas is widened, to encompass virtually a full range of types and classes, with the images sharpened by the fact of their having as a backdrop Mukden in the thirties, the feudal past encapsulated within the great Manchu walls.

> The world beyond seems... distant
> ... And it is, for many decades of thought and action lie between Chinese Mukden and the outside world. (p.198)

Among the women Smedley writes about is another old-fashioned, long-suffering wife. She is much older than Hsu Mei-ling; she has long ceased to try as Hsu Mei-ling tries. Her story is told only in the sketchiest way; she represents the thousands upon thousands of suffering wives. An O-lan without her individual feisty qualities, just another "Little old-fashioned Chinese lady". She is now old, worn out and ugly, and her husband is planning to buy a sing-song girl of sixteen to bring home as his concubine. All familiar enough. But Agnes Smedley is also concerned with the sense of hope in the new generation and the new revolutionary ideas. She introduces the rebellious son, who frightens his father into not bringing home a second wife. Here we have the story of Kwei-chu in embryonic form, but here the note is optimistic. The son wins in the battle against the father because right is on his side, and, "these are the glorious days of sedition in many fields". And indeed in this collection of vignettes Smedley tries to prove her point that "some women are passive and some are not". The sing-song girl and the stereotypical suffering wife are passive, but many of the women depicted are otherwise. And even that old lady is shown to be an intelligent being, deprived by society of her due.

> Her eyes are very bright and intelligent and she sits for hours asking questions about women of other lands. They are intelligent questions, such as intelligent women anywhere might ask… (p.200)

It is almost as if this portrait supplements the very terse delineation of Kwei-chu's mother.

Other women depicted in this piece have not allowed their potential to be wasted. The wife of the revolutionary Li Shing-jen is only drawn in outline, but the brief descriptions of her appearance and demeanour suggest the depiction of an individual by an observant reporter. The woman is described as beautiful by the narrator, but she is, by no means beautiful according to conventional Chinese norms, as indicated by the initial reaction of a Chinese student :

No, she is not beautiful ... Yes, she is ... but not the usual kind of beauty.

But there is no attempt to deal with the individual. The Western reader is made aware of a breed of cultivated, intelligent Chinese women, of the corruption surrounding her and of her deep sensitivity to the political realities of the times. But this is just another fleeting "image", deliberately not gone into beyond the generic.

Perhaps the following account is a particularly succinct summing up of Agnes Smedley's use of generalizing techniques to give a broad perspective of the "new" Chinese women. First a distance shot of the women students striding purposefully and confidently through the streets, the ease and breadth of their strides gaining the more point against the background of years of foot-binding for Chinese women.

> And now and then two or three modern girls swing past, their hair cut short, their hands in their pockets. It is easy to see that they are students, free of gait and manner, self-confident and proud. (ibid., p.203)

Then the focus zooms in on a pair of representative women—representative of the old and the new, standing side by side in a period of transition. No time is specified—Smedley just writes "Once"—because the specific time is irrelevant; the names of the women would be equally irrelevant.

> Once in a tramway a student girl dressed in the usual blue cotton tunic got in with an older woman. Clearly they were mother and daughter. Many decades lay between them. The mother had bound feet and long hair done into a roll at the back of the neck. The daughter was as strong and as tall as a northern Chinese man, with short hair, natural feet, and an intelligent face...
>
> The girl grasped the wooden rod above with one hand and supported her old mother with the other. The only person in the whole car of fifty or more men to arise and offer a seat to the old lady was a young man who, by his dress, was obviously a student. The old lady was surprised into an outburst of gratitude. The other men passengers watched the student in amusement, spat,

and laughed outright that a man should be so weak. He and the tall girl both turned on them with a look of withering scorn. Two of them—amongst fifty. The percentage is too low for south China, but far too high for Manchuria. (ibid., p.203)

Images of change, male and female, pitted against the forces of reaction. They are mainly important as indications of that change, and in the last sentence become a percentage, a statistic of hope for the future. And yet, as I have said before, the reader should think twice before relegating Agnes Smedley's work to the category of partisan propaganda. She wants to show in general terms the resentment and frustration of poor and foot-bound women. But there is intensity and memorable individuality in the portrait of the "miserable-looking foot-bound peasant women refugees from the Shangtung famine" included among "Some Women of Mukden". The graphic description of her sprawled out on the icy street, bracing herself with her hands and using the only weapon at her disposal against the heartless, laughing crowd—violent cursing—ranks as a "literary" gem. Agnes Smedley draws a general truth from this apparently insignificant incident—"Some women are passive and some are not." There are, to Smedley, all sorts of ways of showing resistance. A happy blending of the "moral" and the incident.

When we consider the general Western view of the Chinese in Agnes Smedley's time, these pictures of different and *human* types of Chinese women go a long way towards helping to remove unjust preconceptions and biases. It is a pity that Agnes Smedley's work on China reached—and still reaches—such a relatively small readership, because, in its way, it fills in the gaps left by Pearl Buck in providing a more complete picture of Chinese women in pre-World War II China. I have referred to the very informative work of Harold Isaacs on the subject of American attitudes to the Chinese in the first decades of this century. A little known book, which has appeared recently, throws light on the vague and distorted view held by the ordinary provincial English person. This is an autobiography of an English woman who married a Chinese engineer in

England and then returned to China with him on the eve of the Sino-Japanese War. Esther Holland Jian in *British Girl–Chinese Wife* (Beijing, 1985) relates her youthful impressions of the Chinese, before she came to know her husband-to-be. She refused to go near a group of Chinese students. She told her friend, "'I am afraid of the Chinese," and relates her feelings at the time: "Stories of Chinese hiding knives in their long sleeves and scratching people's eye out with their long nails suddenly came to my mind. Though I didn't believe them as I had when I was young, I was still prejudiced." (p.11)

As individualized, sympathetic portraits of Chinese women, the delineation of Shan-fei and of Chang Siao-hung, the heroine of "The Dedicated", are deliberately general, but for Western readers unfamiliar with images of Chinese women other than that of either the passive, empty-headed inferior or the manipulative dragon lady, the portrayal of two such dedicated, active and heroic figures is indeed a departure. However a reader might discount the "realism" of the figures because of political biases, he or she must at least give Smedley her due in that she has produced portraits of intelligent, thinking, feeling Chinese women who are worlds away from the painted dolls in the typical Western imagination, especially in the 30s. Chang Siao-hung is the more generalized of the two characters, and Smedley has adopted very deliberately a stylized technique to give her the stature of a symbol; the epitome of the revolutionary spirit which is overtaking China and which is bound to break the feudal shackles of the past. She is given a local habitation—Hong Kong—and a name. But the very opening of the story gives notice of the author's generic motives:

> Across the great historical stage on which the Chinese revolution is being played, appears and reappears the figure of a woman.
>
> At first the figure looks delicate and the hands as frail as those of a child; but when one sees more clearly, the slender body, of a little more than ordinary height, looks tough and wiry and the hands but thin from constant labour. The hair, smooth and black as a soft summer's night, is sometimes closely cropped close like a boy's, sometimes grown longer and clasped at the nape of the

neck in a narrow brooch of green. At times the figure is clad in the uniform of a soldier, at other times in the faded cotton trousers and jacket of a woman of the masses; and at still other times in the elegant silk gown of a lady of the ruling classes... (*Chinese Destinies*, p.68)

She then focusses on a figure, and the figure is allowed to speak for herself. Here Smedley is using the monologue technique of old feudal Chinese drama, in which actors step forward to explain what role they are playing. The story as a work of art suffers from this technique. Dialogue meant to suggest an alien tongue is always difficult, as I shall discuss in a subsequent chapter, and the stilted style adopted for her purposes is used as the vehicle for a narrative not only of Chang Siao-hung's personal history but of the history of China from the turn of the twentieth century. Smedley, through Siao-hung, speaks of the old Chinese women stereotypes such as we encounter endlessly in Pearl Buck, such as the idle and greedy matriarch, and the hapless slave girls. The story of Shan-fei runs on almost parallel lines in that both Siao-hung and Shan-fei are rich and privileged girls who yet are fired with a great and passionate conviction that there is a need for change. Shan-fei's mother, unlike Siao-hung's family, understands, aids and abets Shan-fei in her attempts to be free. Both Siao-hung and Shan-fei marry peasant revolutionaries who die for the cause they believe in. "Shan-Fei, Communist" is perhaps the more effective piece of literary writing in that the third person narrative is terser and better structured, not hampered by many digressions into history and overt political comments. Possibly the significance of these two pieces in relation to the presentation of Chinese women is that, while on the one hand Smedley's writing suggests there are class stereotypes, in these two portraits she shows that Chinese women of the upper classes are also capable of compassion and feeling. Of Siao-hung, she writes,

> The face belies the costume [that of a woman of the ruling classes].
> For here is none of the expressionless doll-like beauty, or the cold

> passive indifference, or any of the calculating selfishness or cruelty
> that characterize the faces of women of the ruling classes. (ibid.,
> p.68)

If we look for nuances of characterization and individualizing details, then we would be disappointed. The partisan is more in evidence than the literary artist. And yet in the very lack of individualizing Agnes Smedley gains a universality which creates the effect of one great sisterhood of thinking and dedicated women which knows no barriers of race. Consider the very effective ending of "Shan-Fei, Communist", which enforces the sense of the commonality of "the daughters of earth", in spite of physical distinctiveness.

> Shan-fei is twenty-five years of age. Her skin is dark and her
> face broad; her cheek bones are high. Her eyes are as black as
> midnight, but they glisten and seem to see through a darkness
> that is darker than the midnight in China. She is squarely built
> like a peasant and it seems that it would be very difficult to
> push her off the earth—so elemental is she, so firmly rooted
> to the earth. Beautiful? I do not know—is the earth beautiful?
> (ibid., p.42)

I do not think that any account of Agnes Smedley as a literary artist should be without a reference to "The Martyr's Widow". While "Shan-Fei, Communist" and "The Dedicated" give the impression of the partisan more than the literary artist, "The Martyr's Widow" shows the literary artist at work and the story has a distinctive appeal based on care in construction and style. It is far beyond journalism or propaganda. The setting and the details are precisely and accurately given. The physical attributes of the characters are decidedly Chinese. Dates—for example "May 30, 1925, when the news of the Shanghai massacre flashed through all China"—give a sense of historical perspective. And yet the folly and foibles of the anti-heroine, the martyr's widow, Hwa-chuan, are characteristic of the stereotypical vain, self-centred woman so often found in anti-feminist literature of the West as well as of the East. The techniques used to delineate her and to reflect the corruption of her times through her, show Agnes Smedley the ironist at her best. With more venom but with the same sort of apparent detachment as Chaucer, Smedley the feminist paradoxically uses an antifeminist viewpoint to show how attitudes of women contaminated by conventional values have to change. The story opens with Deng Yin-chiu, Hwa-chuan's husband, sitting in prison awaiting death, which is certain unless Hwa-chuan raises thirty thousand dollars to save him. The use of the flashback is to accentuate the irony, in which indeed the whole story is steeped. Deng is certain his wife will come through,

> He had glowed with joy and sat waiting for the consummation of her promise. (ibid., p.237)

Then we return to the past, the beginning of their marriage, and this description of Hwa-chuan: "She was short of stature, fair of skin, and with small eyes. Hers was a dead stupid beauty, like the face of a doll. She worked hard to preserve a certain prettiness" gives her a degree of particularity. Smedley sets this beauty against the more stereotypical Chinese beauty of Deng's father's concubine who had seduced and totally dominated him, and Smedley shows that Chinese feminine beauty has more than one form. "[The] first woman had been tall and slender, with long black eyes that could burn with passion when he held her to him. Her body had been like a slender bamboo swaying in the breeze, responding to every breath of his desire." The first woman is as silent as Hwa-chuan is garrulous. Here Smedley cannot resist an ironical feminist comment on the sexist point of view Deng has been conditioned to believe in:

> He could recall nothing she had ever said—but then women are supposed to have nothing to say. She was the beginning and the end of his expectation from woman. (ibid., p.238)

In the rest of the story a great deal of the narrator's irony is directed towards Hua-chuan but much of it also at the decadence and the hypocrisy of the so-called "revolutionary" regime. After Deng's execution "the Kuomintang was purified of everyone but the militarists, the landlords and their intellectual apologists. Many of Deng's friends led the lives of hunted animals". The new militarist claimed Deng as one of the "martyrs" and Hwa-chuan, the chief betrayer of Deng, reaps the benefits of his martyrdom.

> Hwa-chuan, the widow, became known as the true and faithful wife of a revolutionary, as a woman who had stood like a rock by the side of her husband aiding him in all his work... Officials called upon her, she was showered with presents and attention. She was asked to honour the government with her presence—to continue Deng's work where he had left it. (ibid., p.247)

In Hwa-chuan's presentation Smedley focusses on the universal, not just Chinese, archetype of the *femme fatale* who uses her sexual charms as a means to obtain political power. We have seen that the association between the *femme fatale* and political power is particularly marked in Chinese history and literature. The power which Hwa-chuan ultimately secures through the familiar pattern of coaxing and sexual teasing of a besotted old man is certainly nothing compared to the power of an Empress Wu. Her methods are virtually a parody of such high-level manipulations as those of Wu Chao or Tz'u-hsi; she uses lies, slander, tears, cajoling, taunts to rid herself of all who stand in the way, including the official's old wife, "mother of his ten children", of "a modern marriage to an old Kuomintang member", "by name Fu Kwang-chuang... so rich that Hwa-chuan's heart almost ceased beating when she thought of him". In telling the story of her rise through the exploitation of her husband's martyrdom, a martyrdom she brought about by her refusal to pay the ransom demanded, Agnes Smedley is unsparing in her irony, directed not just against Hwa-chuan, the besotted old official, the minions who compromise truth for gain, but also against the abuse of the so-called new ideas and doctrines for the convenience of the self-seeking. As in "Hsu Mei-Ling" Smedley plays with words like *modern* and *old-fashioned* to achieve her satirical ends. Here, Smedley uses the technique of interior monologue when she describes the initial infatuation of Fu Kwang-chuang:

Hwa-chuan demurely returned Fu Kwang-chuang's admiring gaze. True, he was married to an old-fashioned woman whom he had left on his estate in Hunan, and true, he had ten children. But in these revolutionary days divorce is not difficult for an official. (p.248)

Smedley narrates Hwa-chuan's final triumph with a masterly use of double-edged words.

Finally Hwa-chuan's long years of suffering for the revolution came to an end. Fu Kwang-chuan divorced his old wife and settled a part of his fortune upon her and a part upon his children...

Following the divorce and the settlement Hwa-chuan walked to the table where a modern marriage ceremony was gone through, the old man proudly at her side, claiming as his own the revolutionary widow of a revolutionary martyr. There were many speeches about the benefits of modern marriage, marriage based upon love, and about the birth of a new society as expressed in unions as this. In this marriage, one speaker poetically cried, 'we have love presiding over the revolution. Could anything be more hopeful for the future of China?' (pp.252-3)

Agnes Smedley had one firm conviction and that was that Communism was the answer to China's problems. She was sceptical of those who took the name of revolution in vain. The last paragraph of "The Martyr's Widow" sums up the sharp irony of the story. Smedley makes Hwa-chuan epitomize vanity, decadence and mindlessness, the worst of all feudal and reactionary vices. And yet,

After the wedding Hwa-chuan spoke with deep feeling to friends who congratulated her: 'Now I feel that I can be of more service than ever to the revolution.' (p.253)

Certainly her "The Martyr's Widow" displays at their best those very "literary" qualities which its author apparently did not want to be identified with her work. And yet, while Smedley individualizes, provides details of names and place and history, gives one or two touches to mitigate the absolute ruthlessness of her central character, and considerably more light and shade to the character of her gullible husband, the readers never lose sight of which side the narrator is on, or on which side *they* should be on. The morality play is played out by recognizably human characters. This is an instance of the successful fusion of the individual and the generic.

Chapter IV

A Highly Controversial Thing:
The Writing of Han Suyin

If Pearl Buck's work gives a limited picture of Chinese women in the 1930s in that she concentrates on the rural backwaters and does not give sufficient indication to Western readers of the great strides being taken towards breaking with the feudal past, and if Agnes Smedley is too fiercely devoted to the Communist cause to give extraneous details about women against the background of a society in transition, Han Suyin gives an incredibly full and detailed account of the period from her birth in 1917 to the end of the Cultural Revolution in China, in a remarkable *tour de force* of five volumes, each with the subtitle *China: Autobiography, History*. The events of her earlier work, *Destination Chung-king* (1941) are covered in the third volume, and *A Many-Splendoured Thing* is contained in capsule form in the first part of the fourth. It is on these seven works that I shall focus, and only on those aspects directly relevant to my topic, namely the conveying of images of Chinese women to the West. My interest is not in her shifting political opinions and allegiances. Her work is controversial because her personality is controversial, and work and personality are inseparable because of her autobiographical mode. Questions of veracity and integrity get in the way of a detached assessment of the obvious literary merits of her work—the flexibility of her style, lyricism, reflected in some of her fine titles taken from imagery from the natural word, the fluidity of her narrative technique and the sharpness of the images she creates.[1]

In Han Suyin's work are contained a myriad of "images" of all types of women living, working, suffering in China in the important formative years from the 1911 Revolution to 1949, when the People's Republic was established—European,

Eurasian children of Chinese fathers; Eurasian children of Chinese mothers, Chinese. And among the Chinese, wives and concubines, reactionaries and revolutionaries, aristocrats and patricians, intellectuals, European-returned, American-returned students, Chinese students, professional people, peasants, servants, the dedicated, the half-dedicated, the downright self-serving, the super-rich and the unspeakably poor. Even without the embellishments and self-dramatization she seems given to, Han Suyin's life has been a fascinating one.[2] Her real name is Rosalie,—or is it Mathilda?—Chou, born of a Belgian mother and a Chinese father, Chou Yentung from a Szechuan landowning family. As a Mandarin and a scholar he was entitled to enter the Imperial Academy, but, largely because of the changes affecting China culminating in the Boxer uprising of 1900, was sent at the age of nineteen on a scholarship to Belgium to study engineering. Han Suyin's mother, Marguerite Denis, was the only daughter of a father of good family who had given up a promising career by marrying a Dutchwoman considered beneath the Denises. She married Han Suyin's father in the belief that he was "a Chinese prince" and followed him to China, where she was to undergo the most intense physical and emotional suffering and torment.

Han Suyin was one of eight children born to the couple, one of four survivors, an elder brother, Son of Spring, and two younger sisters, Tiza and Marianne. She was determined from the early age of twelve to be a doctor in order to help towards alleviating the intense suffering around her. She studied Chinese and science while waiting for a place at Yenching University. Then in 1935 she left Yenching at the age of eighteen on a scholarship to continue her studies at the University of Brussels. She distinguished herself academically, but gave up her scholarship in 1938 to return to China in order to be there in China's time of need. She met on board ship Tang Paohuang, son of a rich Confucian Mandarin family, who was returning from three years of study at Sandhurst. She married him and he later rose to the rank of general in Chiang Kai-shek's army. She trained and served as a midwife in the interior of

China during the Sino-Japanese war. From this experience she wrote, with the help of the American missionary Marion Manley, *Destination Chungking* in 1940. In 1942 she followed her husband to London where he had been sent as military attaché. By this time she had adopted a daughter, Yung-mei, a girl sold, as so many others were in those terrible times of poverty, by starving parents. In 1945 her husband was recalled to active service in China. Han Suyin chose to remain in London with Yung-mei to complete her medical studies. After her husband was killed fighting the communists in Manchuria in 1947, Han Suyin spent a year as house surgeon at the Royal Free Hospital before taking the decision to "watch and wait" at the "gateway to China" (*Birdless Summer*, p.350) by accepting a doctor's post in Hong Kong. There she wrote the Eurasian love story which was a record of her own experiences with Ian Morrison, son of the legendary George Morrison or "Chinese Morrison". *A Many-Splendoured Thing* brought her international acclaim and success as a writer. Since that time she has written many books, both novels and non-fiction. Her combined autobiography and history of China are in five volumes:

The Crippled Tree	1965
A Mortal Flower	1966
Birdless Summer	1968
My House Has Two Doors	1980
Phoenix Harvest	1980

(*My House Has Two Doors* was originally published as one volume under this title. In the Triad Paperback edition it is published as two.) The volume of her work on China and the Chinese (and herself, since she intertwines her history with the history of China) is enormous; one is impressed by the energy and vitality of her writing and the immense sense of commitment, and in my case, particularly by her total lack of self-consciousness in relating her own history. There is no doubt she is a popular writer. Her name became a household word when audiences worldwide cried over the doomed lovers in *A Many-Splendoured Thing*. For years the world identified Han Suyin with the *cheongsam*-clad, elegant

Jennifer Jones. And yet she is generally not looked upon as a serious writer, deserving in-depth critical study. During the Cultural Revolution she was linked with Pearl Buck. Both were accused of writing malicious things against China, and Han Suyin of pornography as well. Even today she is not highly regarded by Chinese "intellectuals" in Hong Kong and abroad for a complex of reasons which I shall try to go into. She poignantly describes the plight of the Eurasian over and over again in her work. Having taken her decision to return to China from Belgium in 1938, she writes,

> ...I was going on a journey to a war, and no one could tell me why, and now even I wondered why, I had forgotten why. But I pushed on. I would not look back.
>
> 'But you do know why' said the other self in me. 'Because you cannot live without China, you dumb so-and-so. Maybe you cannot live in China, maybe you are only a Eurasian, a dirty half-caste, as some people say, but you cannot live without China. For without China you die. I simply die, inside of you...' (*A Mortal Flower*, p.360)

The cynical Belgian railway agent, Joseph Hers, astounded with her decision, blusters, "You are Eurasian, not Chinese. Like all émigrés, you want to be more Chinese than the Chinese themselves." The Chinese possibly resent her intense desire to identify with China, and as a great deal of what she has to say about China, its modes of thought, its squalor and poverty, especially before 1949, is unpleasant; they resent what they consider to be an exploitation of China's miseries for fame and fortune. And, to my mind, the repeated protestations of commitment make things worse.

But I have already considered the case against Pearl Buck earlier: it offends the Chinese sense of "face" that she should only give a picture of the worst and most backward aspects of China. This is in itself offensive, whether done by a Chinese, a Eurasian or an American. There are some Chinese intellectuals who resent Lin Yutang for books like *My Country and My People* because they overlook the informative aspect and see his efforts as exploitative. I am in full sympathy with this view. And it is true that the customs and practices of one race become quaint and odd when explained to another race or races.

Throughout Han Suyin's five volumes are earnest professions of her attachment to China and endless attempts to explain why she did not fully commit herself to the revolutionary cause in 1949. And yet the personality of the author which she reveals as she attempts to reveal the heart and soul of China in her writing suggests willingness to compromise truth, to give up integrity in order to achieve desired personal ends. She wrote *Destination Chungking* with the help of American missionary, Marian Manley, during the Second World War, when national solidarity and American sympathy and aid were essential. *Destination Chungking* is the story of a Chinese girl and her heroic Chinese soldier husband who face untold suffering in the name of patriotism under the leadership of an inspiring and inspired leader, Chiang Kai-shek.

In later years, Han Suyin is able to comment blandly on the "fairy book fabulation of the narrative". She had allowed herself to be persuaded into publishing a book meant to project a favourable "image" of China at war, a book which would not "shock American women... the women are getting interested in giving money for China... but American women are a bit Puritan." (*Birdless Summer*, p.152) Having shown herself capable of compromising artistic integrity for pragmatic reasons, one cannot help, perhaps unfairly, having some sniggling doubts about her literary honesty elsewhere. She relates incidents from childhood in minutest detail, taking care to include her own emotional, often extremely intense, responses. In the first of the series she writes of her experience in trying "to run after" her own childhood. She claims to have a perfect auditory memory. So precocious is the young Suyin that one is astounded at being reminded that the volume closes with the author-rememberer being only eleven years old!

For better or for worse the Chinese even today, unless they have grown up in the West, tend to be far less given to self-revelation: the idea of laying bare the soul to a vast public is repugnant to most of us. I remember many years ago, in a Chinese poetry class in a convent school run by American nuns, thirty-nine other Chinese girls and I, quite Westernized because of my family background, listened to our Chinese literature teacher expound on the merits of the love poems of the Sung poetess Li Ch'ing Chao. She was writing of herself pining away for her absent husband, and how her person had become as slender as a cucumber. This was some thirty years ago, but the response of my contemporaries to these open confessions of attachment was one of derision. One of my less disciplined classmates shouted out what she felt was the appropriate second line of a couplet:

My person as thin as a cucumber,
My skin as thick as cowhide.

The fact that in Cantonese the two lines rhyme perfectly reduced the class to gales of laughter. Reticence, reluctance to reveal all, which has, possibly unjustly, earned the Chinese race the accusation of being inscrutable and cunning, would cause a number of Chinese readers, no doubt, to be repelled by the "un-Chinese" nakedness of many of Han Suyin's revelations. Her careful documenting of her irresistible sexual attraction, the accounts of the men she spurned, may not particularly appeal to the Chinese reader, although many taboos and barriers have been broken down by Chinese women writers during and after the May Fourth Movement, writers like Ding Ling. Still the narrator is very much the central character and her personality is focal to her story, and on this personality and its complexities and sensitivity Han Suyin lavishes an excessive amount of verbiage. The resultant persona is not particularly appealing. She records a letter, written by her father to her Third Uncle, in which he writes:

My First Daughter is shallow and easily temperamental, always changing her mind… my Second Daughter is much like a Chinese woman, quiet and subdued, affectionate and devoted… (*A Mortal Flower*, p.38)

…intended, almost certainly, by the author as a compliment to herself and her independent qualities of mind and spirit.

Rumours about her relationship with Joseph Hers, the Belgian mentor of her youth, the man who, in a sense, shaped her destiny by giving her a scholarship to Belgium, were rife. While insisting on a platonic relationship, she acknowledges she "made eyes at" the ageing womanizer in order to attract his attention. "I want a scholarship," she tells a friend, "How do you think I could have got his attention if I had not made eyes at him?" In the same way that she used Hers, she can be said to have exploited her affair with Ian Morrison, fictionalized as Mark Eliott in *A Many-Splendoured Thing*.

She caused a scandal by publishing the story of her sublimated many-splendoured love affair with the married Ian Morrison. She describes the frenzy of despair she was plunged into after his death in Korea, and how, as a purgative exercise she had to write their story.

> Writing was now a frenzy; not solace or opiate, but compulsion, insidious mastery of the white page waiting. As the book grew I could not bear to get away from it. (*My House Has Two Doors*, p.57)

This is all very well. But she was clearly an emotional exhibitionist, eager to show parts she had written to her friends and anyone willing to peek, no—openly look—into her private life (and poor Morrison's) even before the book went to press.

> [The book] became a great joke with all my friends. 'Let her get on with it, at least it makes her happy.' Mary Mostyn, to whom I showed a few pages, thought the style clumsy, Cherry was not interested. Someone else called it verbal diarrhoea... Only the Pulitzer Prize winner, Keyes Beech, back from Korea said, 'The lady can write.' (ibid.)

When the book did come out in England in May, 1952, a great deal of hostility was exhibited against it by reviewers. Chief among the critics was *The Times*, of course (because the hero, Mark/Ian had been their Far East correspondent), and *The Observer*. A correspondent of some fame who had been Ian's great friend felt her book destroyed a myth he had propagated about Ian, namely that he had been devoted to his family. He felt it bad for

Ian's children. Thus, in spite of its phenomenal popular success, and as a novel it is extremely well-written, with passages of "verbal diarrhoea", true, but also some of extraordinary lyrical beauty, the moral issue fills the scrupulous commentator on Han Suyin's person and hence her work (her work seems to me to be inseparable from her person) with some misgivings. She made use of Hers, and, in spite of passionate, ecstatic professions of unending love for Ian Morrison, she can be said to have used him rather unscrupulously. In her own defence she said, "I have done what all writers do, write about their love and praise it." But not usually at the expense of the living.

And, in any case, "to kiss and tell" is not generally acceptable behaviour, especially to tell vast readerships, to become rich and famous thereby, and at the same time satisfy vanity. The author relates her meeting with Jawaharlal Nehru at the British High Commission in Delhi.

> He started immediately talking about *A Many-Splendoured Thing* which Lady Mountbatten had given him to read. 'I think great loves should be kept private,' said he.

And, because of the circumstances, the brevity of time between the death and the detailed account of the love, one tends to agree with Nehru. Her account of her second marriage and almost unspeakably cruel exposure of her second husband's inadequacies and his frustrated love of her, down to the frequency with which he required intercourse (with someone else since she was unwilling) suggest strongly the earthiness of the Wife of Bath. But the Wife of Bath didn't get any money for her revelations and, as a character, her intimate tales of married life were meant only for the other pilgrims.

The point I am trying to make is that Han Suyin perhaps has not endeared herself in general to Chinese readers because of a certain "shamelessness", the less acceptable because she so often identified herself with the Chinese. There can be no doubt that she finds China fascinating, feels this link with it. Deciding for a second time, in 1949, to relinquish security and a peaceful life for the sake of China, she writes passionately of her motives:

But I could not contemplate living 'in peace' in England while tremendous China, like the phoenix, was being reborn from the consuming pyres of this massive conflict. I could not... I would not abdicate, give up, turn my back on China... (*Birdless Summer*, p.350)

She turned to tremendous advantage her love affair with Ian Morrison, though no doubt she loved him intensely. Might it not be the same in the case of her intense love affair with China? China has contributed a great deal towards making Rosalie Chou, Han Suyin, a writer with an international reputation.

And yet, having said so much on the debit side I must give credit where it is due. Han Suyin undoubtedly became the best known popular writer of the twentieth century, of novels, autobiography, history, reportage about China. When I commenced my research on this work, the question I was most often asked was, "And what will you do about Han Suyin?" Her combined autobiography and history of China was hailed as an important contribution to international understanding. Bertrand Russell said of the first volume, *The Crippled Tree*,

During the many hours I spent reading it, I learnt more about China than I did in a whole year spent in that country. (Blurb for Triad Edn)

In an introductory note to her first volume she informs the reader she is not writing fiction:

The characters in this book are not fictional, neither are the events. So far as research can make it so, historical accuracy has been maintained. Here and there however minor characters have had their names changed in deference to their feelings.

And if one were to set aside some of her subjective comments the five volumes do give a coherent and informative account of the sequence of events that took place in China from 1885 to 1979. During the 50s and 60s and indeed into the 70s her profile was very high. On the basis of her work, mainly *A Many-Splendoured Thing* and to a less extent *The Mountain Is Young* and by virtue of the fact she was allowed to return to China frequently, she went on endless lecture tours in the West, talking about China. She presented to the West an "image" but in spite of the Chinese dress she favoured and her insistence on her Chinese roots, I do not think informed Western readers ever really saw her as "Chinese"; those who knew her work could hardly miss her insistence on her mixed culture. She does not look particularly Chinese: she acknowledges this often in her work. And those who know her as a person attest to her aggressive, strident manner and her racy speech. If this is seen as an "image" of Chinese woman, then it is a very atypical one; and broadens the range of possibilities further.

I find the first three volumes of her work on herself and China most illuminating in terms of giving a graphic, fascinating— sometimes the fascination is the fascination of horror—picture of China up to 1941 when China was in the throes of her struggle with Japan. She was then, apart from her three-year absence in Belgium, actually living there, in touch with many classes and types of people. Though in some ways cut off from the Chinese by her Belgian blood, she was nevertheless able to speak (she had acquired a writing knowledge of it in her teens through private lessons) the language. So was Pearl Buck, but Pearl Buck was not in touch with the Chinese in the same way. As Rosalie Chou, she was recognized as a daughter of the family in the family seat at Szechuan. She had the familiarity with the Chinese that arises from being part of a large feudal family, however her European blood might have distanced her. She is able to describe trips to Szechuanese opera and to little food stalls for Szechuanese specialties with her many cousins. Agnes Smedley did not speak the language and was in China for a much shorter period of time, when her views had already more or less been formed. She saw China through the eyes of a Communist partisan from the start.

Let us consider her in relation to some American women apologists for China. Anna Louise Strong had gone to China in the 1920s. She had chronicled the early Revolution in some books; when the 1927 massacres started she escaped from China via the Gobi Desert. She went to Russia, but went back to China in the 1940s during the war with Japan, and was received several times by Mao. She went back to live in China and was a guest of the government in the late 1950s. She poured out books interpreting the new China to the West, sending out her "Letter from China" to hundreds of Americans. Agnes Smedley, Anna Louise Strong, Helen Snow, all were strong, dedicated apologists for China, Smedley and Helen Snow giving notable insights about the plight of Chinese women. But, like Pearl Buck, they were, in a sense, more alienated, from the people they were apologists for, less able than the half-Chinese Han Suyin to get to "the heart of the matter" in so far as Chinese mores, cultural attitudes, traditional and changing, to and of Chinese women were concerned. There was a dearth of writing in English about Chinese women by Chinese women before writers like Maxine Hong Kingston and Bette Bao Lord. Huilan Koo, wife of Chinese diplomat Wellington Koo, actually published her autobiography in New York, but the book was suppressed by her husband and withdrawn from the market because it was considered improper for a woman of the upper classes to write about herself. And we cannot discount the very voluminous nature of Han Suyin's work; she goes through shifts of viewpoints. Her political views have not always been considered sound, but they are not my real concern. My interest is in Han Suyin the literary artist recreating for the West a panorama of life in China in the first four decades of the twentieth century, and as a woman, focussing sympathetically on all classes and types of women in the China of that time.

She wrote and spoke throughout the 1950s and early 1960s at a time when the West, especially the United States, was disinclined to hear or read anything good about it. When Kung Peng, wife of Chiao Kuanhua (who was later to be foreign minister), an old school friend and then a high-ranking official, expressed dissatisfaction with Han Suyin's article "Peking Revisited" published in America because it was not all "gush and praise", she defended herself with "It's already difficult enough to have anything good about China printed... *one cannot write for a Western audience as one does for a Chinese one.*" (*My House Has Two Doors*, p.250) I am aware she is here speaking within a context, but it does seem likely that Han Suyin has always deliberately moulded her material and her style towards the tastes of the Western reader. Generally, when she is writing of China and the Chinese she uses strong brush strokes, with pulsing intensity. *Destination Chungking* was "tidied up" by the American missionary, Marian Manley, when Han Suyin felt unsure of her English. She describes her response to the book years afterwards,

> Today reading the book emerging out of this cooperation… I can pick out the parts that are mine, the immediate concrete detail, the drag and drift of people, the smells and the heat, the landscape and the exactness; but, as the writer Nora Waln, whom I met later in England and who reviewed the book, rightly observed, a veil of beautiful writing had been cast upon events, softening into a beautiful patina, nothing protruding that was ugly and raucous and crude. The squalor, the sufferings of China, the horrors and the injustices were neatly polished with smooth compassion and diminished in their enormity (*Birdless Summer*, p.149)

Many of the descriptions of China we find in the work Han Suyin wrote later on her own are indeed "ugly, raucous and crude". The narration of its problems and the sufferings of the people "large… sweaty and human", (expression used in *My House Has Two Doors*, p.276) Pearl Buck succeeded in reaching a vast Western readership and audience. She individualized the Chinese in a way which had not been done in fiction before, but the characters do seem protected by the fact of their being exotic and remote. The horror and the suffering is to some extent smoothed over by compassion and the detachment of a narrator who is not one of them. Agnes Smedley conveys in more objective terms the injustices, the agony and the glory of the Chinese people in struggle and at war, but in her vignettes of Chinese women, either the stylization or the irony, sometimes shields the reader from the full injustice and horror.

If we focus on Han Suyin's contribution to portraiture of Chinese womanhood, then we find that the reader meets an entire spectrum of women with whom the author came into personal contact within the course of her varied and interesting life—from Huilan Koo, wife of Chinese diplomat Wellington Koo, Kung Peng, wife of Chiao Kuanhua, Jiang Qing, through her Chinese classmates at Yenching, some of whom became prominent either in the Kuomintang or Communist governments, her fellow midwives who worked alongside her in the Chengtu clinic, old-fashioned wives and concubines related to her by blood or otherwise, young "sisters" and cousins, progressive or reactionary, the *amahs* who took care of her and her family, to representatives of the surging, suffering masses of Chinese women—prostitutes, sing-song girls, destitute peasants, factory girls with hands gnarled and in agony through working at the silk filatures. As Han Suyin narrates it, before the changes of 1949, China was a "world's convention of agonies", especially for its women.

Han Suyin professes to espouse the cause of women worldwide and her life is a testimony to what a woman can achieve in spite of prejudices and apparently insurmountable obstacles. And certainly her heart went out to the suffering women of China. She lays claim to being a very skilled calligrapher, but her knowledge of Chinese etymology may be less sound: her explanation of the origin of the Chinese ideogram for woman is as much based on emotion as scholarship.

> The very ideogram for 'woman' denoted subjection, the bar across, horizontal burden of her heavy breasts, the protuberant hips and the crossed bow-legs, not quite quadrupedal, but almost.[3] (*Birdless Summer*, p.168)

Her picture of women in the 30s and 40s, although the first three volumes of her China series did not appear until 1965, 1966, and 1968 respectively, complement the pictures of women drawn by the American apologists of China, most of whom she knew, and with the notable exception of Emily Hahn, admired. She has a broader canvas than either Smedley or Buck; the greater human interest of Buck but not the diffuseness and in many ways the blood and guts of Smedley when describing suffering Chinese women. And yet for all her avowed sympathy and familiarity with Chinese women, no Chinese woman is foregrounded. This is perhaps in the nature of the narrative method. Everyone is seen through Han Suyin's Eurasian consciousness, and for all the names and details and authenticity of setting, the reader encounters, I think it would be fair to say, very few Chinese women drawn in the round. Two Chinese men are allowed to speak for themselves through their diaries and letters. These are the author's father and her Third Uncle. The Father's disappointments and frustrations can be read between the lines of his bland unemotional style, and the Chinese courtesy of Third Uncle is evident in his treatment of the events relating to his foreign and difficult niece. After Han Suyin herself the woman figure who is most carefully drawn and whose presence dominates even after she withdraws from the scene after 1949 is certainly the author's Belgian mother, Marguerite. Han Suyin claims that she strives for spareness of style, aiming "to give the feeling of a scene in as few words as possible, not building up, but stripping down". This may be true but in a number of instances she uses the device of repetition, and in delineating her mother, scenes are repeated, with some variations in detail. Over and over we find in the two first volumes scenes of her mother's sense of alienation and desperation as she is rejected both by the European community and by the Chinese whom she learns to despise; scenes of conflict between the desperate mother and the obstinate child who is the author herself. The repetition builds up a general aura of helplessness and futility—the European woman against the backwardness, the poverty and bigotry of a China still caught in feudal times; the Eurasian child venting her feelings of isolation through tantrums and recalcitrant behaviour. And always there is the China of the early decades of the twentieth century, vast, unwieldy, sweaty, human, dominating the lives of mother and daughter.

A few lively images of Chinese women do stay in the mind. In particular I should like to discuss two "sets" of women: those in the Chengtu home of her Third Uncle and her fellow midwives in the Chengtu maternity hospital. Then there are the pictures of Miss Hsu, who gave in to the demands of society, of Caroline, who could be seen as a more fully-drawn picture of Agnes Smedley's Chang Siao-hung or Shan-fei, and the strangely—or perhaps not so strangely—shadowy figure of her adopted daughter, Yung-mei.

The description of Chinese New Year festivities spent in the bosom of her "large feudal family" in *Birdless Summer* is written with zest. Everything and everyone seem suffused in the glow of unreality, whatever terrible things are happening in the world beyond the walls of the family compound. She has described the same event in *Destination Chungking*, and for once, the details and the responses of the author are virtually identical in the two accounts.

The account of her "big family" runs from pages 144 to 180 in *Destination Chungking* and takes the writer from Chinese New Year's Eve through the fifteen days of celebrations. In the more sombre mood of *Birdless Summer*, the description is somewhat abbreviated, but Han Suyin affirms she enjoyed her family. In passages reminiscent of Pearl Buck she explains Chinese customs and traditions; the Westernized Chinese reader tends to feel a twinge of irritation, almost as a reflex, when they read such explanations, because rightly or wrongly, they see a note of patronage in this type of explanation. I wonder if it is not because, not really secure in their acquired ways and behaviour, they subconsciously feel ashamed of their people's old and different ways. And yet people who have truly acquired a happy assimilation of East and West begin to take pride in their own time-honoured traditions and customs. A superficial reading of this type of writing so easily lends itself to parody, as some of my own students have indulged in. One particularly adept parodist did a hilarious send-up of the Chinese New Year feast, with innumerable "Third Uncles" and "cousins on Fifth Grandmother's side", "aunts thrice removed" and so on. But careful reading of Han Suyin shows the details are accurate, the writer is an enthusiastic participant in the festivities and has a genuine desire to explain her Chinese ways to the Western reader; for example, she carefully explains the patrilineal system of recording and descent, in which the family name is all important. She tells of the traditional ways and explains with a great deal of elaboration and detail the complicated relationships within her family.

The Chinese members of this family fall to some extent into the types we have encountered in previous discussions. Sociologists have defended the concubine system in China because of its usefulness to the military men who had to go to the front or the landed gentry who kept more than one household. The concubine(s) would keep the man company while the "big wife" would take care of the main household. Florence Ayscough does a rather naïve exposition of the system in the book, *Chinese Women Yesterday and Today*. (London, 1938) In Han Suyin's account of her Third Uncle's domestic arrangements in the 1930s–1940s we have an actual demonstration of how this method actually works in practice. Third Aunt, the "big wife", runs the household in Chengtu and Yao the concubine, the household in Chungking, and a harmony prevails that would be difficult for the average Western reader to understand. There are unusually detailed descriptions of the wife and the concubine and the narration of a quite heartwarming little story that gives readers some insight into the true nature of comradeship and loyalty that can spring up between wife and concubine and indeed between concubine and concubine in old feudal families. Concubines call one another "sister", and, often, because there is no longer cause for possessiveness since the "old master" is no longer possessed by any of them, there is genuine sisterly solicitude and friendship. I have seen this—my father-in-law had eight concubines. In writing of her Third Aunt, Third Uncle, the concubine Yao and yet "another woman", Han Suyin writes with lively humour of the "quadrangle" relationship.

> I liked Third Aunt immediately and so much; she had hair polished like black jade, a smooth white skin, beautiful small hands. Even today, at sixty-seven, she has those lovely hands, though her skin is darkened with the sun and her hair is beginning to turn white. She had tiny bound feet, and she wore mourning for Grandmother for three years. Third Aunt was so small that when she sat in a chair her feet dangled off the floor, and this is how

I remember her, sitting in a chair too high and too large for her, patient and folded patently upon herself. She knew all that had to be done for a large house and clan, and though she was never anything but gentle, she was also capable. She did not mind Yao the concubine, who was insignificant-looking, rather ugly, did not push herself forward, and as long as she had opium to smoke was able in her own way. Yao the concubine ran the Chungking house easily, for she was a Chungking woman; Third Uncle had found her in a house of pleasure, and she had nursed him through an unspecified illness whose symptoms and signs she related to me most gleefully, but which I could never identify. He had bought her out, and she became his housekeeper. He had very little to do with her, but for thirty years looked after her needs, chiefly in opium, and never stinted her for money to buy clothes. Yao was not profligate, but careful, and sombre, as was Third Aunt; she did not drink nor did she bring disrepute upon the house, and her opium habit was discreet, she did it in secret, and never cooked more than three pipes.

Several months later Yao the concubine and Third Aunt were to become active allies, the reason being a temporary infatuation which Third Uncle underwent for a film star. The film star was beautiful, she was an 'outlander', from Shanghai (or so she said), and very expensive; it was this last point, and not the fact that she might or might not lavish her favours upon Third Uncle (and this was never made clear), which alarmed Third Aunt and Yao the concubine. They both went about with glum faces, Third Aunt muttering that Third Uncle was under a witchcraft spell, had been given a love philtre by that 'foreign' woman from Shanghai: then sighing and going on with her duties, with dour mouth and knitted brows; Yao more explicit, more garrulous, being a coarser person, terrified that her source of opium might be cut off, saying that the 'star' was a prostitute, and that she knew who was the procurer, that it was a racket, of which the star was the bait, to destroy Third Uncle and blackmail him. But soon all was well again, the star did cost too much, and became more and more demanding; Third Uncle put an end to it. His office at the bank and his living-room in Chengtu and also the rooms in the hill house at Ta Erh Wo in Chungking, where he went to stay after the house in Woodcutter Lane in Chungking was bombed later, in May 1939, had blossomed with photographs of the star, generous-busted, dimple-cheeked, dreamy large eyes raised to heaven, and the lot coloured by hand. 'So expensive,' grumbled Yao the concubine. Third Uncle would take these framed likenesses down and discourse lengthily on the precept of good looks, making it sound like a philosophy of pulchritude. 'Consider this face, for instance. You notice the proportion of forehead to chin, indicating a moral character of considerable strength... Notice also the eyes, how they are set... the astrologers say that the breadth between the eyes must be as much as the eye itself...' He was never lewd, or immodest, but rhetorical and what, at the time, Yao Niang called 'That cheap bone' and Third Aunt 'Star what?' And suddenly there were no photos, no more lectures on the laws of good looks; Third Uncle shut himself up in his study and practised calligraphy; then came out, called for his sedan chair, and that very evening all the photos disappeared and no one ever heard mention of the star again.

Apart from that slight episode, in all the years I knew Third Uncle and Third Aunt, there was no rift to their harmony and that tolerant companionship which is marriage; Third Uncle made fun of Third Aunt's lips; Third Aunt would blush like a young girl when Third Uncle spoke to her. She would sit, waiting for him; she would hover, listening to him, as we did, for hours. Today, they are both old, but together; after the Revolution Yao the concubine was cured of the opium habit, and died of tuberculosis after some years. Third Aunt looked after her, and now Third Aunt, who in spite of her small bound feet can walk miles and is full of zest, goes every day to a lecture on politics, on the Thought of Mao Tsetung; she is so interested and avid for more that she arrives half an hour before the group is due to meet. Third Uncle nurses his bad knees and stays at home, waiting for her. And Third Aunt is as happy in the comparative poverty which is theirs today, as she was when she had so much more, so many houses and so many relations to look after, when Third Uncle was a rich man. (*Birdless Summer*, pp.103-105)

I have quoted this passage at length in order to show that China, even in feudal times, with its arranged marriages, its unfaithful, chauvinistic men, could not always and altogether break women's spirits. The usual details that would strike the Western reader are included—Third Aunt's glossy black hair and incredibly smooth skin, her diminutive stature, her bound feet are all part and parcel of the stereotypical "dainty Chinese lady" image. Addiction to opium is another touch of "local colour". The film star, rather than the sing-song girl, reminds us this is set in a more urban area than *The Good Earth*. Han Suyin also anticipates in her narration the greater fulfilment of Third Aunt under the new scheme of things brought about by the events of 1949.

She also tells the story of sixth Aunt, another bright interlude in the midst of feminine misery and suppression. Some arranged marriages are indeed made in heaven. Sixth Aunt and Uncle were fortunate enough to have been matched off by their parents after he had fallen in love with her secretly. Not every Chinese man, even in those benighted times, was a tyrant and a lecher.

Sixth Uncle and Sixth Aunt were also a happy couple; theirs was a love marriage. All unknown to their respective families, Sixth Uncle had briefly perceived Sixth Aunt at the park on a festival and fallen in love; and behold she it was who was chosen for him! They never got over this good luck, it enriched their married life for all its years. Sixth Aunt was very beautiful. Even after twelve children, six sons and six daughters, she remained slim-waisted and doe-eyed, her skin pale and even. Her body was completely hairless, even at thirty-five; for many a mature woman in Szechuan is thus hairless, nothing on pubes or in armpits, but with most luxuriant heads of hair.

Sixth Aunt, who was 'modern' (had she not married for love?), had herself sterilized after the twelfth child, as she said it was enough. She remains slim, smooth-faced and dark-haired even today, and Sixth Uncle is still so much in love with her he cannot do anything without first running to tell her about it. They shocked a good many people because when Chengtu was bombed by the Japanese in 1940, they let their children go to the shelters by themselves, while they walked behind them, hand in hand, something never seen in Szechuan before the Revolution. (ibid., p.105)

This passage (and the passage about Third Aunt, Third Uncle and the Concubine Yao), except for the erotic detail about hairlessness, with so much folksy optimism, could well be something out of *The Reader's Digest*. Contrasted sharply with these passages are some of the stories told of the women who came as patients to the hospital where Han Suyin worked as a midwife. She gives a description, clinical in its detail, and we must remember we have a trained physician writing, of the fetid, unhygienic conditions which prevailed in China around the time of the Sino-Japanese War. Poverty and ignorance, we are reminded, know no national or racial boundaries. She compares her experience of midwifery years later among the poorest of Dublin to her Chengtu experience: "Same odour of poverty, same prolificity of babies, even the fleas and the lice were the same." (ibid., p.158) Nor is the dirt limited to the poor, "though they lived in what were called mansions, the noisome neglect and dirt, the spitting and hawking were almost less bearable, coupled with the satin hangings and carved beds". (ibid., 159) Shades of Jacobean drama.

In this part of the narrative Han Suyin parallels Agnes Smedley in her accounts of Chinese soldiers marching—blood and guts, stench, and human excrement. The reader is not spared. But Han Suyin, who in her two earlier volumes has described, in sometimes irritating and what strikes the reader as self-aggrandizing detail, herself as "the little girl of feeling", tremulous with intense vicarious suffering over a dying hedgehog or a wooden horse which has lost its tail, has now grown into a woman of feeling. And in her account of the different types and classes of women who come to the hospital to have babies delivered she maintains a controlled objectivity, but she does make use of impassioned authorial comment to show her great anger at the injustices suffered by women, not just Chinese women, but in the context, Chinese women in particular.

The story of Spring Wave, the favoured concubine who falls into disfavour even before giving birth to a little girl, underlines once more the dependence of poor women on the fickle lechery of infamous men. Here a Lotus Blossom with a difference, for Liu the warlord is not human and kind like Wang Lung of *The Good Earth*. And here the reader is not shielded by the consoling thought that this is fiction. The story of Spring Wave is narrated from the point of view of the midwife who knows only what she has heard of her and sees her only in her professional capacity as an assistant in the delivery of her child. The description of the woman conforms to that of the many good-time girls raised to wealth by beauty.

> [She] was beautiful, with a lovely face, which she daubed with rouge and caked powder, making it nearly an actress's mask. Her make-up stopped at the high collar which topped her silk dress. Her sleek black hair, the pride of the women of Szechuan, she wore with little bangs on the forehead and a large bun on the nape. Her hands were small, as were her feet. (ibid., pp.159-160)

The physical beauty overlaid with artifice is familiar enough; also familiar is her insecurity, her fear of her "master".

> She was self-assured but not arrogant in her pride of place as the favourite of the moment. The warlord came with her, and there was a flutter of zeal and too many smiles when he was about, for his presence, whose porous benignity did not conceal a habitual snarling temper, evoked obsequious trepidation and unacknowledged fear. He let it be known that this concubine was highly favoured and we worried lest something should go wrong. (ibid.)

And indeed something does go wrong—not with the birth but with Spring Wave's status. Even while she is going through labour in one room of the Lui Palace, separated from the adjoining bedroom only by a screen, Spring Wave can hear the giggles and screams of a new favourite, in bed with the warlord. And, as if to bring her paragraph to a blandly worded but terrible climax of failure for the poor displaced favourite, Han Suyin writes,

> ... and when her child was born it was a girl

Here Han Suyin applies a technique which is indeed spare, almost in the Smedley mode to tersely tell the fate of Spring Wave and of all women dependent on unreliable men:

> A month later she was back at the hospital for her postnatal check, as sprightly, beautiful and slim as before, but a little haggardness had webbed very finely her thin temples, where pale blue veins showed, and there was new shrillness in her loud voice. The warlord did not come with her, and a year later it was the next concubine who had a child delivered by our midwives at Lui the warlord's mansion. (ibid., p.161)

Then without comment, in the detached style of reportage, she inserts a short paragraph which intensifies the idea of suffering beauties...

> And then there was the case of the warlord, who only two hours after his concubine had given birth, insisted on intercourse with her... We were called in haste, but she died bleeding. (ibid.)

From the temporarily pampered, Han Suyin moves way down to the destitute. Here we have a compassionate rendering of two counter-images to the savage warlord and his pampered concubine.

> The very poor would also call at the hospital... I remember one such case; a young girl, so young, so thin, biting her lip, making no sound, during the painful first birth, in a lean-to against the city wall, on a cold rainy night of January; only a mat rent with holes for ceiling, kept upright by two bamboos; we held an oil-paper umbrella open above her and our heads while the delivery went on. The stones of the city wall were her pillow, a grey rag flapped behind us in the wind and threatened our sterile equipment, and that was the door; only the darkness, probed by our torches, defended and concealed her on the wooden plank on which she lay; there was no blanket, no sheet, no mat, no pillow, nothing.

Her husband was a rickshaw coolie and he helped us by sheltering us with his body from the rain, he held her in his arms when the pains were strong, and murmured words of endearment to her; when the child was born there was no piece of cloth to wrap it in, only the tattered dress the woman wore on her nakedness, only the tattered top and trousers of her husband; and so the man took off his trousers to wrap the baby in them, but he would need his trousers to work, to pull his rickshaw the next day, so what would they do? We left a towel (though towels were precious) for them to wrap the baby in. They would have to sell the baby as soon as the cord dropped off; perhaps the mother would hire herself out as wet nurse.

The midwife who did the delivery fumbled in her inside pocket and gave the new mother some money, and muttered it was to buy the *tzaotze*, the gruel given to women after parturition, which is supposed to stop bleeding. The young girl thanked her, nestled her baby close with heartrending tenderness, her husband saw us off; he was young and lean, and very quiet… (ibid., pp.161-2)

The story of the young pair, rickshaw coolie and wife, is poignant in the extreme. We have indeed come across descriptions of such abject poverty in Pearl Buck, Agnes Smedley and other writers; here, as often elsewhere, the degradation of total deprivation is ennobled by their courage and mutual affection. But then even Wang Lung the farmer only became depraved after attaining wealth and leisure. The nakedness of the coolie fits in with the motif of nakedness throughout the descriptions of the surging masses; the beggars with their rags. This is genuine poverty—true

loop'd and window'd raggedness.

This story is told with overt commitment and sympathy although even the bare outline would speak for itself. The author concludes with an impassioned comment:

My heart burned within me; oh surely, for these, a better day must come, a star must rise in the east. (p.162)

For all the details, one detail is left out—the sex of the baby. It is called "the child", or "the baby". After all, to people who had nothing, the sex of a child they would have to sell was of no consequence. One *could* see such writing as cheap, obvious and exploitative. And yet such cases were common: babies *were* sold and women did hire themselves out as wet nurses: indeed my own brother had a wet nurse during the War; the wet nurse's baby, blind from malnutrition, now lives and works in the Ebenezer Home for the Blind in Hong Kong. Then perhaps one can overlook the author's emotional excesses and see the poignancy of the scene, a poignancy which lends greater significance to China's subsequent struggles. In her fifth volume, which takes China to the end of the Cultural Revolution in 1979, Han Suyin writes hopefully of a "phoenix reborn from its ashes". (*Phoenix Harvest*, p.302) Those from the West who glibly remark that Beijing is "ghastly" or China is "ghastly" because of the level of air pollution or the yawning gap between rich and poor should perhaps bear in mind the improvements in the quality of life for the masses. But in the 30s ignorance and bigotry still made the lives of the vast majority of women unspeakably painful. There is more than a touch of black comedy in the grotesque aspects of the story of the poor superstitious country woman who had the great misfortune to bear ten daughters when daughters were regarded as the greatest liability.

There was the country woman who came a long, long way from Chingsien, eighty *li* or more, to be delivered of her tenth child, because all the others had been daughters; and a neighbour of hers had been to the hospital and had acquired a son; this woman thought she too could obtain a son by coming to be delivered at our hospital. She rode in a rickshaw all the way and this must have cost a good deal; and as she lay on the obstetric table in labour she told Miss Hsu what had happened to her baby daughters: the first was alive, and also the third; but the second had been strangled at birth by the husband and so had the fifth and the sixth; the seventh had been born in a bad year, a year of famine when her belly skin stuck to her spine, and the husband had smashed her skull in with his axe; at the eighth female child the husband had been so angry that he had hurled it against a wall; the ninth was a year old and had been given away to a neighbour and now here was something in her belly... oh let it be a son, a male child.

As the pains came and went, Miss Hsu, stethoscope upon the woman's belly, asked: 'What happened to the fourth?' We went through the whole list of infanticides again and again, and every time the woman missed one out—the fourth. As the pains became worse (and labour was not easy, for her flesh was exhausted; her belly muscles had parted so that the womb could almost be seen under the skin; and we were prepared for a haemorrhage which is usual after many births), the woman began to sob and told us how the fourth had been killed. She had been so frightened when it was born and it was a girl that she herself had pushed it in the big toilet jar, and there it had suffocated.

And now we hoped, we all hoped. All the midwives by now had heard the woman's story, and all the other patients, and some sat up in bed straining with the woman straining on the delivery table, turned in spirit towards it, waiting, waiting for the miracle, for the son which would truly consecrate the hospital as a miracle-working place. But this did not happen; the tenth was another girl. 'Such a beautiful little sister, look,' said Miss Hsu as the woman lay mute, her eyes fixed on the ceiling, in a frozen stare. 'Look at her. She is so pretty.'

'It is a girl, another girl.' Perhaps she had not paid enough; she unwound the belt round her which she had pushed up under her breasts so as to free her belly for the work it had to do. And there was another twenty dollars in paper, and she said: 'All, that is all I have, for a boy.'

'But a girl is just as good as a boy,' said Miss Hsu to her; and for the next few days we all told her how good it was to be a woman, and how a woman now could do so many things, even become a doctor, or a midwife, and how pretty her baby was. After five days the woman went home, and she wanted to leave the baby behind, but this could not be. Miss Hsu placed the baby, wrapped tight in its swaddling clothes in the approved Szechuan fashion, in its mother's arms and said, 'Take care of her, she will bring you luck.' Then she walked with her to the door, still trying to persuade her, while the hospital servant went to call a rickshaw. Many rickshaw or wheelbarrow men would not carry a woman that had given birth to a child only a week or ten days before. They would only take a mother if the baby was a full month old, thirty days, when all evil was reckoned purged away. Often Miss Hsu would send out the servant to call a rickshaw, only to find the man pick up his shafts and go away when he realized that he was to carry a woman with a week-old baby. Then Miss Hsu would get angry and cry out: 'And where did you come from? Did not a woman bear you? Have you no mother?' to the back of the departing man. But in Little Heavenly Bamboo Street there were rickshaws who were used to carrying pregnant and new mothers, and laughed at the refusal of the others. So a rickshaw was obtained for the woman, an obliging smiling man, who also persuaded her to keep the baby, and told her: 'These are new days, a woman child is also good, look at all those doctors here.' Afterwards the porter told us that all the way home the woman was telling her story and that she did not dare to go back to her husband with yet another girl, and that on the way home she would find a convenient ditch, and throw the baby into it; but we never knew whether she did this or not, for neither the porter nor the rickshaw man would tell us. And some of the midwives thought we should have kept the baby; someone might have turned up to adopt it. (ibid., pp.165-67)

The story seems almost too outrageous, the husband too brutal to be true. Indeed it was stories of infanticide which caught the imagination of the West and contributed to China's barbaric image, and gave missionaries and, worse still, imperialists, an invidious excuse to assert their moral superiority and hence their right to govern on our behalf. But the truth has to be faced and even today with so much progress having been made towards education and enlightenment we still read reports of infant girls being put to death in backward rural areas. Yet if we look at the account of this unhappy woman we find signs of hope for the future. The women delivering the child are capable and independent. Even the rickshaw men and the porter are embued with the ideas of the "new days". What is more, in the telling of the story, in spite of the horror of the multiple murders we are given a sense of the community of good will within the hospital and among the rickshaw men outside it, a sense of man's humanity to man, in spite of the greatest inhumanity.

We are told that some of the midwives felt they should have kept the baby girl. Someone might have adopted her. Han Suyin herself adopted a baby girl through the midwives she knew in the hospital. And Yung-mei, the girl purchased by Han Suyin, had an interesting fate. The Western reader is given a detailed account of the care and love which the author lavished on this beautiful child who came to her physically and emotionally battered and scarred. The West reads accounts of the hundreds upon hundreds of girls sold into slavery or prostitution or both, but here the emotions of seller and buyer are explained and gone into. The child is seen as very human, not passive as one would expect something sold as chattels might be. The mother chose to sell the third daughter because at a year and a half old she would be able to bear the separation better than either the older ones or the three-month-old baby. And the mother was educated, could read and write. She sold the baby because it was better that she should live rather than die of starvation. All this is told in a matter-of-fact way, but when the toddler herself is presented the description becomes overtly more emotional. Far from being a passive object the child shows all the emotions and responses of a child in such a state and such a condition. The other descriptions of her childish responses to gifts proffered, to shows of affection are done very movingly and with a recognizable (at least to Chinese mothers) "realism" which attests to the "truth" of the narrative at this point. We have for Western readers an "image" of a Chinese baby girl, with its cries of "Don't want, don't want,"—with its "lovely eyes and serious face". The author remains devoted to the adopted daughter, named Yung-mei by her husband. We have an account of Han Suyin's life as a diplomat's wife in London, with Yung-mei's welfare a matter of paramount concern to her; the child's unfortunate experiences with "crazy" old nannies because so few nannies were available during the War, and of the author's finally finding Gillie, an ideal nanny who made innumerable sacrifices for her Chinese charge. The "little Chinese girl" is seen from the first as an independent spirit, and she appears at intervals in the narrative even after she leaves the author's side for school in England. We read of her traumas as a child in England, of her long bout with tuberculosis, the legacy of her deprivation as an infant. In the text is an occasional direct comment from her. Joseph Hers, Han Suyin's old mentor, bitter and twisted in his old age, reveals the carefully-kept secret of her adoption and there is a temporary period of estrangement between mother and daughter. A trip to China and her "roots" have a therapeutic effect on her in that she learns there were millions in China like her—only less lucky. She marries, then divorces, an American producer, Sidney Glazier, and is the mother of a Eurasian daughter, Karen, who according to the author, is startlingly like herself. We are given her adoptive mother's summation of her character: in spite of her "apparent frailty" she is "Chinese-tough". (*My House has Two Doors*, p.515) As always, the perspective is that of the narrator. This is in the nature of Han Suyin's autobiographical narrative method, but her relative reticence about someone who so clearly means so very much to her may well be intentional. It is the image of Yung-mei as a child which strikes the reader, and details of the transaction humanizes the process of traffic in human beings. "There were millions of such cases all over China; millions of such children, so common no one even thought it anything but normal that children should be sold in times of famine." (*Birdless Summer*, p.233) In spite of this cold fact, the Chinese are well-known to be enormously fond of children. Images of colourfully-clad, rosy-cheeked and really delightful children have been made familiar to the West today through the media. The story of Yung-mei provides the necessary balance to the accounts of little girls abused or sold or killed. The midwives all make much of the child, and gifts are lavished on her. The author makes the comment, applicable to virtually all cases of children sold:

...I knew the mother was not doing this gladly, but because she had to, and it was better than killing the child, as some did, so that it might escape misery... (ibid.)

Yung-mei is one of the lucky ones. Some Chinese women, equally independent of spirit, have yet to bow to the pressures of society because of fear and insecurity. This is true of course of all women, and indeed of human beings, irrespective of time and race, but Han Suyin gives a memorable portrait of Miss Hsu, head teacher of the midwives. I have recorded Harold Isaacs's criticism of Agnes Smedley's characters as being like poster figures from morality plays, and we have seen that while this criticism is not an entirely just one there are some Smedley characterizations, like that of Shan-fei and Chang Siao-hung in which individualizing, shading and nuances are given up in order to enforce a message. The delineation of Miss Hsu shows the extent to which Han Suyin eschews methods of caricature and humanizes her figures. And yet we could equally say that the story and evolution of Miss Hsu are meant also to bring out a moral truth: that individuals often have to make compromises and concessions to unhappy realities. Here too Han Suyin combines the highly individualized and the generic.

When we first meet Miss Hsu she is a calm, independent and highly competent woman; we see her taking her student midwives with her into the mansions of warlords and the hovels of coolies to deliver babies, always competent, and with the appropriate soothing words when a daughter is born. We see in her the image of the woman who has learned to fend for herself, who possesses the calmness that comes from inner peace and resignation. Then the image changes. She becomes all flustered and unsure, for she, "the charming and clever Miss Hsu" becomes caught in the dilemma between the fierce but painful independence of the single state, and the servitude of the wedded one.

The person who had cajoled Miss Hsu into premarital pecuniary preoccupation was a lady with eight children, a frequent visitor to our hospital and enthusiastic about the whiff of anaesthetic which banished all pain... On her days off Miss Hsu played mahjong with her and other friends. Miss Hsu had delivered her last little boy, and this had made the woman gratefully devote herself to Miss Hsu's change of status. She promoted herself matchmaker to such effect that very soon Miss Hsu blossomed into a fuzzy permanent, put rouge and white upon her face, encased her half-bound feet in altogether hideous modern shoes, talked in a distracted manner and, what was worse, began to lose her mild, equable temper.

Before her spirit had begun to dwell upon the importance of being wedded, Miss Hsu had been the most unruffled person one could meet. Now she began to throw tantrums. Marian Manly did not approve of the project, because the man whom Miss Hsu was going to marry was 'old-fashioned', and not a Christian, and Miss Hsu would not only no longer be able to practise midwifery, nor to teach; but also might lose her Christianity. She would have to adapt to that soul-eroding idleness which was the life of the better-off women, busy with a thousand trivia, yet with a host of servants: lengthening each task to make the day seem shorter; filling the hours with gossip, smoking the water pipe, playing mahjong, breeding children, then immediately giving them to wet-nurses to care for; and to express all this was the word *shua*, which meant that there was always time to dawdle away, a doing nothing, a loitering, bland and formless, and no counting of the drifting hours or the days.

Miss Hsu would be clasped into these longed-for fetters, day-long week-long mahjong parties, and these would take the place of useful hours of midwifery...

Miss Hsu was palpably unsure, in dread, weighing the loneliness of the older woman coming upon her, against the unbliss of marriage and living with a man and having to endure not only intercourse, to which she professed repugnance (as all women did, for what 'moral' woman would confess to *liking* sexual intercourse?), but his certain infidelities; for if he did not continue to frequent brothels or indulge in a concubine, that would prove that he was 'wife-fearful' and his male friends would jeer at him.

Hence those moods altering her former self; but relentlessly she was being borne every day nearer to matrimony; her hair now became blacker; her heavily plastered face showed more wrinkles than had ever been perceptible when it was lightly powdered; she smiled at mirrors, talked of black-market gold for teeth-fillings, essayed a youngish gait, resurrected some influential relatives.

And then it turned out that Miss Hsu was very worried about one thing, which was her virginity. She had, it was known to only very few, been raped when a child of thirteen by her maternal uncle—a by no means uncommon occurrence in large clan families—and now wondered whether the warlord would mind... certainly she would never tell him. Marian suggested that she should not tell the warlord anything. 'Anyway he has not been a saint,' said Marian, who always became very angry at the double standard. But this point of view carried no weight. A man could do what he liked, a woman never; and if she had been raped she was spoilt for ever, and had better die. But then Miss Hsu's friend thought of an obvious way out, which was to stain a towel beforehand, and place it where post-wedding inspection would effectively prove pre-marital intactness, a device which had been used in an old Chinese novel. Preparations now went ahead, subtly and underground, for the not-yet-announced betrothal. Miss Hsu did not meet her husband-to-be; it was all done by the marriage-broker, her garrulous, enthusiastic and determined sponsor.

How this match-making came to be tied up with buying land later became obvious; in the general turn about of her personality, Miss Hsu was capsizing, throwing overboard the sober ballast of her life as a midwife, a salaried teacher, a respected member of a hospital, a spinster, and plunging into the oceanic muddle of money-caring, security-riddled gentry wifedom, with its cortege of valuations and worth; and the most important asset was land. Miss Hsu's status in the world would depend on the number of silk dresses, fur-lined dresses, coats and shoes she owned, the number of times she could afford to have a permanent for her hairdo, the servants she would be able to commandeer and keep, and above all whether she was a 'landed' person or not. In fact, this purchase was all part of the new image in order to make Miss Hsu acceptable even unto herself.

And this destroyed the pleasant sweet Miss Hsu we had known, and out of the wreckage was born a shrewish small person with rouged cheeks and screaming voice, a metamorphosis achieved not at once, but in several stages, of which one was buying land...

Miss Hsu duly entered upon marriage. Though I missed her wedding, I heard about its aftermath from others: that Miss Hsu was giving mahjong parties, that Dr Manly had not attended the wedding, which gave Miss Hsu no face and much anger, so that she eschewed coming to the hospital, but invited the midwives to her home instead.

Miss Hsu must be an old woman now, but the fixity of images once perceived does not allow me to modify her round face with the frizzy permanent, nor the rich pigeon murmur laughter which was hers... (ibid., pp.173-76)

The account is informative in that it gives details of customs and traditions relating to women in a Chinese feudal society. I have left out a long digression on the importance of mahjong playing in a wealthy married lady's life. The medieval custom of the post-wedding inspection is alluded to more than once in the five volumes, and indeed prevailed up to very recent times. Poor Miss Hsu becomes a victim of the narrator's irony here—a hapless victim of society's demands and expectations. And yet for all her newly acquired darker frizzy hair, her powdered and berouged face and her new "youngish gait", she is not a figure of fun, but one who is essentially sympathetic. How many human beings have what it takes to be "heroic"?

At the beginning of her voluminous "history, biography" Han Suyin avows that the facts she records are as "accurate" as she can make them, and she also makes the claim: "The world needs the artist who records, with dispassionate compassion, more than the missionary who proclaims with virulence unreal crusades against reality..." (*The Crippled Tree*, p.17) High-sounding words of self-approbation. We have noted the violent attacks against her for her lack of "accuracy" and moral integrity by Simon Leys and Lydia Dan Li-t'i. I am not particularly concerned with point-for-point accuracy in her telling of the story of Miss Hsu. And yet she records with more than just "dispassionate compassion". She manipulates her material for her own ends, if her end in this case is merely to illustrate the strong power of the "real", as opposed to the ideal. This is, of course, the literary artist's right. But she insists she is recording history, dealing with facts, until it serves her purposes, whatever they may be, to retract, to justify a change of stance which renders previously expressed opinions a pack of lies. She dismisses rather cavalierly the "fairy-tale fabulations" of *Destination Chungking*, and self-righteously defends her support of the events of the Cultural Revolution in earlier works: Lydia Dan Li-t'i, childhood friend of the author, bitterly resentful because of alleged lies about her mother and herself, suggests that Han Suyin should have used her considerable talent to write straight fiction, rather than to satisfy her fantasies by pretending to write history or autobiography. (See Endnote 2) The story of Caroline alias Lisan, because it is told twice, more clearly than the story of Miss Hsu, illustrates Han Suyin's novelistic powers of shaping material to serve her own purposes. Her loyalties are not as straightforward nor as constant as Agnes Smedley's and her characters, generally speaking, more complex in terms of good or evil. Caroline, like Smedley's Shan-fei and Chang Siao-hung, is dedicated to the communist cause, but she is depicted as a much more humanly fallible figure, with many more facets than either Shan-fei or Chang Hsiao-hung.

Caroline is called Lisan in *Destination Chungking*, and, according to the author, her story as told in her earlier work, is "but an attenuated, transformed version, all unpleasantness eschewed" (*Birdless Summer*, p.197), but the bare outline, and even some of the details are the same. She is trying to reach Yenan but is unable to get through Kuomintang territory once she gets to Chungking from Shanghai. While waiting for an opportunity to break through Kuomintang lines, she lodges in a little room in the house where the author and her first husband, Pao, are staying. Lisan's beauty is of a delicate variety, and unlike many Communist sympathisers of the time, she has long hair "bobbing down her back and on her shoulders". (ibid., p.196) Women who dared to have their hair cut short were dreadfully victimized in the 1927 massacres. The narrator also refers vaguely to Lisan's beautiful silk garments, so inappropriate in wartime, and especially for a trek to Yenan. Lisan's beauty contributes to the romantic aspects of the narrative. Pao's brother officer, Ensui, is a dedicated member of the Kuomintang with views diametrically opposed to those of Lisan. He falls in love with her in spite of himself, and she seems attracted to him. The result is a relationship not unlike the cliché one we find in Doris Day-Rock Hudson films of the 1950s and 1960s. All this is eliminated from the more sombre *Birdless Summer*. The episode of the author rescuing the cat is much more elaborate in *Destination Chungking* and the person who emerges as compassionate, sympathetic and heartwarming is, of course, the author. She is in the un-Chinese womanly position of being perched on a roof with an axe while the disciplined and sychophantic Pao is entertaining a fat, pompous and hateful superior officer who is filled with hypocrisy and old-style Confucian concepts about the place of women. Pao explains her absence by saying she is cooking—"traditional" activity sure to gain to approbation of the superior officer. Meanwhile the lady has to crouch on the roof to keep herself from view., All the ingredients of an American situation comedy. The introduction of Lisan into *Destination Chungking* apart from the superficial fact of adding interest to the narration seems to have the larger purpose of introducing a humanized image of an idealist who believes herself dedicated to a very worthy cause: Lisan is presented as charming, educated and vivacious, albeit immature and somewhat shallow. *Destination Chungking* concludes with an account of a gathering in the author's Chungking home, which gives Han Suyin an opportunity to present the clash of conflicting ideologies through her characters: the doctrines of Confucius, of Mencius, of Christianity, of simple privilege and of Communism are discussed in relation to China's needs. Lisan is a rather imperfect spokeswoman for the Communist viewpoint. In this early work the last glimpse we have of Lisan is when she leaves, after giving offence to the General. She leaves, full of a sense of the drama of her own fate. The author's account of Lisan's departure is certainly not without irony:

Lisan came out of the house, a coat over her arm. She came slowly down the steps, as though making a stage entrance. She paused for the exact moment of suspense, then said, 'I am going away.'

'Where will you go?' I asked.

'To—friends...' Her face quivered.

'You have nothing to fear, Lisan. It is quite unnecessary for you to go.'

She shook her head. It was for her a great dramatic moment. She would be able to say afterward, 'I could not stay. After I had defied a high official—told him the truth. I would have been arrested. I left that night—alone—on foot...'

We stood up stiffly, making an awkward leave-taking. Lisan and Ensui avoided each other's eyes; there was no reconciliation there. She tilted her chin stubbornly. 'I shall find a way yet to go to Yenan. If they turn me back, if they arrest me, I shall make the attempt again. They cannot stop me unless they shoot me!' This for Ensui's hearing, bravado to his taunts.

Kefan and I walked with her to the gate. At the last moment Lisan flung aside the veil of restraint between us with an impulsive gesture. 'Why do you not come with me? You cannot be happy here, repressed and hedged about by this kind of life.'

Kefan smiled at her. 'My work is here.'

I said, 'I have always wanted to go to the north-west. But it would be flight. Here we stand against the drift, our efforts often cancelled by reaction. We make little advance, but we stand. Someone must. We still believe the future belongs to us.'

She looked at me with incomprehension and shook her head. 'Well... good-bye... I shall send someone for my things. I don't think I am coming back.' Looking very small and lost, Lisan walked away. We did not go with her farther; we understood she had a longing to go away from us.

Then Ensui said under his breath: 'I suppose she will tramp all the way to Yenan in those thin-soled slippers, and wearing silk and her lips reddened!'

(*Destination Chungking*, pp.247-48)

The compassionate summing-up of Lisan's character comes from the philosophical Wen Hsien-sen, dedicated to the teachings of Mencius:

> Even if she flames up in false heroics, there is a core of sincerity in her. She is unhappy. She is seeking for something, for truth and meaning. (ibid., p.247)

In the almost fairytale aura which envelopes the people and events of the first novel the reader gets the impression that, although Lisan leaves, "looking small and lost", nothing permanently wrong can really befall the characters. In the darker world of *Birdless Summer* the introduction of Lisan as Caroline has an additional sobering purpose, namely to underline and further develop the manic qualities of Pao. Han Suyin has moved a very long way from the young love and married tenderness motifs of *Destination Chungking* to the almost unbelievable horror, persecution and unhappiness of married life with the rigid, Confucian-trained, feudalistic and militaristic Teng Paohuang. The facts remain essentially the same: Lisan, now Caroline, an extremely pretty young girl, comes to live in a tiny room in the same house as the author and her husband. In the earlier work the narrator refers more than once to Lisan's beautiful silk garments. Ensui also speaks disparagingly of her "thin-soled slippers". Now Han Suyin, evidently better schooled in how to attain literary effects, concentrates on her red shoes. Her red shoes, mentioned many times, and seen as a danger when the Kuomintang agents are on her track, become almost a symbol of her non-conformity, her bravado and her defiance, also her frivolity, lack of maturity and her naïveté. In *Birdless Summer* Lisan's most unprepossessing characteristics are less dwelt on. She is still fastidious about food and impatient with the servant, but the narrator makes excuses for her on the grounds that these are habits acquired from having been born and raised a rich girl. Caroline is less petulant and childish than Lisan, but the more "sophisticated" or, according to one's point of view, "seamier" side of her experiences, is brought in, namely her love for Jonathan, the English lecturer, a Communist and his subsequent jilting of her. She rouses the instinctive anti-subversive suspicions of Pao, and her jibes become the occasion for one of Pao's worst and most unattractive performances. The episode becomes a means for the author to dwell on Pao's deeply ambitious and reactionary character, to illustrate yet once more why for such a long period she is so terrified by him that she becomes a spiritless, despicable coward. Pao unscrupulously goes through Caroline's papers and reports her to the secret police, headed by Tai Lee. Caroline's sudden return becomes the occasion for one of Pao's many, many tirades against liaisons with foreigners, against wives who disobey their husbands or are negligent of their duties according to the Confucian ethic.

The story of Caroline, told by a more cynical narrator, who no longer has to humour foreign allies, becomes also the means of bringing out another point:

> Perhaps it is wrong to expect writers always to be aware of the anguish and sufferings of the people they write about. (*Birdless Summer* p.207)

Some American diplomat, whom Caroline gets to know through the students to whom she teaches Chinese, promises to enlist the help of Emily Hahn, who will write about her case. Caroline naïvely believes that friendship with foreigners will be some sort of protection because of the Chinese government's fears of a bad press. But Emily Hahn, whom Han Suyin clearly does not admire, lets Caroline down badly, according to the narrator:

> Then one day Caroline came in tears, holding in her hand a copy of the *New Yorker*. The magazine had been given to her by an American diplomat. Inside was an article about Caroline by Emily Hahn. But it was not a pretty piece of work. It made deft fun of Caroline, of her ideas, of her candour. (*Birdless Summer* p.207)

The story of Lisan-Caroline seems to have served different purposes in the two works. In both versions one might say that the narrator has retained the sort of objectivity she boasts of. In spite of her lyrical and idealistic eulogy to Chinese coolies, which provides the finale to *Destination Chungking*, Han Suyin does not seem easily taken in by human beings. Caroline has many very human failings: as I have noted before she is not Smedley's "Shan-fei, Communist" or Chang Hsiao-hung, of "The Dedicated." She is an altogether human, rather naïve, vulnerable young girl in red shoes.

Chapter V

And Sometimes The Twain Shall Meet: The Mixed Liaison in Hong Kong Fiction Written in English

I. Towards a Definition of "Hong Kong Fiction"

Before proceeding any further, a definition of the term "Hong Kong fiction" is called for. Can we talk of *the* Hong Kong novel or *the* Hong Kong short story as critics talk about Asian-American literature as a genre apart? A decade or so after the middle of the 20th century there emerged in fiction written in English a sense of the unusual dynamics of this rather unique place; of the psychological pressures on the inhabitants living in a borrowed place on borrowed time. Novels like John Gordon Davis's *The Years of the Hungry Tiger*, Lee Ding Fai's *Running Dog* and Anthony Cooper's *The Sanctuary* brought out the clash of the capitalistic and communist ideologies. Christopher New's two novels, *The Chinese Box* and *Goodbye, Chairman Mao* depicted the realities of politics on human lives. Lee Ding Fai ended her novel *Running Dog* (1980) with:

> The future is a mind-blocking preoccupation with most people in Hong Kong, the consideration of which often colours their major decisions. Some people emigrate not because they themselves desire a new way of life, but because, for the sake of their children, they feel duty bound to provide a more stable and secure background for their development. Against the unthinkable worry of drastic political changes in the future, the city builds and grows like a stem surging to catch the last rays of the sinking sun. With the construction of huge commercial complexes and flyovers that swirl above narrow streets, people who have gone abroad often come back dazzled by the new face they see. But then just as a man knows about the blemishes hidden under the clothes

of the woman he has lived with for a long time... Most of their generation... are tolerant and try, in their own way, to work out a compromise of acceptance for themselves. As for their children, they do not dare to speculate.

The language might not be particularly felicitous but the message of the uncertainty which plagued Hong Kong's upper middle classes for many years is adequately expressed. After the signing of the Sino-British agreement the picture of the future became clearer. The economic and social mores of the place were also captured in quite a number of novels. An impressionistic description of the single-minded passion for money-making which apparently dominates Hong Kong was given in the opening chapter of John Gordon Davis's *The Years of the Hungry Tiger* (Corgi Books, 1976):

> ...and factories and the workshops and the sweatshops and the great tai-pan trading houses and the banks from all around the world and the import-export agencies and shops shops shops and the money-making everywhere and the lucky Chinese names on the signboards and neon signs everywhere and the sweatpots and fleshpots and the bars bars bars, and the many many smells. (p.21)

Another "Hong Kong theme" constantly brought out in fiction was the question of the relationship between races, and we can see changing perspectives—from Somerset Maugham's *Painted Veil* (1925), when Chinese characters appear merely as houseboys or other types of servants, part of the colonial backdrop for the events involving English people who could just as well have been in Singapore or Malaya or "Tching-Yen" (the name for an imaginary colony adopted by Maugham in the face of libel suits)—to much more complex studies of the race and power structure of Hong Kong in works like Robert Elegant's *Dynasty* (1977) and James Clavell's *Noble House* (1981), though perhaps you did occasionally see a regression from such sophisticated attitudes, as notably in Anthony Cooper's novel, *The Sanctuary* (1984), which carried an outmoded colonialist view of race and particularly of inter-marriage between the races. The issue of racial relations and the intricacies of an anachronistic colonial machinery were simplified in a paternalistic, almost fairy tale fashion by Austin Coates in *Myself A Mandarin* (1968). In spite of his undoubted good intentions and his many modest disclaimers, Coates appeared to see himself as a Solomon come to save the benighted natives.

Another favourite motif—and this appeared over and over again in the work of Anglo-American writers who (to my mind unfortunately) had a virtual monopoly over writing about Hong Kong in English—was the aimlessness of expatriate life in general, with its endless rounds of cocktail parties, visits to bars and passionless pursuit of sex, described usually from a male viewpoint. This had been done before in tales of colonial life, as in Maugham's short stories. But in more recent times this theme developed a new and interesting slant, in keeping with the more liberal tendencies of the times. The end of ennui, purposefulness and joy came with finding the right Chinese girl. This is Richard Mason's account of his feelings of suffocation at a cocktail party and the glimmer of hope that he simplistically saw as coming from the look in the eyes of a worn-out Chinese houseboy:

> ...I began to grow bored, and to feel a creeping claustrophobia in this hygienic modern flat, amongst the high-fidelity loudspeakers and the martinis and the hygienic theories of art. Then the Chinese house-boy, who was not a boy at all but an elderly man, came to refill my glass, and while he was doing so I noticed his eyes—small deep withdrawn Chinese eyes that belonged to a world infinitely remote from everything else in this room. It was as though all at once a window had been thrown open and I had breathed fresh air... And I knew that I had come close to the answer I had been seeking. If I had married Kay or the pretty girl in the cocktail dress who was saying 'Of course it's the theatre I miss', I would have been shutting myself in this room and bolting the windows and doors. But marrying Suzie would be like taking a flying leap from the sill. (*The World of Suzie Wong*, p.268)

And this brings us to the motif of the mixed liaison and the obstacles engendered by such liaisons. In novels with happy endings like *The World of Suzie Wong*, love conquered all; in those with unhappy endings like *The Years of the Hungry Tiger, Miller* and *The Chinese Box* we saw the Anglo-American hero shattered, totally destroyed by the loss of his Chinese love. To this topic I shall return in a subsequent section. My concern in this first section is still to circumscribe the scope of my study by defining "Hong Kong Fiction" written in English. I have so far talked in terms of theme. New immigrants to America from Hong Kong were making their homes in new and already established Asian American communities, but Hong Kong writers made no significant contribution to the growing body of "Asian American" literature, although film-makers like Wayne Wang made an impact on Western filmgoers with films like *Chen Is Missing* and *Dimsum*. It is perhaps interesting that the first novel to deal with the plight of immigrants in Britain came from Timothy Mo, whose father was a Hong Kong solicitor and who spent his early years in Hong Kong and who still returns frequently. The characters in *Sour Sweet* made their passage to Britain from Hong Kong and though the female characters are, strictly speaking, Northern Chinese, we could see the work as concerned with Hong Kong people cut off from their Hong Kong milieu. There were novels, like Le Carré's *The Honourable Schoolboy* and Ian Stewart's *The Peking Payoff* which feature Hong Kong settings, but since they did not deal essentially with the "Hong Kong experience", as it were, they lie outside my study.

Leaving aside the question of subject matter there is the question of authorship. If the criterion falls on the author, then how are we to define "Hong Kong person"? And I don't mean a definition in terms of the political jargon then current. In *The Years of the Hungry Tiger* (p.462) we find this dialogue uttered in the midst of the 1967 riots:

'Aren't you worried about all those Chinese?' the American lady next to me said.
'Madam,' I grinned, 'I am Hongkongese.'
'I thought you were British,' she said.
'Only my parents.'

So there are British Hongkongese, as well as American and Chinese, Australian and Indian and so on. Generally speaking, published writers who wrote *about* Hong Kong as opposed to merely mentioning the place in passing as any other bit of Oriental exotica, tended to be Anglo-Americans, native users of English. While some may not have shown the same degree of commitment to the place and its unique culture as the "Hongkongese" quoted above, they did know the place. Many, like Christopher New and Anthony Cooper, lived and worked here and had done so for a good many years. Others, like Robert Elegant, had made a study of Hong Kong; indeed Elegant had been a student of Asia for almost three decades. Yet others, like James Clavell, exploited a superficial knowledge of the place gained from frequent stays and, as he stated in his acknowledgements in *Taipan*, through his Hong Kong friends. They succeeded in giving an aura of verisimilitude to the many readers who did not really know Hong Kong. Han Suyin and, to a less extent, Timothy Mo, achieved international reputations. They wrote about Hong Kong and they have a half-claim to "Chinese-ness" of race. Both had lived in Hong Kong. But it would not be entirely accurate to say English was a second language for either. Indeed Timothy Mo, in conversation with me in London, vigorously refused to be identified as a "Hong Kong writer". He could neither read nor write Chinese and could barely speak Cantonese. A cursory glance at the Heinemann Educational Books (Asia) Brochure on its *Writing in Asia Series* showed that the only writer listed who fulfilled the criteria of being a local Hong Kong Chinese and writing *about* Hong Kong in English was Lee Ding Fai. The writer of *Running Dog* (1980) is actually a woman, despite her masculine-sounding pseudonym.

I have given a rather long, but I think necessary, preamble to my study, which focuses on a selection of works which fulfilled my tentative definition of "Hong Kong fiction".

My choice of a corpus was not based on literary merit. Indeed the selection ranges from works which received international acclaim to those that could hardly lay claim to being "literature" and had little interest beyond the topical. In 1983 Timothy Mo, in a note to me, wrote, "The lack of literature from and on Hong Kong expatriates and locals—as opposed to the many potboilers—is an interesting question." He was referring to writings in English. The over-fastidious may well regard some items I selected as "trash". The majority of works in my corpus were written by *Western man*. Hence the potential barriers to understanding were not only sexual but also racial. Han Suyin's *A Many-Splendoured Thing* and Lee Ding Fai's *Running Dog* are notable exceptions. The author of *Sour Sweet* and *The Monkey King*, in terms of understanding his Chinese woman characters, had the advantage of a Chinese father and stepmother and first-hand knowledge of a Chinese family living in Hong Kong.

II. The Importance of Social Context

(i) The Question of Race: "Expatriates" vs. "Locals"

Within the Hong Kong context, political and social conditions, until around the decade preceding 1997, fostered an image of subservience for not just Chinese women but the whole Chinese race among the expatriate community. The situation can best be understood if one compares it to the situation depicted in *A Passage to India*. The idea of privilege by virtue of race persisted in some writers' writing until fairly recent times. Even the "liberal" writer, in his very disclaimers of complicity in the social order, admitted his belief in the existence of his privilege. Harry Ricketts, in a collection of little-known, rather light-weight sketches which resulted from three years as a lecturer at the University of Hong Kong, entitled *People Like Us*, wrote with rather heavy-handed satire about the situation. In his short story "All That Went Out with Kipling" (the title is already significant), a colonial type, obviously disapproved of by the narrator, says,

> Don't misunderstand me, there are plenty of rich Chinese, but there are no poor Europeans... Socially speaking I think you'll find that the *gwai-los*, as we're called, and the locals stick pretty

much to their own sides of the fence. It's simpler for everyone concerned.

An interesting study of caste and class among the English community was made by H. J. Lethbridge in *Hong Kong: Stability and Change.* (Hong Kong, O.U.P., 1978, pp.163ff) He quoted from Arnold Wright and H.A. Cartwright, authors of a compendium on Hong Kong and the Treaty Ports of China. "Among Englishmen who have never visited the outlying portions of the Empire the idea prevails that social distinctions are forgotten in the presence of the stern realities of life in the colonies, and that 'all sorts and conditions of men' are united in the bonds of brotherhood by a common feeling of expatriation. But, though this idea may not be without justification in the backwoods of Canada, the bush of Australia and the veldt of South Africa, it is certainly a travesty of the conditions obtaining in our Crown Colonies. Nowhere, perhaps, is it more completely repudiated than in Hong Kong where society is cast into innumerable divisions and subdivisions." (*Twentieth Century Impressions of Hong Kong, Shanghai, and Other Treaty Ports of China*, London, 1908, p.341) *The Painted Veil* focused interest on the British community and tensions resulting from the social divisions operative before the Japanese war: officials, merchants, members of the professional classes and Europeans in supervisory or low status occupations generate at least part of the interest in the novel. But in my study I do not go into a detailed sociological exploration of the social origins of these expatriates and the rise in both the standard of living and self-esteem for most of them consequent upon their expatriation. This Lethbridge does very lucidly and interestingly. In the novels I was concerned with, while there was clear stratification in the expatriate European community, the stratification in terms at least of external recognition is based on wealth and position in the adopted community, rather than on class antecedents or educational background. Veronica wrote in 1907 a series of sketches for *The Hong Kong Weekly*. One devoted to marriage is written in a humorous and mildly satirical vein. She asks of a possible marriage partner:

"Has she her aspirates under control? Most of the women here do. Does she use crested note-paper? Most of the women here do. Is she connected with the Peerage? Most of the women here are. Has she private means? That is the most important point of all." If one were to take in the implications of this frivolous sketch one would see that Europeans in Hong Kong saw themselves as members of an elite—"as an upper class elite in the English sense—sharply distinguished from a European petty bourgeoisie and a Chinese *lumperproletariat* and working class". (James Lethbridge, ibid., p.164) Many social changes took place after the Japanese occupation, and unemployment in Britain, among other factors, changed the type and classes of people seeking employment in Hong Kong. But, while pretensions to the practices and life style of the upper classes in England had been eroded, works of fiction published as late as the 1980s still show a vision of an expatriate entity, a European community separate from the Chinese and, by and large, enjoying a life style far more privileged than the vast masses of the local population.

It was true, though, that the expatriate community was aware, and growingly so, of the very wealthy Chinese "taipans", with their glamourous daughters, bejewelled wives, antique collections and fleets of limousines. And these glitterati appeared as cameo sketches, for the most part, in fiction. But, except through the media or business or professional contacts, the average expatriate man had little opportunity to really get to know such people personally or at first-hand. On the other hand, the surging masses, living in cramped conditions in resettlement estates and milling about in Mongkok or Causeway Bay, lent credence to their vision of themselves as being privileged people. Most Anglo-Americans, up until relatively recent times, worked for the trading companies, many for the established 'hongs' like Jardine Matheson, for the civil services, taught at the universities or in the English language secondary schools, or else were journalists. The majority were provided with housing in large (by Hong Kong standards) flats, passages, home leave, privileges accorded to local people in the same positions only not long before the 1997 handover—and then not all of them and not all the privileges. The situation changed almost more rapidly than one could take it in. The "localization" programme, whereby expatriates were replaced by local people where possible in "key" positions, accelerated and "decolonialization" as a lead-up to 1997 advanced in all fields. The old British-dominated "hongs" passed into the control of powerful Chinese magnates, the new taipans. But the situation reflected in the works in my corpus, for the most part, is that of the 50s to the early 80s, before Margaret Thatcher's visit to Peking with all its repercussions. With some notable exceptions the Chinese women the average expatriate male was likely to encounter would be his professional and/or social inferiors—secretaries, airline hostesses, bar girls, salesgirls, waitresses and *amahs*. Added to this was the popular image of Chinese women in the minds of the English-speaking world outside Hong Kong. If the writer was trying to cater for a mass market, his fictional Chinese woman had to live up to some stereotype, or the attempt at "realistic" portraiture might paradoxically have created the reverse effect.

It must be admitted the failure of racial integration was as much due to the prejudices of the Chinese. In spite of travel, education and residence abroad, in spite of having all the trappings of being Westernized, even the relatively young members of the middle class frowned—and still frown—upon marriage to a *gweilo* or *gweipor*, that is, a Western man or woman. Inter-marriage has become much more common with the ever-more popular practice of sending children overseas to be educated. But it is still a standing joke among middle class families that the danger of this type of arrangement is the risk of having a *gwei* son-in-law or daughter-in-law. In Lee Ding Fai's *Running Dog*, the daughter of the family, Siu Wah, has gone to the prestigious Smith College in the U.S.A., on a scholarship. Consider this exchange:

'And how is Siu Wah? Does she write home often?'

'Not as much as we wish she would, I am afraid, children are forgetful'... Chen said some of his friends' children are worse. Not only do they write in English. Imagine having to have your son's letter translated to you!'

'Well, it's no worse than their wanting to marry foreigners, I'm sure,' the sister-in-law reiterated one of her favourite fears for the Chen family. (p.74)

The World of Suzie Wong opens with the meeting between the narrator, Robert Lomax, and Suzie on the Star ferry. Suzie pretends to be a very rich taipan's daughter and claims her father will beat her if he knew she has been fraternizing with a *gweilo*. (p.10)

With the rapid changes taking place in the social, economic, and indeed, political power structure of Hong Kong, it would seem that, by the last decade of the century, there should be less reason for Western man to feel so much more privileged than the average educated professional local. But a new bolster for his sense of superiority had developed: this was his foreign passport. While it might be true that some Hong Kong women desire a foreign (preferably American) husband and the right of abode in his country, the truth has been grossly exaggerated. In any case this ego-boosting myth coloured the presentation of Chinese women vis-à-vis their Western lovers, and strengthened Western man's self-image of being the superior partner. In *The Years of The Hungry Tiger*, the wedding reception of a bar girl and an American consulate official is described. "It was big news in Wanchai 'Local Girl Makes Good.'" Mimi, the bride, is clearly considered by all, narrator included, to have made the catch of the century, although his satirical attitude towards the patronizing paternalism of the American Consul is evident:

He [the Consul] gave the blushing Mimi a big kiss. 'Welcome to the Yoo Ess Ay!'

'Thank you, sir,' Mimi blushed happily.

'Now now,' the Consul wagged his finger; 'none of this sir crap, you're an American now, yessiree, you call me Al!' (p.130)

This is of course an extreme case: the blushing bride was already thrilled by the prospect of getting out of the brothel. America is a bonus.

And so the inflated sense of expatriates being associated with the good life—spacious and gracious flats with harbour views, carpets, fitted kitchens, cars, boats, travel abroad, as contrasted with squalor and cramped, unhygienic living conditions and habits, persisted. The Peak vs. Wanchai. The Mid-levels vs. Causeway Bay. Plus the foreign passport. The most outrageous presentation of this supposed contrast appeared in Anthony Cooper's *The Sanctuary*, which was published in 1984. What was surprising here is that the author was clearly aware of 1997. He overtly pledged, in his own person, in the preface to his work, his commitment to Hong Kong, and yet the work itself made no concessions to the shifting power, economic and social structure. His American heroine insisted that the commitment of his civil servant protagonist was only to a Hong Kong that existed then, but would soon be no more. The whole "philosophy" of marriage to a Chinese girl was startlingly anachronistic, reminiscent of the attitude prevalent in Maugham's short stories of the East. Indeed, Cooper specifically mentions "Young Guy", the character in Maugham's "Force of Circumstances", who married an English woman while on home leave, returning to Malaya to face all sorts of complications. He finally had to return to his "Kampong whore" (Cooper's term).

Cooper's "philosophy"—and I know I am committing here the critical error of equating character with creator, but the intensity and the unnecessary length with which the different aspects of his whole "philosophy" were propounded suggested a degree of total commitment on the part of the author—was put into the mouth of his protagonist, James Waltham, a Colonial civil servant like Cooper himself. The reasons included the undesirability of Eurasian children, the essential Anglophobia of the Chinese race so that when a person married a Chinese girl he "might get some of the heart but never, never the soul". The most telling passage in terms of what I have been talking about—the advantages of marrying Western men, and the splendours of expatriate life in contrast to the squalor and uncouthness of the Chinese way of life—is this one:

But I've seen it happen! A mixed couple seem very happy; then, at Chinese New Year or some other festival, the man's in-laws and Chinese family come round by the bus-full to his nice home. They make the most god-awful din, drop rubbish all over the balcony. And while they do it they look askance at their daughter and wonder whether living so close with a round-eyed long-nosed foreign-devil barbarian is worth life's meal ticket she got on her wedding day. Every time it happens a bit of the man dies inside because he knows no matter how much he loves his wife he could never break through to her Chinese core. No non-Chinese can. (p.70)

In the only novel in my corpus which was written by a Chinese woman, one of the focal points of the plot is a triangular love situation: a beautiful Chinese girl with a degree from Smith College and her two suitors—Yau Man, a Chinese refugee with little formal education who has become a multi-millionaire industrialist and Charles Felton, journalist, graduate of Harvard and Columbia. Lee Ding Fai, who herself came from the middle class and had received a Western-style education, presents a well-informed picture of the living conditions, habits and mores of up-and-coming Chinese families. The Chens move from modest comfort to the splendours of a professionally decorated flat. Her novel shows awareness of the complexities of the stratification of Chinese society in Hong Kong. She is aware it is not just a simple two-tier structure of "taipans" and "the others"—the spitting hoards who show an inordinate addiction to chamber pots (cf. *The Years of the Hungry Tiger*, p.274) and shouting on that unfamiliar instrument—the telephone. (cf. *The World of Suzie Wong*, p.62) She also gives a vision of society where there are ways of living and homes more luxurious than expat quarters with great views of the harbour, the obligatory Tientsin carpet and more often than not, institutional furniture.

The Chinese world of Yau Man in the latter part of the novel is in contrast to the expatriate world of Charles Felton, but the contrast is in reverse to the stereotyped one. Yau Man seems to represent a world of unimagined luxury, where all material things are possible—banquets with over 1,000 guests, luxury flats, fully furnished, to be handed over to a discarded mistress to assuage guilt, lavish round-the-world trips without the help of leave passages. Charles Felton's world seems very bland compared with Yau Man's. In a world of cream-coloured Jaguars and other luxury cars, Charles Felton commandeers a second-hand Toyota! It is a pity that Lee Ding Fai, who obviously has a clearer perception of the Hong Kong milieu as it exists for 99% of the population, is unable to write with greater force and sensitivity and with a more flexible style and to reach a wider audience. It is in this novel that we have the presentation of a ludicrous caricature of an English executive working for Jardine Matheson as seen through the eyes of a perceptive, educated and intelligent young woman, well able to deluge him with ironical remarks which are lost on the dense and self-centred specimen of an outmoded colonial type. The tone of patronage is maddening and yet has a terrifyingly "familiar" ring.

'You went to school in America, didn't you?' he commented blandly. 'A lot of Chinese students want to go there, I understand. It's easier, I suppose. Of course, their college is really a school to us.'

She sipped her drink, and returned a shrug and a slight smile.

'I wouldn't mind going there to have a look myself, though there are other places that one would rather go first... So where exactly were you when you were there?'

'In a school called Smith somewhere in the wilds of Massachusetts,' she replied.

'Really, how interesting.'

His obnoxiousness fascinated rather than offended her. He was like a kid turning up his nose at another boy's possessions. And he talked about his work and his company as if, without it, Hong Kong's trade and commercial interest would come tumbling down to the ground.

'It's a good thing for us you've decided to come here,' Audrey said, flashing him an innocent smile...

He was fun to listen to, and it amused her to see how he accepted her gentle mockery as guileless remarks. As a dinner date his obnoxiousness could be tolerated because she did not have to take him seriously. In a work situation his haughtiness and insensitivity would have caused endless conflicts. There had been times when she felt like shaking him and telling him that his 'I am the master here,' attitude only showed what an ignorant fool he really was. But then she did not feel enough affection for him to want to reform him. He would learn his lesson sooner or later, perhaps the hard way.' (pp.147-9)

Han Suyin's powers as a novelist are of course far superior and her portrayal of the consciousness of the Eurasian woman doctor (herself) in *A Many-Splendoured Thing* is far more sensitive than Lee Ding Fai's portrayal of Audrey's vision, but Han Suyin's consciousness is that of a Eurasian born in the North, educated in China and Europe, in Hong Kong by political accident, and not that of a "Hong Kong Chinese".

(ii) The Question of Sex: Men vs. Women

In discussing social context I have for the most part concentrated on the racial aspects—of expatriate life versus local life. What of the position of women in Hong Kong? European women here run the gamut from top taipans' wives through the wives of middle management to embassy wives to deserted wives who drift about making a precarious living some by dubious means. There are single professional women, many working as teachers, nurses, physiotherapists. And many portraits of clear stereotypes appear on the pages of Hong Kong fiction. Even my superficial survey of images of European women give me the impression that they are exaggerated and, paradoxically, largely biased in favour of the Chinese women. This is certainly the case in *The Years of the Hungry Tiger*, *Miller* and some of the women who are glimpsed fleetingly in Harry Rickett's collection of sketches.

But my concern is not just with portraiture of Hong Kong women but specifically of Hong Kong Chinese women and in this essay, with Hong Kong Chinese women involved in romantic attachments to European men. Eurasian women do appear in Hong Kong literature. Han Suyin is the best known example. Otherwise they tend not to be central characters. Wallace, the central character in Timothy Mo's *The Monkey King* (1978) is Eurasian-Macanese, but he is male. Many of the characters in *Dynasty* are Eurasian, with varying proportions of Chinese blood. The Sekloong dynasty, into which the English woman Mary Osgood marries, is believed to be based on the Eurasian Sir Robert Hotung's dynastic family. In *Dynasty* there are mixed marriages of every conceivable combination, to show the cosmopolitan nature of the clan and their vast empire. The genealogy table provided by Robert Elegant already gives us indications of how many powerful connections the Sekloongs have built up through interracial marriage—a grandson-in-law who is an American Under-Secretary of State, a grand daughter-in-law who is the daughter of a legendary Japanese tycoon. But in the majority of Hong Kong novels, Eurasian women figure largely as secretaries, mostly girls-Friday, competent and capable, as in *Noble House* and *The World of Suzie Wong*, in which, for example, we find Miss Ruggeroni, the Macanese assistant of The British Consul in Macau, the lady who has "the dreamy yearning voice of a Eurasian who belongs nowhere". (p.280) Indeed, in the years after 1949, with the influx of refugees from China, there could be found many Eurasian men and women, many with Portuguese blood, working in banks. The women tended to work in airlines and as secretaries, and because their English tended to be better, on average, than the English of their Chinese counterparts their services tended to be in demand by European companies. Hence the sort of stereotype you find in *Noble House* in the person of Claudia Chen—jolly, grey-haired, all-knowing, extremely shrewd. (p.66) In the same novel we have the more fully drawn Portuguese-Chinese love interest Olanda Ramos, and she is drawn according to the Oriental sultry siren stereotype.

As for the status of Chinese women in Hong Kong society today, it would appear that, for the professionally trained person, discrimination is no worse than anywhere else in the Western world; it could even be argued that the situation is a little better. Current statistics show larger enrolment of women than men in top universities and women here are not behind those in the West in making strides towards equality. One stereotype among Hong Kong Chinese is the "strong woman" or literally "female strong person", based on a few real-life models in the professions and trade. I started this section off by referring to stereotypes. Rightly or wrongly human beings all over the world tend to think of other human beings in terms of stereotypes, and Hong Kong Chinese are no different. Indeed a night's viewing of locally produced situation comedies and skits will show the large number of such female stereotypes—the Westernized women, the mahjong-mad wife, the "philanthropic" *tai-tai*, the wise-cracking *amah*. Needless to say a great novelist has to go beyond the stereotype, and to make full use of the literary devices at his disposal to create character.

III. Literary Antecedents and Media Stereotypes

Apart from considering the social context, the writer of Hong Kong fiction may well be tempted to look for "models" for his Chinese women characters in Western literature as well as from the Western media, but as I have tried to establish, there are few fully drawn, individualized and memorable portraits of Chinese, or indeed of Oriental, women in the literature of the West until the early decades of the twentieth century. And even then, apart from Pearl Buck, the writers who did attempt sympathetic portraiture, like Agnes Smedley and Emily Hahn (e.g. *China Only Yesterday*, London, 1963; *Hong Kong Holiday*, New York, 1946) did not enjoy a wide circulation. The conclusion one is forced to, then, would appear to be that the writer of "Hong Kong fiction" had no real literary models to fall back on in the depiction of Chinese women. What was available were certain stereotypes, popularized largely through the media. And the most persistent and tenacious stereotype was that of the sex object, the alluring "dream girl from the East".

The corollary of my suggestion that there is an absence of literary models is the claim that, in a sense, writers of "Hong Kong fiction" were breaking new ground in their attempt to give three-dimensional portraits of Chinese women. It may be of interest to note, though, that the portrait of Phuong, the Vietnamese girl, in Graham Greene's *The Quiet American* (1955) precedes the portrait of Suzie Wong by two years, and even a cursory reading of the two novels will reveal some resemblances between the two heroines, though it seems fairly obvious that Phuong is the more sophisticated literary creation.

IV. Literary Modes in Relation to the Presentation of Character in Fiction: Narration, Description, Comment, Dialogue.

Dialogue, description, commentary, narration, are used by the writer of fiction for many purposes. (See I.A. Gordon, *The Movement of English Prose*, 1966, p.162: "Viewed (so to speak) anatomically, a novel consists of four prose 'systems': dialogue, narrative, description, and commentary. In many twentieth-century novels, the systems overlap and run together.") They work together to advance the plot, to create background, to contribute towards "theme"—but it is on their function in portraying character that I wish to focus. Of these methods in the creation of illusion in a work of fiction, the presentation of speech has a distinctive role: it is in this element that the closest "imitation of reality" is likely to appear to take place, if only because the author's presence appears to be least obtrusive. Apart from being functional, dialogue has, of course, a distinctive and intrinsic interest. In *Speech in the English Novel* (London 1973), Norman Page raises fundamental questions concerning the nature of speech in fiction and its relationship to real-life talk. He confronts the problems of giving the illusion of real speech, "as proceeding from the mouth of an actual person" (David Lodge, *Language of Fiction*, 1966, p.47) without actually reproducing, as from a tape recorder, real speech. As with other "prose systems" (I.A. Gordon's term) of fiction, speech has to be the result of a process of purposeful selection. "The writer of dialogue… seeks to create by the use of one medium the effect of language used in another, and if there is a means by which this can be accomplished, however incompletely, it is certainly not by the slavish reproduction of the features of actual speech" (Norman Page, ibid., p.10). When a writer writes speech which differs from the norms of standard English he generally makes use of certain fixed conventions. If the dialect is an English one, for example, Cockney, and his readers "know" what it sounds like, then only a limited number of signals in the printed text should be sufficient to create the desired effect. In Shaw's *Pygmalion*, the speech of Eliza Doolittle's pre-phonetics lessons is presented briefly in the form of an "eye" dialect; then, after an explanatory note, Shaw abandons the effort and reverts to ordinary spelling. But in a play, dialogue is written to be spoken again. In a work of fiction, the author's reader will "hear" what he wants him to "hear", if he is successful in his presentation. In the presentation of foreigners—notably continental Europeans, for example the French, Italians or Germans—speaking English, certain conventions have been accepted. The stereotype French, or Italian or German accent and speech mannerisms are familiar to the average reader of English novels, in the same way that the stock Scot or Irishman speaks in a way accepted by convention. Again, a minimal number of markers in the written text are required. The average Western reader who has not been to China would not be familiar with the "accent" of any of the major Chinese dialect groups when they are speaking English, though they may have an idea of the stylized features on the grammatical level of Chinese speech from media representations of Fu Manchu or Charlie Chan, or Dr No. In presenting the speech of Chinese women the writer has the task of using that speech to assign her to a group, in this case a group determined by race and sex and also to individualize her. The conventions adopted by the writers in my corpus differ, and the differences are dictated by the author's attitude to the character, and the responses towards her he wishes to evoke in his readers, although his apparent attitude and the reader's attitude in response to the conventions chosen do not always coincide. And a great deal depends on the nature of his readership.

The tradition of using dialect to bring out specific qualities in fictional narrative dates from *The Second Shepherd's Play* through Chaucer's *Reeve's Tale* and Shakespeare to Fielding and other eighteenth century novelists and later. The associations of dialectal speech are many: they bring out the comic, the provincial, the idea of integrity or lack or sophistry and sophistication. (In this connection see Norman Page, Chapter III and A.E.C. Letley's unpublished M.Phil. thesis on *The Use of Dialect in the Work of John Walt,* University of Hong Kong 1980) in which she asserts strongly that dialect is used to bring out integrity of character.

For my purposes, for "dialect" read "non-standard", and specifically, the varyingly non-standard levels of English spoken by Chinese female characters. The Chinese servant, the *amah* in the expatriate household, is a stereotype in Hong Kong fiction. They are there to take sides with "the good guys", often the expatriate heroes in love with Chinese women, and to speak with homespun wisdom against the "baddies", often the expatriate wives. They speak pidgin, represented by certain stylized conventions on the level of grammar and lexis. The *amah* in *Miller* uses only the simple present tense: "I make plenty strong." Her parts of speech are confused, and her command of items of the vocabulary limited. She says, "White wine with fishy", and when corrected by Miller, she admits her mistake and makes her statement clearer by using also the Chinese equivalent for *prawn.* "Yes, prawns—ha." She uses *housie* for house. The question of the accuracy of her "dialect" or "idiolect" is not at issue. The impression given is one of servitude and lack of education. The associations are comic and the limited nature of her expressiveness would make her boring, unsympathetic—in all ways inadequate. The example of Joseph, the old Yorkshire servant in *Wuthering Heights* comes almost immediately to mind when one thinks of dialect speakers in English fiction. In the first edition of *Wuthering Heights* (1847) the dialect speech of Joseph is of exceptional vividness. Emily Brontë had made an unusually bold attempt at fidelity. She made a substantial effort to suggest the sound quality of a broad Yorkshire speech through spelling variants. This resulted in difficulties of comprehension for most readers. Charlotte Brontë asked the publisher of the 1850 edition to modify the orthography in order to make Joseph more accessible to the general reader.

Similarly the creator of major Chinese characters who are speaking a non-standard English has to steer a careful course. Needless to say similar problems arise whether the character is male or female, but whereas marked deviance from the norms of speech, generally speaking, diminishes the status of a male character or gives sinister or comic overtones, Western readers tend to be more tolerant to deviant speech in female characters. There are connotations—like the French accent of *femme fatales*—often of exotic allure, or at worst, a certain "cuteness". A heroine who speaks a strongly marked pidgin for the duration of the book may well give rise to the wrong responses from the audience, but the author has at the same time to cater for conventional expectations. To the complex issue of how Chinese women characters speak in English language fiction I shall return in the following chapter.

V. The Hong Kong Chinese Heroine in an East-West Relationship: The Techniques of Portraiture.

A good number of Hong Kong novels include a liaison between a Western man and a Chinese woman. If the love interest is not central to the novel, it is still included almost as if it were an obligatory part of local colouring. In Christopher New's *The Chinese Box*, the love between the English academic and the Chinese ballet teacher-cum-spy is pivotal to the narrative. In his second novel, *Goodbye, Chairman Mao*, it is more incidental to the narrative of personal tragedy set against international intrigue. The Chinese origins of the wife give the "excuse" for the exotic Hong Kong setting so familiar to the author. *Taipan*, set in historical Hong Kong, features the liaison between the taipan Struan, and May-may, and this is all part of the excitement and adventure of carving out a trading empire in the exotic East. The half-caste descendents of this liaison add colour and intrigue to Clavell's later novel, *Noble House*. In the stories of Harry Rickett's collection, *People Like Us*, we have a brief, and, quite frankly, meaningless vignette of the breaking up of an apparently shiftless English youth and a rich Chinese girl. The following exchange is, one supposes, meant to tell a great deal about such relationships:

'Well, are you happy I'm going?'

'What do you think?'

'I don't know. My friends told me Europeans had no feelings?'

'What else did they say?'

'That you get what you want and then you don't want it any more.'

'Nice friends you have.'

'You don't know them.'

'Whose fault is that?'

'I really loved you.'

'Would you like some more tea?' He ordered more tea and coffee.

'It's someone else, isn't it?'

'I don't want to talk about it.'

'Is it what I said about going with other people?'

'You give me no freedom.' (p.10)

It is perhaps worth referring to the totally unstereotypical East-West liaison depicted by Timothy Mo in *Sour Sweet*; the central concern of this novel is with Chinese immigrants from Hong Kong adjusting to life in Britain. It is comic, original and poignant, reflecting the author's combined gifts of humour and sympathy. Mui, formerly a Hong Kong domestic servant, has migrated to Britain to join her younger sister and her family. Mui is presented as comically plump and short and physically totally unprepossessing. The last thing the reader would associate with this unexpectedly resourceful Chinese woman would be sexual desire. The family runs a Chinese take-away and deep into the night Mui takes out trays of food to loud and usually burly lorry-drivers. Her disappearances become longer and longer. She grows fatter and fatter and it turns out that she is actually with child. The identity of the father is left untold. And indeed the author makes the readers feel that this knowledge is not important, only incidental, in the same way that race in this particular case is also incidental. An anonymous Western man and a Chinese anti-heroine and anti-siren.

From the few examples I have referred to it is clear that the "norm" of fictional East-West relationships is Western man plus Chinese woman. Reversing the sexes would be exceptional. This is certainly not necessarily a reflection of the "norms" of contemporary Hong Kong society. But most of the writers are Anglo-American men and the stereotypical norm suits their vanity, and, generally speaking, satisfies the expectations of an international readership.

Han Suyin wrote movingly of the love between an American woman, and a Chinese intellectual, Dr Jen Yong, in *Till Morning Comes*. The two are swept apart by the events of 1949. A best-seller in the late 1980s was *Son of the Revolution*, a documentary of a Chinese student and his English teacher, an American woman, and their love in the midst of political turmoil. The autobiographical documentary was jointly authored by Liang Heng and Judith Shapiro, now his wife. But these works are not examples of "Hong Kong fiction". I have already mentioned the multi-racial marriages in the cosmopolitan world of Robert Elegant's *Dynasty* where no laws of fairer races attracting the darker or vice versa operate. But the usual formula in "Hong Kong fiction" is Western man plus Chinese woman.

I wish now to consider three novels in my corpus which can be called "love stories" in that the central concern is the working out of a love relationship. Of equal, if not more, interest to the reader would be all the exciting and history-making events taking place in Hong Kong between the 1950s and the years leading up to 1997. A great proportion of narration, comment, description and dialogue went towards creating "background" and in localizing the story, but the plot on which other "interests" were hung is essentially one that centred on the affair between an Englishman and a Chinese woman. The three novels are, in chronological order, Richard Mason's *The World of Suzie Wong* (1957), John Gordon Davis's *The Years of the*

Hungry Tiger (1976) and Geoffrey Thursby's *Miller* (1983).

Each writer lived and worked in Hong Kong and "knew" the place; Geoffrey Thursby lived and worked here till his death in 1985. He was a journalist, the publisher of *Hong Kong Business*. Richard Mason worked for the British Council and knew other parts of the East as well as Hong Kong. John Gordon Davis was a Crown Counsel in Hong Kong when his first best-seller (about Rhodesia), *Hold My Hand, I'm Dying*, was published. Each man wrote of the place and its people with a deep degree of sympathy, as projected through their narrators. All three novels reflected the motif of "renewal through the love of a Chinese Woman" that I have referred to in my attempt to define "Hong Kong fiction". The expatriate woman is used as a foil in each case—a symbol of betrayal, materialism and neurotic self-interest in *Miller*, and to a less extent in *The Years of the Hungry Tiger*; as a symbol of joyless routine and convention and artifice in *The World of Suzie Wong*. But true to the self-image of Western (and possible masculine) superiority, each protagonist saw himself as (at least potentially) the protector, patron and saviour of the Chinese lover. It seems superfluous to say that of the three heroines—Suzie Wong, alias Wong Mee Ling, Tsang Ying Ling and Tina Lau—Suzie Wong is the best known, thanks to the film and the success of Nancy Kwan in bringing the character to life, and thanks also to the rather sensational nature of her profession and the Wanchai milieu.

But, difficult as the task may be, let us separate the film from the book and concentrate on Richard Mason's manipulation of the means available to the novelist in the portrayal of his Chinese heroine. Richard Mason adopted a first person narration in his novel. The narrator is Robert Lomax, a self-taught aspiring painter who has come to Hong Kong after resigning his job on a Malayan plantation in the hope of finding inspiration and fame. Because he has a limited budget and it is the cheapest place he can find, he sets up in the Nam Kok Hotel, haunt of prostitutes catering for the hordes of sailors on rest and recreation in the heyday of the girlie bars and brothels of Hong Kong's Wanchai district. He befriends all the "girls", whom he depicts largely through description and commentary but also through dialogue and in some cases through incident. While characters like Wednesday Lulu, Big Alice and Minnie Ho were individualized to varying extents, it is Suzie on whom the greatest care in portrayal was lavished.

Legend has it that the model for the Nam Kok Hotel was the original incarnation of the now-redeveloped Luk Kwok Hotel in Wanchai; more than one *habitué* of the place claimed to be the real-life Suzie Wong. (In *The Years of the Hungry Tiger*, John Gordon Davis set a wedding in the Luk Kwok and introduced a character who insisted that she was Suzie Wong, in spite of repeated scoffs.) But whether Suzie was indeed "drawn from life" is not altogether relevant. Mason drew on all the resources of the novelist in creating a character who was at once the embodiment of many stereotypes in literature about women and yet *intended* to be a very endearing individual. A great deal of work has been done on images of women in literature, especially as they appear in books written by men[1]. Analyses have uncovered such stereotypes as the virgin and the whore; the mother (angel or devil?); the submissive wife, the domineering wife; the bitch; the seductress; man's prey, the sex object; the old maid; the bluestocking; the castrating woman[2]. It is interesting to note that Suzie incorporated in one woman the images of virgin and whore (an apparent contradiction that Mason painstakingly tried to reconcile and delineate in a number of passages in the book), the mother, the largely submissive but at times domineering (from good intentions) wife, and also another pair of apparently contradictory images—the seductress who is also man's prey, the sex object.

A close look at the opening chapter in the book will show Mason used narration, comment, dialogue and description to illuminate character. But the perspective is entirely that of a foreign male, seeing Suzie, at this stage, from the outside, and trying to understand, but not always showing a great deal of perception, a fact which can perhaps be excused on the grounds he has only been in Hong Kong for "a couple of months".

The novel opens with narration and description. The Chinese girl is introduced against a backdrop of strong, concentrated local colour; details being selectively given to build up the "Chinese-ness" of the place with many—too many even for the late 1950's—ethnic types and stereotypes— "women in cotton pyjama suits... men with feet slippers and gold teeth... old man in a high-necked Chinese gown... stroking his white, wispy, foot-long ribbon of beard". The list goes on with a baby slung on a woman's back, coolies in blue tattered trousers and the remnants of shirts, Cantonese fisherwomen in comical straw hats and shiny pink suits. One detail is intended to bring out the apparent contradictions of this meeting point of East and West. A youth is also among the crowd waiting for the ferry. He has horn-rimmed glasses and is studying a graph in a book held close to his nose. "The book was called *Aerodynamics*." Against this highly coloured background we see her. "Her hair was tied behind her head in a pony-tail, and she wore jeans—green knee-length denim jeans."

His first comment anticipates his surprise at all the paradoxes and contradictions in her life and her nature.

"That's odd, I thought, a Chinese girl in jeans. How do you explain that?"

From the point of view of my analysis, what makes this comment particularly significant is that it draws our attention to how strongly perception is affected by the racial stereotype. The narrator is characterized as well: he is seen as the naïve recently arrived expatriate steeped in the myth of inscrutable Chinese womanhood.

Suzie's first action is to buy a newspaper coneful of melon seeds from a street vendor for ten cents. Then she absently picks the seeds "with red-painted nails". This elicits the comment:

Probably some wealthy taipan's daughter, I thought. Or a student. Or shopgirl—you never could tell with the Chinese.

The comment furthers the impression of the naïvety of the narrator. If the reader judges by Chinese "norms" of behaviour, especially of the 1950s, no wealthy taipan's daughter (or self-respecting student for that matter) is likely to buy melon seeds from a street vendor, and is even more unlikely to actually pick at them in public—much less offer some to a male stranger, and a *gweilo* at that, on a ferry. Her actions and her revelations regarding her virginal status, her father's possessions and her arranged marriage would strike the knowledgeable readers as entirely out of keeping with the accepted stereotype of the "rich Chinese girl". Indeed her long discourse relating to her virginal state causes even the narrator to wonder whether this is "typical". And if the girl were indeed unconventional and avant-garde and Westernized, one may well question her unquestioning acceptance of the arranged marriage and her pride in her virginity. Then there is the question of her English. But all this scepticism would not be present in the minds of the great majority of international readers. Seeing Suzie through the perspective of the naïve observer, as yet uninitiated into the mysteries of Chinese women, the equally uninitiated reader sees her actions as disarmingly natural and child-like. Suzie herself, playing the role of a taipan's daughter, shows her unsophisticated image of the Chinese taipan, the vision of an outsider, a stereotype which is a product of her own imagination and wishful thinking. Thus there are a number of perspectives in juxtaposition here: the narrator's, Suzie's, that of the uninitiated reader (which has no reason to diverge from that of the narrator), and that of the "knowing" reader (which may or may not converge with that of the author).

The description of physical beauty reinforces the impression of innocence: the narrator writes of "the mischievous innocent look in her eyes". "Her face", we are also told, "was round and smooth, her eyes long black ellipses, and her eyebrows so perfectly arched that they looked drawn—but in fact they had only been helped out with pencil at their tips. Her cheek bones were broad, with hints of Mongolia." (pp.6-7) Her physical attributes are alluded to frequently later on in the novel. She is willowy and sinuous rather than voluptuous and buxom. There are no universal norms of female pulchritude and Mason, to his credit, made no attempt to "Westernize" her appearance to make her irresistible appeal plausible to his wider audience—as John Gordon Davis and Geoffrey Thursby did in the cases of their Chinese heroines. Suzie's beauty is based essentially on the Chinese stereotype. The description of her perfectly arched eyebrows is perhaps particularly significant. They are the sort of eyebrows immortalized in descriptions of archetypal Chinese beauties—in Po Chu-i's poem *The Song of Eternal Sorrow*, for example, Yang Kuei-fei is described as having "moth brows"—or, more poetically rendered "eyebrows as delicate as the moth's fine silken feelers". (See Chan and Gray's translation, *Renditions*, Chinese University Press, Autumn 1980, p.81) She has the long, smooth dark hair hanging straight down her back, such as you get in the prototype Chinese beauty—as well as, unfortunately, the caricature of this beauty as the sultry Oriental siren in the Western media. The fact that Suzie is Shanghainese can also be seen as Mason making use of a stereotype, both in Chinese as well as Western society: those Westerners who know of the pre-revolutionary Shanghai have an image of it as "sin city", full of delicious vices, and Shanghainese women, in Chinese society, enjoy a reputation for being stylish and *avant-garde*.

The direct descriptions of her appearance in her many moods are almost always accompanied by usually rapturous commentary on the part of the narrator, strengthening the impression of the disarming nature of her charms. This is reinforced by the narration of events which show her in relation to other men, events in which she is seen as both seductress and man's prey, their sex object.

Let us return to the opening chapter and consider what is possibly the most significant single element in the portrayal of Suzie: her speech. The author makes no attempt to mark deviant pronunciation by means of deviant orthography except in one notable instance when he exploits as it were a phonetic cliché of Hong Kong English—the "typical" substitution of 'l' for 'r'. In fact, this is a Cantonese rather than a Shanghainese error. But it is associated with the Chinese stereotype, regardless of dialectal region of origin.

'... What is your name?'
'Wong Mee-ling.'
'Mee-ling—that's charming.'
'And you?'
'Robert Lomax—or Lomax Robert, your way.'
'Lobert.'
'No, "R".'
'Robert.' (p.8)

In *Sanctuary*, the hero James Waltham, makes a not very funny joke in dubious taste which plays on the substitution of 'l' for 'r'. Questioned about his "lust", he replies that in Hong Kong "lust" is what gets on Chinese cars. To return to Suzie, we assume from this exchange that her English pronunciation has the phonetic characteristics associated with the pidgin used with Chinese stereotypes in media presentations in the West. Her grammar gives the same impression of pidgin, although devices suggesting its substandard nature are not consistently used. There are direct translations of Chinese structures—the classic "No talk". Articles are left out—as in "You sailor?" But "No, there is a car to meet me in Hennessy Road." She virtually always uses the simple present tense, in conformity with the expected patterns of pidgin English: "Oh I forget how many cars"; "I get married soon." Her vocabulary is small. Her failure to come up with the English term for the state of "You have not made love—not with anybody" is, of course, significant beyond giving exemplification of her limited competence in English. It is for bringing out her candour, "the naïvety of a child". (p.7) It also reinforces the double image of her which is dwelt upon in the rest of the novel—that of virgin and whore, virgin though whore. Though there are just enough markers in Suzie's speech to set it off as pidgin, the markers are not consistently and insistently used. She can, for example, utter perfectly grammatical sentences:

"No, I'm too scared to drive. But I don't mind tramcars, you know—I like riding in tramcars."

And at the very close of the novel, she demonstrates control over all her verbal structures, using contracted forms as well.

'Who's that?'

'My husband… you'<u>ve</u> got the tickets?'

'You'<u>re</u> sure'? You have<u>n't</u> lost them?'

As is evident from the opening chapter the narrator did not want Suzie's pidgin to grate on the readers' nerves, underlining too forcibly the stereotype rather than the individual. Indeed in their first encounter the author assigned to Suzie very short snatches of direct speech. She uses minor sentences—answers, repetition of what has been said, catalogues. When she intimates details of her future, gives the imagined picture of her arranged marriage and speaks of the high moral standards of Chinese girls vis-à-vis their European counterparts, this was recorded by the narrator as indirect speech, which, though attempting to reflect some of her idioms, is in perfectly correct English. Mason invested Suzie with some distinguishing markers in the area of word choice. The Cantonese sound "hah" occurs as an indication of not having heard properly, as an implicit request for repetition. Mason may have noticed the propensity among the Chinese—and Cantonese particularly—to give nicknames based on physical attributes. "Tall man Leung", "Fat Man Chiu", "Pock-marked Lam" these are often used openly and in direct address with connotations not of malice or ridicule but of intimacy and affection. Suzie persistently calls Betty Lau, "Canton girl", the "rival" she stabs with a pair of scissors, with the "typical" Shanghainese contempt for the "provincial" Cantonese. She calls the neurotic American in frantic pursuit of her "the butterfly man" because of her instinctive feelings concerning his fickleness.

In a passage of description cum commentary, Lomax looks at the sleeping Suzie and muses:

I wondered if she was dreaming, and what Chinese dreams were like. I hoped they were like Chinese poetry, full of wicket-gates and rock-pools and chirruping cicadas, and warm rice-wine and love.

A tame Western stereotype image of Chinese poetry. Mason possibly has in mind the simplicity and repetition in the language of some Chinese love poems, when he has Suzie, brokenly in her English tongue, use the same images of mutuality in love more than once.

> Go to bed with sailor—nothing happens inside, nothing happens to heart. Go to bed with you—everything happens. I love. I feel beautiful. I think, 'My man,' you think, 'My girl.' We belong. (p.36)

Banal—embarrassing, perhaps. But I suspect the author intends it to be poignant, even poetic.

The heroine of John Gordon Davis's *The Years of the Hungry Tiger* is Tsang Ying Ling. The narrator is Jake McAdam, a successful young British policeman in the Hong Kong police force. Davis has created a "domestic" canvas. While the focus of the novel is on the love story of McAdam and Tsang Ying Ling, a communist school teacher, the novel is as much an adventure story set in Hong Kong and China in the years 1962 to 1967, the years starting from China's Great Leap Forward to the Cultural Revolution. Against a background of earth-shaking events, espionage, riots, the liaison between the British policeman and the Chinese "communist" school teacher takes its course to its tragic ending. Ying Ling is presented through the perspective of a man who falls madly and besottedly in love with her. His love for her overcomes all professional caution and common sense. There can be little doubt that Davis wishes to make Ying Ling a truly beautiful and desirable woman, but more, a very special woman, to make it credible that the ambitious, worldly-wise McAdam should be willing to give up the world—his entire world, professional, social, emotional—for her. Davis seems to want to invest his protagonist with something of the grandeur of a tragic hero—a man who loved not wisely but too well. And the woman must be presented as a worthy object of that love. Unlike Suzie, whose main characteristics, physical and otherwise, are more or less presented in the first chapter, Ying Ling's characteristics are revealed gradually. The portrait begins with the narration of action, an incident which gives an important clue to her character.

Let me begin by noting that John Gordon Davis quite clearly wants to depart from the existing stereotypes of Oriental women. The plot requires her to be Chinese and communist. Her Chinese-ness adds a great deal of interest and local colour, but the devices which have gone into her portrayal seem to come as much from Western ideal images, one being the heroine of *Lassie*, the young Elizabeth Taylor in *National Velvet*, author of "Nibbles and me", Nibbles being a pet chipmunk, and Rebecca of *Rebecca of Sunnybrook Farm*, transplanted to a squalid little room and roof-top. But I am anticipating.

The narrator first meets Ying Ling when he is in charge of an operation to stop the unending tide of illegal immigrants from China. He is stationed at Takuling at the border. Into the closed area comes Tsang Ying Ling to "survey the situation" and to bring buns for those illegals in hiding from the police. This is the first reference to Ying Ling: "and there, coming along this cross-trail was a young Chinese woman, and a dog. She was carrying a big China Products shopping bag." (p.73) The dog and the China products shopping bag are essential elements in her characterization. This first episode establishes her independence, courage, humanity and her own brand of patriotism. Her physical appearance strikes the narrator—and the reader—in stages. We first see her as just "a young Chinese woman". Then after their initial confrontation, the narrator notes "She was tall for a Chinese girl, with a squarish face and she had slanted, deep brown eyes." More angry exchanges. Then Miss Tsang is taken away from the closed area in a police Landrover. While in the Landrover, the narrator looks at her, and we are made to share in his vision through a stream-of-consciousness technique. "Her jeans had paint on them, all the colours. She was very pretty in a somewhat severe sort of way. Twenty-three? Two short pigtails. Wide full mouth. Good nose. Tall for a Chinese girl. Big breasts for a Chinese. Northerner, Shanghai way." (p.76) The description is still fairly detached. Her sensual appeal is noted early. The conflicting images of sex object and bluestocking are conveyed.

She had long full legs. She didn't look much like a communist school-mistress.

But this is a convention well established in Western popular culture: the schoolmarm whose sex appeal is released along with the shedding of her spectacles and the loosening of her hair from the confines of a bun (or in Miss Tsang's case, pigtails). As the narrator falls more and more deeply in love with Ying Ling, the reader is given more and more intense descriptions of her beauty, over and over again.

The narrator encounters Ying Ling a second time when she, as a member of the S.P.C.A. reports a case of extreme cruelty to animals. The Heavenly Restaurant serves brains of live monkeys. Ying Ling displays qualities which to some readers may suggest a self-righteous girl scout, a do-gooder quite determined that every possible wrong be righted. A picture of earnest determination. The following exchange reinforces the image of Miss Goody Two-Shoes.

'Are there any more animals in the kitchens, on the lower floors?'
'No, sir,' the Inspector said.
'Yes!' Miss Tsang said vehemently. 'There are pigeons.'
I said, 'I am afraid eating pigeons is not an offence in this Colony, Miss Tsang.'
'The cages are too small,' Miss Tsang said.
'All right,' I said, 'I'll look at them on the way out, perhaps there's a cruelty charge.'
'Yes, cruelty,' Miss Tsang said. (p.172)

The author uses the two initial encounters to characterize Tsang Ying Ling as a high-minded but rather naïve lady and prepares us for her rather simple-minded and misguided idealism, of which we are given many examples, and which finally leads to the unhappy ending.

As I have stated, the picture of her physical attractions is slowly unfolded. The author uses her account of the happenings at the Heavenly Restaurant, written up as a police report by the narrator, as a device for giving the reader a summary of her life story to date. Like Suzie Wong, she is not Cantonese, but from Chungking. This confirms my impression that Western male writers find women from Canton less fascinating than women from the North. Perhaps it has to do with the unfair stereotype of the "Southern barbarian", unsophisticated and raucous. Ying Ling is twenty-six when they first meet and by the end of the novel is thirty-two. Tina Lau, the heroine of *Miller* is in her thirties, a divorcee and the mother of a young daughter. None of the writers are working with the archetypal giggling nymphet of a Chinese woman character. Hong Kong society, represented by the millions who watch Chinese television, appeared to be gradually giving up the age-old tradition of very young female idols, but only gradually; they still have some way to go before they can emulate the West in its adulation of women in their 50s like Joan Collins, but they seem to have abandoned the notion summed up in the Chinese adage: "A man at forty is like a flower; a woman after thirty is like left-over tea leaves." But I digress. Let me now return to the more detailed description, combined with the narrator's commentary:

> She stood up, straightened her skirt over the flat belly and thighs. She had ink on two fingertips and her plaits were a bit ragged and she looked tired now it was all over. Her lips were full and her face was squarish and purposeful and she smiled at me for the first time. *Her eyes were large and the eyelids had the double fold like a European's, which is unusual in a Chinese*, and they were softer now she was satisfied I had done the job properly, and when she smiled at me like that briefly I thought she was beautiful. (p.176; italics mine)

In his abandonment of the Western stereotype of the Chinese woman, the author makes every effort to "Westernize" her appearance, keeping none of the features considered "typical" of Chinese beauties. He takes note of her "un-Chinese" characteristics explicitly: she is tall for a Chinese, has big breasts for a Chinese. He dwells on her big brown eyes often in the course of the novel. Her square face and large mouth would, according to traditional notions of feminine beauty, be regarded as liabilities rather than anything else. My first reaction is that John Gordon Davis is in a sense cheating. He wants to appeal to an international readership. He wants features, physical and otherwise, which would strike a familiar chord in his Western readers. Ying Ling is just a Western woman in the guise of a Chinese communist school teacher because both her race and politics are essential to the plot of the novel. But consider the images of Chinese persons in Hong Kong and on the mainland in the much earlier novel, Maugham's *The Painted Veil*. They are seen through the immature perspective of the shallow English heroine, Kitty, who previous to her marriage, has never left Europe nor allowed the Chinese to impinge on her consciousness. She finds the flat, yellow faces and narrow slanted eyes of the Chinese children in an orphanage, and of a Chinese general, utterly repugnant. The portrait of a Manchu lady, a former princess, is almost done as a caricature, with a painted, utterly "foreign" face. No standards known to the author or his compatriots are operative here, although one may say there is a degree of patronage in the "sympathy" with which her story—her violent, and apparently unaccountable, passion for the unprepossessing English customs inspector—is told. John Gordon Davis is at least trying to portray a Chinese woman who has individual physical traits, and anyone who has lived among Chinese people will know that not all Chinese women look the same: nothing about Tsang Ying Ling's appearance would make her a physical impossibility. Some Chinese girls are indeed tall, even by Western standards, are well endowed, have big brown eyes and long legs, square faces and generous mouths. This doesn't fit the Chinese traditional stereotype—much less the Western concept of the dainty almond-eyed lady with "cherry-like" mouth. But the Chinese ideals of female beauty are changing, moving for better or worse towards the Western mode, although the conventional view dies hard, especially among the older generation and country folk. Timothy Mo's heroine in *Sour Sweet*, Lily, is portrayed as having an appearance attractive to the *gweilos* in London, but she is thought ugly and ungainly by her dour husband from the New Territories.

On Lily there were two opposing views. Chen did not think she was pretty. She has a long, thin, rather horsy face and a mouth that was too big for the rest of her features, and also a tiny mole just under the rim of her lower lip on the left side, which fell into a dimple when she smiled, which was frequently, too frequently to be consonant with Chen's passive ideal of female pulchritude. She was also rather busty and her hands and feet were a fraction too big to be wholly pleasing to her husband. It was her face, though, which really let her down (Chen had decided), being over-full of expression, particularly her bright black eyes which she had a habit of widening and narrowing when listening to something she found interesting. Probably there was too much character in her face, which perhaps explained the lack of Cantonese male interest better than any particular wrongness of an individual feature or their relationship to each other. Westerners found her attractive, though. Lily was unaware of this but Chen had noticed it with great surprise. That was if the second glances and turned heads on the street were anything to go by.

Chen wasn't disturbed. He knew what he liked and Lily didn't conform to the specifications. This he knew with a certainty as absolute as his knowledge that the food he served from the 'tourist' menu was rubbish, total *lupsup*, fit only for foreign devils. If they liked that, then in all likelihood they could be equally deluded about Lily. He did once attempt to see what exactly it was the English saw in her, trying to look with new eyes, starting at her well-shaped calves, and moving up in stages to her glossy but too short hair, but still couldn't detect the remotest hint of any sexuality, however exotic and alien it might be.

Perhaps they could see from her general bearing what she was like in bed, in which case they might be more astute than he gave them credit for, because in all conscience he had no complaints on that score, none at all. (p.15)

Thus, on deeper reflection, John Gordon Davis is not cheating. He is honestly *trying* to create a Chinese woman whose beauty and character win totally the heart of his narrator. She explains why she is a Communist, and the narrator adds commentary.

'I am Chinese.' Then she sat back and was more serious and her face was equally beautiful. A beautiful Chinese woman, strong face with such eyes. (p.214)

Her actions present many contradictions, so that a reader may well regard her with exasperation rather than admiration. A great many details relating to Ying Ling are meant to be endearing to Western readers; her love of animals, for example: there are Mad Dog, Percy the cockatoo, a mouse called Puku, a hamster and an aquarium of assorted tropical fish. She also has a love of growing plants, and can coax them into growing in the most unlikely places. But she is not just a Walt Disney character. She drinks, smokes (Red Victory cigarettes) and is fond of black coffee, and has the traditional feminine fondness for frilly, sexy underwear. There is no dearth of details, and yet the impression one gets is not that of a living woman, but a very conscious creation of an author anxious to present a fusion of East and West in one character. Perhaps this simply underlines the difficulty of successfully delineating a Chinese heroine. Paradoxically the drastic movement away from the stereotype has not moved Davis any nearer the verisimilitude we assume he is aiming at.

In the matter of Ying Ling's speech, Davis boldly sets aside any conventions associated with the stereotypical "foreign" speaker of English. She was educated in Manila and attended a teachers' training college in Hong Kong. The written representation of her English speech is not set off by any markers of deviance. Her first utterance is marked by a degree of unidiomatic pomposity, but it is generally true to say the very faint markers of foreign-ness, and these are rare in any case, occur only on the lexical level. Her lover, McAdam, also speaks Cantonese. When they converse in Cantonese, the reader is told that this is the case, but the occasions when they do not speak in English are rare. At their initial encounter, the author makes sure to establish his own set of speech conventions for Ying Ling.

> I said, and as soon as I said it I felt foolish, 'I must congratulate you on your English.'
>
> She did not look at me. 'Why not? You speak good Cantonese.'
>
> Go to hell, I thought. (p.77)

Apart from setting up the convention of Ying Ling's English, we have here a manifestation of the rightly contemptuous response of educated Chinese women (and men) to the patronizing attitude of Europeans vis-à-vis their ability to speak their language. Ying Ling makes jokes in English; she reads T.S. Eliot and Dylan Thomas in the original; she paints in both the Western and Eastern styles; she deep-sea dives.

Her creator does make a few conscious attempts to bring out her Chinese-ness, at least "foreign-ness". She hesitates over the English term "extra curricular".

'All teachers work hard, I think. But we have more'—she thought for the word—'outside duties?'

'Extra-curricula.' (p.193)

One incident that tends to stick in the mind relates to the supposed earthiness of the Chinese, and Ying Ling is no exception. Ours has traditionally been an agrarian economy and every effort had be made to increase crop yield. Davis tries to suggest a naturalness to bodily functions which, incidentally, is also a feature of the fabliaux characters of Chaucer.

I imagined her doing her graceful Chinese shadow-boxing in the dawn, slow motion, more like a ballet dance, watching for the sunrise, and the look in her eyes; and singing as she watered her flowerpots with a mixture of her urine and water from her red chamber-pot which she kept under her bed for this purpose. She was quite unabashed about telling me such things. She even considered collecting urine from other people in the house where she lived, but decided against it because she didn't have enough flowerpots or chamber-pots. She considered getting more of both, lying with me in the back of the station wagon, 'It is a pity to waste all the urine.'

'Oh, quite.'

'It just goes into the sea. But it is so good for flowers.'

'Indeed.'

'In China everybody must save their urine and shit, you know, to put on the fields, it is the law.' It shook me when she said this in English, though not in Cantonese. The Chinese swear a great deal.

'And a very good law too.'

'It is very important because we have not yet got factories for fertilizer. If we had always done this, under the previous

governments, China would be a rich country today.'
Seven hundred million Chinese,' I said, 'that's a lot of urine.'
'And shit,' she said.
'*And* shit. The mind boggles; terrifying.' (pp.232-3)

Opening with a description of her graceful shadow-boxing—a touch of the sublime—the narrator descends quickly to the ridiculous. The narrator shows gentle ridicule and tolerance in his share of the exchange, as if he were humouring an earnest but simple-mind, albeit lovable, child. A Chinese reader—and I am here using myself as an example—is apt to take deep offence at this passage on first reading and to find insulting the depiction of Tsang Ying Ling's subsequent insistence on introducing the chamber pot routine to the "penthouse" she shares with McAdam. "The Chinese swear a good deal" is made as a general statement. The expatriate policeman in Hong Kong usually commands a racy brand of "gutter Cantonese" through his contacts with underworld elements. One of the most insistent (and offensive to most Chinese readers) features of the speech of many Chinese characters in James Clavell's *Noble House* is their propensity towards swearing. They intersperse every speech with obscenities. But even if we move in very very broad generalizations, as the narrator, McAdam, does, it is only a certain social sector of Chinese men who "swear a good deal", and usually only in the company of other men and Chinese oaths do not usually involve the excretory processes. It would be quite surprising to hear a schoolmarm talking directly and with such relish about urine and shit. Is the author being deliberately insulting to the Chinese in general and his Chinese heroine in particular? *Probably* not. This episode can be regarded as part of his effort to "sinicize" his character, to insinuate his inside knowledge of Chinese people as a bilingual who responds instinctively to equivalent terms in the two languages, though one may well draw the conclusion that the inclusion of this episode is ill-advised in the wider context of his portrayal of Ying Ling. An unsympathetic or just neutral reader may very well see this as an endorsement of one of Anthony Cooper's objections to interracial marriage, his vision of the Chinese as uncouth and unhygienic, spitting over the balcony, stinking up the bathroom and so on.

And yet this same woman portrayed as being so earthy in the matter of the chamberpot is credited with some very sound and balanced views on interracial marriage. In the "Hong Kong novel", and *The Years of the Hungry Tiger* is no exception, marriage to Western man in general is considered an unqualified boon for a Chinese woman. But the other side of the coin is presented through Tsang Ying Ling:

'What would your friends think? I am a curiosity. People in England stare at me in the street. When I go into a shop...'

'Chinese live all over this world.'

'But what about *me*?' she insisted. 'Where is my culture? My people? My books? My songs? My jokes? My language? I am a yellow Englishwoman! And our children half and half... I disagree with you that most marriages between Chinese and Europeans are successful. I do not think so. Because of culture. The Chinese girl is trying to be a white wife with all her husband's white friends. Conversation. Jokes. Interests.' (p.264)

This coincides with the views explicitly expressed and implicitly brought out by an incident in Lee Ding Fai's *Running Dog*, in which the Chinese heroine finds her romantic attachment to her first love, an American journalist, palls because of the realities of adjusting totally to American culture and his American friends even while physically still in Hong Kong. She feels constrained to be constantly alert to American references, and feels left out when they allude to the latest "in" American item. John Gordon Davis, then, tries to present the downside of marriage to a Westerner through the Chinese heroine.

The use of Chinese motifs, where possible, are used by writers about things and people Chinese to help in portraiture. The motif of Fa Mu Lan, the woman warrior, is utilized in Maxine Hong Kingston's *Woman Warrior*. In the depiction of Ying Ling, Davis uses the motif of the trees with interlocking boughs to symbolize lovers whose love is eternal, a motif made familiar through poetry. Before a much dreaded year-long separation Ying Ling plants two pine trees on an outlying island as a symbol.

> We had planted the pine-trees. Side by side all alone on the top of the ridge, so that when they grew up their branches would just touch each other. They are still there. (p.397)

Ying Ling responds to inanimate as well as animate nature. The butterfly is a favoured motif in Chinese poetry and philosophy. In a gush of happy excitement she tells McAdam,

> I was buying an orange and a butterfly came and sat on my hand. Wasn't that beautiful! (p.232)

Geoffrey Thursby's *Miller* is an altogether forgettable novel and his Chinese heroine, Tina Lau, an altogether forgettable character. The love story of the protagonist, a fairly successful English businessman, Robert Miller, married to a perfectly horrendous caricature of an expatriate wife (an ex-shop girl, peddling sausages in a chain store in London and now queening it in colonial splendour) and Tina Lau, deserted "wife" of Chinese-American bigamist and mother of a young daughter, is played out against a background of high finance rather than of politics and high risk espionage. Geoffrey Thursby was by profession a journalist and was familiar with Hong Kong's business scene. His novel tries to capture the excitement of Hong Kong's business world, deals involving astronomical figures, dynamic taipans, expatriate and local, male and female. To give focus to the frenetic goings-on in the world of takeover bids and treachery among company men, Thursby centres the plot around Miller's love for Tina Lau. He embezzles in order that her daughter can have an expensive heart operation in America, is found out, sentenced to imprisonment. All for love—but as the cliché ending would have it, Chinese lover, young daughter and loyal Chinese *amah* are all killed in a car crash as they are on the way to visit Miller, thus making a travesty of his great sacrifice.

Tina, the Chinese lady of the piece, falls far short of Suzie Wong and even Tsang Ying Ling in terms of depth of characterization, not to speak of depth as a *Chinese* character. Miller meets her at a barbecue given by an American couple. The guests include many Americanized Chinese. His first awareness of her is when he hears an American—and if one is thinking in terms of fictional stereotypes—a fairly "typical" American greeting her with the words, "Oh, hi, Tina... Wow! You look something." With this "introduction" Thursby clearly wants to establish the ravishing physical appearance of the character. Then there follows direct description, with brief commentary.

> Miller turned to see a tallish Chinese woman, her black hair curling up from her forehead in front, sculptured into her neck at the back, he guessed in her early thirties, a little fleshy, perhaps, but shapely, in worn, but well-cut blue jeans, and soft red silk blouse. Her skin was pale, and she had a delicate, narrow nose for a Chinese, and a broad, intelligent-looking forehead. (p.147)

The use of commas to link the different parts of the description is, one gathers, meant to suggest that all this is going on in Miller's consciousness and that he is taking in all these features together. Like John Gordon Davis, Geoffrey Thursby modifies Tina's appearance towards the Western. She is "tallish" and "had a delicate narrow nose for a Chinese". Tina, we learn from her later account of her life, is an ex-fashion model. She attended a convent school. Her hair is more Vidal Sassoon than Suzie Wong. Her clothes are the epitome of Western chic. In the subsequent narration, amply interspersed with comment and description, Tina's very stylish outfits are described in what must strike most readers as excessive detail. But then Tina is an ex-fashion model and Geoffrey Thursby's wife, Marguerite, a well-known dress designer. To return for the moment to Tina's "narrow nose", narrow "for a Chinese", one is rather astounded at Thursby's misinformation concerning physical features relating to different Chinese districts. His heroine claims:

> 'Mother was Chiu Chow. She touched her nose. 'I got my narrow nose from her.' (p.152)

It seems unimaginable for any Chinese person to make such

a mistaken attribution. Whatever the stereotypical physical characteristics, rightly or wrongly, ascribed to the Chiu Chow, narrow noses would not be one. In assigning such a blatantly stupid comment to Tina, the author makes the knowledgeable reader respond to her, and to him, as frauds. And indeed, any reader responding to the portraiture of Tina as a whole, may feel cheated.

We are *told* that Tina is Chinese but there is little in speech or action that supports this contention. We seem to have to take her Chinese-ness pretty much on faith. She does not seem to have a Chinese name. Once it is established that she has been educated in a convent school (the best place in those days for a girl to learn good English, as Tina herself asserts on p.52), the working out of the dialogue seems to be based on the assumption that her English is the same as Miller's. At least no effort is made to suggest any form of deviance or inadequacy on any level: pronunciation, grammar or lexis. She speaks not just correctly but with native fluency. The author does take pains to remind us of her ethnic origins by having her assert her Chinese-ness in words once every so often by giving a "Chinese" point of view. In response to Miller's question of whether she liked cheese, for example, she replies,

I adore it… My father used to say Chinese who don't eat cheese could never hope to understand Westerners. (p.211)

I'd like a son… I suppose it's the Chinese woman in me. A Chinese woman gives her husband sons. (p.280)

Her pre-school age daughter goes by the again irritatingly "cute" name of "Mickey"; if she has a Chinese name, the reader is never told it. The initial description of the child is also done through the consciousness of Miller.

He had a quick impression of a small, finely boned suntanned Chinese face—coal black hair in pigtails, red bows, dark blue dress. She is holding on to a tattered black minstrel rag doll called Zacker. (pp.179-80)

It is again only through direct comment and description we are reminded of her ethnic origins. For example:

The little *Chinese* girl surveyed Miller with her black eyes. (p.180 – italics mine)

Otherwise Mickey's speech and actions would strike the reader as emerging from an unsuccessfully created child character, and so many portraits of children, even in far better novels than *Miller*, are badly executed. Mickey could be any other precocious miniature adult, whose actions and words are no doubt meant to bowl readers over completely by their disarming candour and directness. Through the mouths of babes and all that. We are told she speaks to her monolingual baby-sitter in Cantonese, but otherwise she is portrayed as speaking nothing but English, and the English she speaks is impeccable, stereotypical only in that Thursby tries to incorporate some of the direct and guileless things that the stereotypical "lovable" child in literature is meant to say. Her mother explains proudly, "She speaks good English. I've seen to that." (p.180)

One is led to the impression that Thursby thinks he has moved away from the stereotype Chinese heroine of the pidgin English and the sylph-like shape. He has even introduced a weight problem! To be fair to Thursby he has in many respects drawn from "objective reality". But he has moved from the Anna May Wong media stereotype to another, a female stereotype in the Hong Kong mode. A hyper-Westernized Hong Kong girl educated in a convent school. Speaks very good English. Ex-model turned travel agent (other fashion- or travel-orientated jobs are possibilities), dressed entirely in Western clothes, is known by all (presumably even poor old monolingual great grandmothers who sadly mispronounce it) by an English name (often of her own devising and highly ingenious, like Harpic or Anglie or Detergent). Her child (or children) also going under Chinese name(s), as cunningly innovative as possible; proud that she has "seen to" her child's (or children's) English. To the chagrin of Chinese readers Miller has based his heroine on a Hong Kong stereotype, known to local Chinese as the "convent school" girl, a type most local Chinese hold in contempt, although the descriptive name is not altogether fair. This type reached its height of development in the late 1950s through the early 70s, and though fast becoming an anachronism, still survives, although the numbers of exponents are greatly depleted. The stereotype is not enriched by depth and modified by selection. I cannot see how Tina Lau can invoke very positive responses from a Hong Kong reader. As for Thursby's possible international reader, there are so few characteristics that genuinely set Tina apart from a Western woman that rightly or wrongly there is bound to be some foiling of expectations.

VI. New Stereotypes for Old or Old Wine in New Bottles?

In the three novels I have looked at, the Chinese heroines are depicted with what one must suppose as varying degrees of loving care by their creators. Each is presented as the object of supreme love and sacrifice. In two instances narrator is fused with lover, and in the third, narrative, comment and description are given in many parts of the novel through the consciousness of the lover. On a surface level, Suzie Wong seems to follow most closely the old stereotype and in turn to fossilize and reinforce that stereotype in the minds of Western readers. Tsang Ying Ling and Tina Lau seem to represent conscious efforts on the part of their creators to move away from the stereotypical Chinese heroine. And yet, in all three cases, for all the details meant to give verisimilitude and individuality, as love of animals or of cheese, the three women share one overwhelming characteristic—fierce loyalty to their Caucasian lovers. They are caring and considerate, and in spite of the always unequal relationships in terms of material advantages, the authors take great pains to make use of incident, comment, dialogue and description to show the absolute disinterestedness of the Chinese lover where material advantage is concerned. The Western hero is loved for himself alone. Could this situation—now a virtual cliché in novels of this type—have arisen because most (in the case of the three I have discussed, all) of the authors are Western males? They are consciously or subconsciously giving expression to their fantasies about subservient and worshipful Oriental women. This is coupled with the fantasy that they are as great white gods able to dispense largesse, material, emotional, sexual. And this is the picture one tends to end up with: Western man as patron and giver.

Take the following examples:

After Tina had picked up the travellers' cheques, Miller said 'It's going to be cold in New York, my love. We've got to get you... warm clothes.'

'Robert, we'll be all right.'

'No,' he said, 'You must have warm clothes. Let's go over to the Hilton. There're some nice shops there, places like Dynasty'... Miller bought Tina two woollen suits—one black, the other cream and brown—and three silk blouses, one plain, one with a tie, the third with a ruffle. Then he found a black overcoat and made her take it... (Miller, pp.297-8)

Suzie Wong is depicted as the constantly distressingly, embarrassingly grateful recipient of gifts and favours—from a pink Japanese umbrella to gifts from London for all her former "colleagues", which she dispenses with great pride as husband, benefactor, patron and lover stands at her side beaming indulgently and fondly as one might at a clever and generous child. Tsang Ying Ling protests at the thought of McAdam setting up a flat for her, but after some hesitation, wallows in the decadence of a "big fat bed" and a "Western bathroom" with abandon. Again the reader is presented with the picture of the generous Western lover pressing upon his reluctant Oriental mistress all the material advantages that his resources can provide. In a particularly offensive scene, we are shown Jake McAdam and Tsang Ying Ling disputing the ethics of Tsang living "like a bourgeois" then going "to school to teach about communism, and outside people are sleeping in the street!" (p.259) The narrator seems not to be offended by her hypocrisy, quite the contrary, and there are no authorial comments to suggest John Gordon Davis's view. In a tasteless mixture of the stereotypical Oriental sex object and the new style cosmopolitan woman of the world and sophisticated wag, with a bit of her own particular ideology thrown in for good measure, the author gives another picture, but a slightly more complex one, of White Man as the giver.

'God, you're beautiful. I'll buy you some dresses to go with them [high-heeled shoes he has bought her].'

'No dresses. It is a waste. You only make me take them off!'

'Go and buy some dresses. I'll pay for them.'

'No dresses. Small sexy things for us, okay, but not big things like dresses.'

'Think big!' I said. 'Think *petite bourgeois!*' I bought her a couple of pairs of fish-net stockings and a red suspender belt. I loved to see her in such things. She had a beautiful body. She enjoyed wearing them for me, being sexy.

Another time I bought her half a dozen pairs of pretty scanty panties. Some of them were hardly there at all.

'Gweilo pants!' she jiggled two pairs in front of her, delighted. 'I always like barbarian pants!' Quick as a bunny she yanked up her skirt and yanked down her China Products jobs, tossed them over her shoulder and wriggled the Paris model up her lovely legs, wriggled her hips and let the elastic go with a snap. 'Voila!' she tossed the skirt from side to side grinning, like a can-can girl... (pp.272-3)

It seems that, whatever good intentions they may have, with regard to the creation of a "new" Chinese heroine, Western male writers of the Hong Kong novel found it virtually impossible to move away from the stereotypical Oriental siren whose great aim in life is to please Western men. *Taipan* deals with historical Hong Kong, starting when the Chinese island became a British colony in the year 1841. The relationship between May-may and Struan is not complicated by the changed and still ever changing set of conditions relating to politics, economics, society, race and sex. May-may is an outrageously compliant sex object who would offend the sensibilities of any self-respecting woman; she also gives away a great deal of the author's attitudes and intentions. She speaks pidgin with a touch of Struan's Scottish idiom and pronunciation.

'I kowtow because you give me the hugest fantastical face on earth... How you like birthday present, heya? Is that why you marry your poor old mother? ...Yin-hsi is very accomplished. She is nice in bed?'

Struan's eyes crinkled with amusement. 'I did na make love...'

'What? ... She's in your bed and you dinna make love?' (p.683)

May-may's sole object in life is to give Struan pleasure. In a novel about Hong Kong after the middle of the 20th century, the author has some new premises forced upon him, and I have tried to reflect how concessions had been made, but Western Man's stereotypical concept of the essential Oriental mistress, I have noted, dies hard. In *Suzie Wong*, set over a hundred years later, in a world where the relationships between the races and the sexes are less simplistic, the Western writer has to acknowledge the existence of educated Chinese women. But consider this picture:

Ben [an English man of the old colonial school] rose without a word, left the house and drove down to the club. There he deliberately set about getting drunk. Soon he was joined by a ship's surveyor called Wildblood... who was married and had children but was reputed to sleep with his Chinese servant. Ben despised him. Ben noticed Wildblood's eyes follow someone across the room. He looked round. It was Moira Wong, a slim beautiful girl of twenty-six who was a qualified doctor. She had been brought in by Bill Harper, an up-and-coming young left wing politician.

'Not bad,' Ben said approvingly. Wildblood grunted, pretending to notice her for the first time. He was always at pains to conceal his interest in Chinese girls and to imply he would not touch them with a barge pole... 'I've never had a Chinese girl,' Ben said.

'Well, keep off them. They're all gold diggers—hard as nails.'

...Moira Wong and her companion were eating a Chinese dinner at a nearby table. Ben watched them... And now, as he watched Moira Wong wiping Harper's chopsticks for him and then helping him to some choice morsel, a new truth burst upon him with a blinding flash: that oriental women had a femininity that western women had lost—that they were dedicated to building up masculinity, whereas western women were dedicated to its destruction. (p.94)

The author's disdain of the old colonial attitudes are made clear in the novel. The hard gold-digging Chinese stereotypes are indeed found all over the pages of Hong Kong fiction in English, from bejewelled, be-Diored, demanding *taitais* to rapacious mistresses clad in $40,000 mink coats, to ultra-chic and super efficient lady tycoons. But these are only part of the background, the local colour. The love interest, the "heroine" is inevitably loving and self-sacrificing, the product essentially of the average Western male fantasy about the exotic and submissive Oriental beauty. If it is not the author's own fantasy, it is a case of his pandering to the fantasy of his international male readership.

In one striking aspect there has been updating and "liberalizing" of the love relationship between Western man and Oriental woman in that the woman is now regarded not as a poor substitute for a white woman because of their dearth and the white man's exile in eastern parts. Maugham's short stories of Malaya were based on the premise that expatriate men made do with native women only until they could bring back some white bride after home leave. But the value judgments have now changed in "Hong Kong fiction". There are many foils to the self-sacrificing, lovable and lovely, submissive Chinese heroines in the shape of self-centred, demanding emasculating European women, usually wives, who are more subtly (for example Catherine McAdam in *The Years of the Hungry Tiger*) or more grossly (Joan Miller in *Miller*) depicted. I have mentioned the motif of renewal through the love of a Chinese woman. The myth of the submissive Oriental woman as the most desirable sex object has been updated. The heroines are regarded as having minds and hearts, are regarded as interesting, invigorating and stimulating friends and companions. The extent to which the fictional preference for the Oriental partner is a reflection of the situation in real life depends of course on many variables, not the least important being the individual men and women. But speaking very generally, the Western male attitudes in

Hong Kong fiction seem to reflect to some extent the real-life situation existing at the time when it was a flourishing genre, at least here. Dr Mildred M. McCoy (formerly Senior Lecturer in the Department of Psychology, University of Hong Kong) did extensive research on the psychological responses of expatriate women in Hong Kong. Her report was published as a Centre of Asian Studies, University of Hong Kong, monograph entitled *Attitudes of Expatriate Women Living in Hong Kong: questionnaire, surveys, a research report* (1983). It appears that many expatriate women suffered from feelings of inadequacy and insecurity in the face of competition from the legions of dainty and attractive Chinese women.

Let us consider the Western male involved in the liaison. In the depiction of East-West relationships, male authors depict Western men as decidedly superior in terms of physical appeal when compared to Chinese men. This idea goes way back in Western literature involving Orientals. The popular stereotypes of Chinese men in American literature are totally lacking a sexual dimension. This may well reflect their positions in American society up to very recent times. Frank Chin and Jeffrey Paul Chan have written very interestingly on this subject.

> Devil and angel, the Chinese is a sexual joke glorifying white power... Fu [Manchu], a man wearing a long dress, batting his eyelashes, surrounded by muscular black servants in loin cloths, and with the bad habit of caressingly touching white men on the leg... is not so much a threat as... a frivolous offense to white manhood. [Charlie] Chan's gestures are the same, except he doesn't touch, and instead of being graceful in flowing robes, he is awkward and clumsy. His sexuality is the source of a joke running through all of the forty-seven Chan films. The large family of the bovine detective isn't the product of sex, but animal husbandry... There is no Asian counterpart even for the stereotypes of black studs, Mexican bandits, and native American savages in American popular culture. The prevalent images of Asian men are as comical servants, sexless sidekicks, cooks, laundrymen, or exotic and unmanly Confucian scholars. Even the archetypal sinister villain

is not a masculine image. Fu Manchu's brilliance is intellectual, not physical or spiritual. (Frank Chin and Jeffrey Paul Chan, "Racist Love", in Richard Kostelanetz (ed.), *Seeing Through Shuck*, New York, 1972, p.66)

In this connection it is also interesting to read Elaine H. Kim's "Asian American Writers: A Bibliographical Review" (in *American Studies International*, Oct. 1984, Vol. XXII, No. 2, pp.41-78). The literary tradition which characterizes Asian men as sexless beings at the same time boosts the image of Asian woman as highly sexual beings. The perspective is that of the Western male. Once the stereotypes were established, this perspective became no longer limited to Western male authors. In Chapter II, I have referred to Pearl Buck's *The Pavilion of Women*, which tells the story of Madame Wu, a very traditional Chinese lady of impeccable breeding. At forty she makes up her mind to give up sex. She acquires for her rather gross and emotionally insensitive husband a concubine. Then she is irresistibly drawn, drawn against her will, to a Western priest, a 'macho' type figure with hairy arms. The reader is given a Western perception of what constitutes masculine attraction. Much later chronologically than *The Pavilion of Women* and set in cosmopolitan Hong Kong, Christopher New's *The Chinese Box* opens with a description of the hero, Dimitri Johnson's hairy chest. All this emphasis on hairiness! One of John Gordon Davis's characters in *The Years of the Hungry Tiger* simplifies the whole business of sexual attraction between the races in a mock serious-fashion: it all has to do with hair: Europeans are hairy and Chinese are not. As foils to the tender, understanding and sympathetic British hero-narrator in *The World of Suzie Wong* are presented the unattractive, indeed physically and otherwise loathsome, Chinese men in Suzie's life—her incestuous and repulsive uncle and her elderly, unappealing Chinese patrons in her early years as a prostitute. In *Sour Sweet*, Eurasian male author Timothy Mo portrays the heroine's husband as anything but an object of desire. He is the same height as Lily, with a roll of fat round his stomach, and in spite of descriptions of their activities in bed, Chen strikes the reader as a totally asexual being.

It must also be conceded, though, that in Hong Kong fiction there is also an updating of the image of the Chinese male, or at least a broadening of the range of stereotypes. One such new stereotype can be seen as quite clearly emerging. This is the outwardly highly Westernized man, Harvard or Oxbridge educated, impeccably groomed, highly presentable, incredibly wealthy, a connoisseur of all the good things in life—and here is the clearest sign of updating—including beautiful women. With their ability to fit perfectly into Western society goes their inward contempt of Western people and things. An example is Richard Kwang of Clavell's *The Noble House*, a Harvard educated banker whose intellect is in the Fu Manchu mode, but whose virility is never left in doubt. But these figures are generally there to create a sense of the dynamics of Hong Kong society. They do not operate on the level of the plot relating to love: they are not set up as rivals of the Western hero. There is one notable exception. This is in Lee Ding Fai's *Running Dog*. We are given a portrait of a Chinese heroine who has formed her aesthetic judgments on Western norms. As a teenager she despises her Chinese male classmates for being pygmies. She wants to marry someone big and "masculine". In the competition for her love, the Chinese Yau Man wins and the American Charles Felton loses. Before we hail this as a victory for nationalism, we should look carefully at the description of the Chinese hero: it is amusing to note the author's attempt to "Westernize" his appearance. Like Suzie Wong, like Tsang Ying Ling, like Wei Wei Jen of *The Noble House*, he is from the north and we are told he has neither the small stature nor the allegedly ill-defined features of his southern compatriots. Paradoxically, then, in this rare novel in which Chinese man triumphs over American man in a love triangle, the Chinese woman writer feels constrained to make the victor as like Western Man as possible in physical appearance, thus unwittingly endorsing the myth of his superior physical attraction.

In discussing male stereotypes I may appear to be digressing from the focus of my study, but I feel it necessary to deal with perspectives on the male partner in the mixed liaison and his appeal vis-à-vis Chinese male characters.

VII. Conclusion

World-wide, China has, for a long time, been a source of fascination to those Westerners who have heard about it and for years, Hong Kong was the major means of gaining access to China. Western writers have capitalized on its potential, and novels like *Dynasty* and *The Noble House* reached vast readerships. In many cases the readers had no knowledge of Hong Kong other than what is offered by the novels. Inaccuracies of fact, insulting or simplistic characterization often make Hong Kong Chinese readers embarrassed, but more often positively furious. The better the novels sold, the more authors had relied on tried and true formulae. Certainly sex and violence were essential ingredients of the popular novel. And readers had been conditioned to expect exotic Chinese women, often involved in amorous relationships with Caucasian heroes, in novels about Hong Kong. We have seen that authors failed to escape from clichés in the presentation of these Chinese women. More often than not the author failed in realistic portraiture not through want of trying. It has long been recognized that Chinese women characters are notoriously difficult to bring to life for Western readers. (Perhaps the same would apply to Chinese men, or indeed any "unfamiliar" or "exotic" ethnic group.) As one of his reviewers pointed out, Anthony Cooper was probably wise in his decision to replace the more expected Chinese love interest with a voluptuous American journalist in *The Sanctuary*. Having created May-may in *Taipan*, Clavell in *The Noble House* eschewed depiction of a major Chinese woman character. The predominantly Western male authors were *doubly* handicapped in their ability to execute multidimensional portrayals of Chinese women, confronted by the barriers of both race and sex. Even in Asian American literature up to very recent times there is an absence of female characters. When one does appear she tends to lack the depth of the male characters. (See Elaine H. Kim, ibid., p.63) Ruthanne Lum McCunn's full-scale biographical portrait of Lalu Nathoy, a Chinese immigrant in pioneering days in *A Thousand Pieces of Gold* (San Francisco, 1981) was acclaimed for its sympathy and sensitively. We have a Chinese woman responding to another Chinese woman adapting herself to an alien world. Ruth McCunn is American-Chinese and has not only the language but the creative skills to make the character come to life. It would be extraneous, and indeed childish, to labour the point that Hong Kong Chinese women, indeed Chinese women, like all other human beings, do not comprise a generic mass, but are individualized, though shaped by some common factors and united by certain common concerns. What are needed are knowledge, understanding, sympathy, artistic integrity coupled with creative skills and complete mastery of the English language as a medium for writing fiction. With the possible exception of Han Suyin in *A Many Splendoured Thing*— but she delineates a Eurasian, not a Chinese woman—these qualities have not really met in a writer of "Hong Kong fiction" in English.

Chapter VI

Chinese Women's Speech in Anglo-American Fiction[1]

In examining some of the English put into the mouths of Chinese women in works of fiction, I wish to address two questions. The first is the whole issue of verisimilitude. The second relates to the use of dialogue in the presentation of character. The two are inevitably interlocked since the writer's presentation of dialogue is linked to his or her intentions vis-à-vis characterization. David Abercrombie writes:

> Many people believe that spoken prose, as I would call what we normally hear on the stage or screen, is at least not far removed, when well done, from the conversation of real life. Writers of novels are sometimes praised, for "naturalistic dialogue", others such as Miss Ivy Compton Burnett, are criticized because nobody speaks like the characters in their books. But the truth is that nobody speaks at all like the characters in any novel, play, or film. Life would be intolerable if they did, and novels, plays or films would be intolerable if the characters spoke as people do in life. Spoken prose is far more different from conversation than is normally realized. (Abercrombie, 1965, pp.1-9)

This point is by no means new, but I think for my purposes it is a point I need to repeat. If novels imitate life, the creation of the illusion of real life depends to a large extent on the presentation of speech, because it is through this element that the closest "imitation of reality" is likely to take place.[2] The question then is: if "spoken prose" is removed from the haphazard and arbitrary quality of "real speech", what are the conventions used by the writer to give an illusion of "the real thing", an illusion of real speech "as proceeding from the mouth of an actual person" (Lodge, 1966, p.47) without reproducing from a tape recorder real speech? The question of how different writers attempt to perform this delicate balancing act of interposing a more or less elaborate code of stylistic conventions with the observed features of actual speech has been the subject of considerable discussion and research. To some extent, the sensitivity and intuitive responses of a reader can be relied on for an appraisal of the degree of success with which a contemporary writer—drawing on the same linguistic resources as the reader—is able to give an impression of verisimilitude. But a strict, coherent theoretical and descriptive framework for the analysis of all naturally occurring talk must be available before we can have a disciplined and comprehensive analysis of dialogue.[3] The crucial words are perhaps "all naturally occurring talk". And for literature of the past, this includes all naturally occurring talk of previous periods as well. For my purposes this would nominally have to include the discourse of Chinese women of varying times and types. But here I must qualify my stance. Chinese women characters in fiction are often depicted as speaking in Chinese. This fact makes my inquiry more complicated and that is why I am as much concerned with illusion based on illusion as with illusion based on reality. The representation in English dialogue of discourse in a foreign language is not even remotely related to "the real thing". If the characteristics of the foreign language are even vaguely known to the intended readers, then some of the illusion-creating conventions will be based on these characteristics.

Hemingway's attempt to suggest the Spanish language in *For Whom the Bell Tolls* is well known. But if the language is virtually unknown and as different from English on all linguistic levels as Chinese is then we are confronted by different "rules", if I may call them "rules", and different conventions. These are available analyses of Chinese discourse, mainly in the Standard Language or Putonghua. Y. R. Chao is a pioneer in this field of inquiry. Linguistic study has established that there are substantial differences in basic sentence type as well as in certain discourse strategies between Chinese and English. For example Chao has suggested that 50 percent of the utterances in Chinese are topic-comment types; e.g. "The president's men, they're a bunch of liars." "Blue surfboard, giant squid ate." He has also claimed that the topic-comment utterance is "the favourite sentence type only in deliberate connected discourse" (Chao, 1968, p.83). Others have written on Chinese sentence types and discourse patterns.[4] Helen Kwok has worked also with descriptions of Cantonese for English readers (Kwok, 1971, 1984). And studies of Chinese structures offer one basis for the analysis of common errors arising through "interference". But be this as it may, it would be fatuous for me to suggest that, if a framework for the analysis of all naturally occurring discourse in Chinese were available, the writer of fictional dialogue in English would (a) avail himself/herself of it, (b) that this knowledge could systematically be translated into a semblance of "the real thing" in English, and (c) that readers would respond to this as "the real thing". The whole question of creating the illusion of verisimilitude is such a vexed one that instead of even attempting to provide cut and dry rules, I shall discuss some of the conventions adopted by different writers.

Indeed it is not until the early decades of the twentieth century that we find Chinese-speaking Chinese women of any significance at all in fiction written in English. And it would be safe to say that it is only in recent fiction that we find the portrayal of English-speaking Chinese women, since such oddities, with notable exceptions, were in fact hard to come by in real life until fairly recent times. First, then, Chinese women speaking Chinese in English fiction. Pearl Buck is credited with being a real pioneer in the work of familiarizing the West with Chinese and the Chinese people. She was born and brought up in China, living most of her first 25 years in China before her marriage in 1917, and she spent four years of her married life in Anhwei province. She learned to speak and write Chinese before she did English. She first gained fame as a novelist with her 1931 novel *East Wind: West Wind*. It is written in the first person narrative; the narrator is a beautiful Chinese woman, set in feudal ways and reared in the traditional mode. Her beauty is of the traditional type: heavy make-up, slanty, slitty eyes, bound feet. On the frontispiece of the novel is the inscription "A Chinese Woman Speaks". And how she speaks! Let me quote an example from her opening monologue:

These things I may tell you, My Sister, I could not speak thus even to one of my own people, for she could not understand the far countries where my husband lived for twelve years. Neither could I talk freely to one of the alien women who do not know my people and the manner of life we have had since the time of the ancient empire. But you? You have lived among us all your years. Although you belong to those other lands where my husband studied his Western books, you will understand. I speak the truth. I have named you My Sister. I will tell you everything.

You know that for five hundred years my revered ancestors have lived in this age-old city of the Middle Kingdom. Not one of the august ones was modern; nor did he have a desire to change himself. They all lived in quietness and dignity, confident of their rectitude. Thus did my parents rear me in all the honoured traditions. I never dreamed I could wish to be different. Without thinking on the matter it seemed to me that as I was so were all those who were really people. If I heard faintly, as from the distance outside the courtyard walls, of women not like myself, women who came and went freely like men, I did not consider them. I went, as I was taught, in the approved ways of my ancestors. Nothing from the outside ever touched me. I desired nothing. But now the day has come when I watch eagerly these strange creatures—these modern women—seeking how I may become like them. Not, My Sister, for my own sake, but for my husband's.

He does not find me fair! It is because he has crossed the Four Seas to the other and outer countries, and he has learned in those remote places to love new things and new ways.

My mother is a wise woman. When at the age of ten I ceased to be a child and became a maiden, she said to me these words: "A woman before men should maintain a flower-like silence and should withdraw herself at the earliest moment that is possible without confusion."

I remembered what she said, therefore, when I stood before my husband. I bowed my head and placed my two hands before me. I answered him nothing when he spoke to me. But, oh, I fear he finds my silence dull!

When I examine my mind for something to interest him, it is suddenly as barren as rice-fields after the harvest. When I am alone at my embroidery, I think of many delicately beautiful things to say to him. I will tell him how I love him. Not, you mind, in the brazen words copied from the rapacious West. But in hidden words like these:

"My lord, did you mark this day how the dawn began? It was as if the dull earth leaped to meet the sun. Darkness. Then a mighty lift of light like a burst of music! My dear lord, I am thy dull earth, waiting." (Buck, 1930, pp.3-5)

That this type of dialogue did not immediately elicit mirth but was taken seriously, as indeed the novel was, attests to the naïveté of the 1930's predominantly American readership with regard to things Chinese. I am not here disparaging in any way the very considerable contribution made by Pearl Buck, but focusing on her choice of stylistic devices in the presentation of dialogue for Chinese women characters speaking in Chinese. Whatever response this passage elicits, I am sure no reader would fail to concur with the view that it is foreign and bears little resemblance to any sort of discourse in present-day English. Critics have commented on the Biblical ring of Pearl Buck's prose. As a missionary's daughter she was brought up on the Bible. The rhythm, achieved largely by repetition and syntactical balance, and, very often, lexical choice, gives the flavour of the Authorized Version of the Bible. Critics given to vague generalized comments suggest that though Pearl Buck's characters do not often speak (and she does not write a great deal of dialogue) when they do speak their turns of phrase seem to suggest they are talking in their native Chinese. This is entirely based on the impression of readers unfamiliar with the Chinese language.

I do not think the similarity to Anhwei rhythms (and Pearl Buck was familiar with the Anhwei dialect) can be instrumentally tested, nor would there be any point in so doing. The majority of Pearl Buck's readers would not recognize *any* Chinese dialect if they heard it. It is the alien quality, the deviation from the norm of any kind of English prose, that is the main device. It is grammatical in the strict sense: it is not a question of Earl Derr Biggers having Charlie Chan drop his articles, prepositions, main verbs, and doubling his subjects, indeed speaking a modified form of pidgin. But then the illusion is that Charlie Chan is speaking English. To return to the extract from *East Wind: West Wind*—the illusion of "Chineseness" of the narrative—discourse is as much derived from the content as from the stylistic devices. Ideas relating to the debased position of the traditional Chinese women, their sheltered existence and general ignorance of anything outside their restricted little lives, emphasis on the "Chinese" virtues of "quietness, dignity…and rectitude" and the whole tone of obsequious subservience do their part, as do references to feminine Chinese pursuits like embroidery, and to satins and pearls. The sentences are by no means contorted. Indeed they are quite direct, and there is quite a high proportion of simple and compound sentences. There are no contractions. This absence seems a favoured convention. It is on the lexical level that a distinctively deliberate effort is made to introduce a Chinese flavour. Direct translations which sound archaic and un-English are used—*Middle Kingdom, The Four Seas, outer countries*. The metaphors are embarrassing and florid to a sophisticated reader, but presumably much more so only if the reader is Chinese, and a Chinese woman at that. To an average Western reader of the 1930s "flower-like silence" "as barren as rice fields after the harvest", and all the balderdash about the dull earth leaping to meet the sun may have been perfectly acceptable, indeed informative. Thus do Chinese women talk, with *thee's* and *thou's*, they think.

What follows is an extract of narrative and dialogue from Pearl Buck's best-known novel, *The Good Earth* (1931). It has been translated into approximately 30 languages, including Chinese. It was dramatized as a Broadway play in 1932 and soon afterwards became known to millions around the world as a film starring Paul Muni and Louise Rainer. In *The Good Earth*, the characters, do not "speak" much. Flipping through the pages of a copy of the novel, I was amazed at the paucity of inverted commas. The heroine, O-lan, a stolid and plain peasant woman, sold into slavery as a child and repressed all her life, is taciturn to the point of virtual wordlessness. Her direct, terse dialogue is part of the author's characterization of her. A great deal of the extract relates to the guilty consciousness of her husband, Wang Lung, who has taken a concubine, a former singsong girl, into the house. O-lan resents most the singsong girl's companion-cum-servant, one Cuckoo, a woman who tormented her in "the great house" where she toiled as a slave before her marriage. The rhythms of the Authorized Version of the Bible are again in evidence in the style of both narrative and dialogue. O-lan's speeches are so brief that the relatively long outburst in paragraph seven becomes the more poignant. The rhythm is made distinctive by the use of the coordinating conjunction "and", giving balance and equal emphasis to each part of her lament. The repetition of "too" suggests the monotonous horror of her long-drawn-out ordeal. "Bore her haughty looks", "the great house" (instead of, say, "the big house") and "a score of times a day" throw the lexis out of ordinary prose. The ring is Biblical, in any case archaic, and removed from twentieth-century discourse in English.

> Wang Lung looked east and west. He would have liked to speak out to say in a surly voice of master, "Well, and it is my house and whoever I say may come in, she shall come in, and who are you to ask?" But he could not because of some shame in him when O-lan was there before him, and his shame made him angry, because when he reasoned it, there was no need for shame and he had done no more than any man may do who has silver to spare.
>
> Still, he could not speak out, and he only looked east and west and feigned to have mislaid his pipe in his garments, and he fumbled in his girdle. But O-lan stood there solidly on her big feet and waited and when he said nothing she asked again plainly in the same words,

"What is this slave woman doing in our house?"

Then Wang Lung seeing she would have an answer, said feebly, "And what is it to you?"

And O-lan said,

"I bore her haughty looks all during my youth in the great house and her running into the kitchen a score of times a day and crying out 'now tea for the lord'—'now food for the lord'—and it was always this is too hot and that is too cold, and that is badly cooked, and I was too ugly and too slow and too this and too that..."

But still Wang Lung did not answer, for he did not know what to say.

Then O-lan waited and when he did not speak, the hot, scanty tears welled slowly into her eyes, and she winked them to hold back the tears, and at last she took the corner of her blue apron and wiped her eyes and she said at last,

"It is a bitter thing in my house, and I have no mother's house to go back to anywhere." (Buck, 1931b, p.180)

Agnes Smedley wrote about China at about the same time as Pearl Buck did. She was also American, a journalist deeply committed to the feminist and the Communist causes. As a literary artist she is perhaps best known by her vignettes of Chinese life incorporated in *Chinese Destinies* (1933). These little stories take the form of reportage rather than fiction. Many of her characters are Chinese women, since she was so deeply concerned with their plight. These characters, as often generic as individualized, do not "speak" all that much. When Smedley does make them speak, the dialogue is frequently deliberately stylized, almost as the gestures and dialogue in Chinese opera might be stylized, and its effectiveness may well be in the fact that the reader is aware of the stylization, the absence of deliberate devices to reproduce or even suggest the elements of real discourse. In one of her stories, "The Dedicated", the heroine Chang Siao-hung is described as appearing on a stage. She utters a very long monologue, at the end of which she asserts confidently:

As for my old feudal family, the family into which I was born—
they are to me but a dark and ugly memory, and to them I am but a
fearful dream... They once tried to pin me to a marriage bed with
a millionaire that I might breed more creatures like themselves.
But I chose a man I loved from the ranks of the revolution, and for
permission to live with him I asked no priest or policeman whose
blessings give sanctity to bourgeois marriages.

You wished to know the role I play in China. It is enough to say
that I am a communist for that means I am fighting in the ranks for
a new world. It means that I may one day cease to appear on this
stage of historical events—but it means also that all that I work
for now will be carried to fruition by the revolution of which I am
but a part. Now I will be on my way, for there is much to do and
I never know how much longer I have to do the share allotted to
me. (Smedley, 1933, pp.88-89.)

Chang Siao-hung is clearly less a human character than a
mouthpiece for Agnes Smedley's political convictions. The
language is stilted and formal, for and but enforcing the sense
of its being "spoken prose", and the metaphor of the theatre
accentuates the sense of stylization in the traditional Chinese
theatrical tradition. While it could be argued that there is
considerable dignity in this type of formalized representation it
is equally true that for purposes of fictional narrative it would
be far too inflexible and lifeless.

Agnes Smedley knew no Chinese. Pearl Buck did, and had
undertaken the formidable task of translating the monumental
Chinese novel *The Water Margin* into English under the
title of *All Men Are Brothers*. She must have been affected
by the language of Chinese epics; she claimed that for her
Chinese novels she thought of them first in Chinese and then
translated them into English. But there is no clear evidence of
entire chunks of dialogue directly translated. However, direct
translation of dialogue from Chinese and the embedding
of that dialogue in English narrative is a device attempted
with variations in two versions of the story of the notorious
Empress Wu. I shall quote extracts dealing with the same

incident. One extract is from the historian C. P. Fitzgerald (*The Empress Wu*, 1955). Fitzgerald tries to re-evaluate Wu Chao's real role in Chinese history by applying Western historical research methods to his material, but his scholarly restraint does not prevent him from telling a very vivid story, replete with direct quotations allegedly translated from the Chinese sources. The style of the translated dialogue is of interest. The author's literal translation of nominatives gives a sense of the exotic and strikes a chord of accuracy to those who know Chinese. *Concubines* is presumably a direct translation of the Chinese term 妾 made familiar from Chinese poetry. It is a term of abasement, sometimes used in place of the first-person pronoun by women who were, like Empress Wang, not *concubines* in the sense usually understood. Similarly the full title *Your Majesty* is used instead of the second-person pronoun of address, considered discourteous for many years even in addressing any elder or a superior, let alone an Emperor. The apparently literalness of the translation rests again mainly on choices on the lexical-semantic level, rather than the syntactic—"changing death into life... so that we may once more see the sun and moon", "treacherous fox". The Chinese and English languages share the same connotations for *fox* or *vixen*.[5] The sentence structures of the dialogue are not, for the most part, "deviant". The curse of Hsiao Liang-ti indeed is very expressive in its very directness. The multiple structure reinforces the multiple lives during which Hsiao will be able to exact her terrible revenge.

> Wu Chao had now achieved her ambition... but she was not prepared to leave any remnant of the opposition to watch for a chance of bringing about a change of fortune.
>
> The fallen Empress Wang and the Pure Concubine still lived imprisoned in the side apartments of the Inner Palace. One day Kao Tsung... found their prison, with the door blocked up leaving only a narrow hole through which food could be passed. Kao Tsung was shocked, and ... he called out to the prisoners, saying, "Empress and Hsiao Liang-ti, are you both well?" They answered, in tears, "We poor concubines for our crimes are now Palace slaves, why does Your Majesty still address us with titles of honour?"

Then they said, "Your Majesty has fortunately recollected former times, changing death into life for us, so that we may once more see the sun and moon. We beg you to change the name of this place to 'Court of Remembrance'." The Emperor, moved, replied, "It shall be done at once."

The new Empress, when she heard of it, was filled with rage and suspicion. She at once sent executioners, who, after beating the two unfortunate women with a hundred blows, cut off their feet and hands, and then threw them, bound, into a brewing vat. Wu Chao exultantly remarked, "Now these two witches can get drunk to their bones." After several days of agony the two victims died, and their corpses were then cut to pieces, and decapitated.

When the Empress Wang heard her fate, she bowed several times to the ground and said, "Long life to His Majesty; Wu Chao has obtained favour, death is my lot." Hsiao Liang-ti showed less submissive resignation: when she was told her sentence she cursed aloud, saying, "Ah Wu is a treacherous fox who has brought me to this. I pray that in my future lives I shall return as a cat, and Ah Wu will be a mouse, and then from life to life I shall tear out her throat."… (Fitzgerald, 1955, p.31)

Let us contrast Fitzgerald's conventions with regard to dialogue with Lin Yutang's. Lin Yutang uses an allegedly historical character, the Prince of Bin, as the narrator. Lin repeatedly asserts that while he has based his account on historical fact, he relates the facts as "fiction" with "a strong sense of drama" (Lin, 1957, p.x). The first-person narration is done in a "personal", almost childish style. The sentences are, apparently deliberately, almost always short and simple, compound or multiple. When they are complex they are constructed according to a very straightforward pattern. In the dialogue used in the parallel account of Wu's incredible vindictiveness, we find Lin attempting a more contemporary, idiomatic style complete with contractions. I suspect that Lin, in line with his life's work of explaining "his country, his people" to the West, deliberately thought he would demystify his Chinese characters by having them speak in what he considered to be a modern, racy way, free of the usual archaic conventions. But the effect seems to fall short of what must have been his expectations, and we have a rather ludicrous juxtaposition of the formal and the highly colloquial. Lady Wu's command and its repetition with variations in the question at the end of the extract might have been effective except for the jarring note introduced by the choice of the word *wenches*.

Gowtsung should have left the deposed Empress Wang and Siowfei alone in their confinement. It was his mistake. Soft-hearted and bitten with remorse, one day he went to visit them... He was shocked to find the door securely locked, with only a hole on the side.

He called through the hole, "Empress, Siowfei, where are you?"

After a while, he heard shuffling feet and soft, faint, distressed voices from within.

"We have been disgraced. We didn't think you would still call us by our former titles... For old times' sake, let us out, we beg you. Just set us free. We shall call this place the Hall of Mercy in gratitude."

Gowtsung was deeply touched. "Don't worry. I will do something about it."...

He did not know that he had been shadowed. When Lady Wu returned, the emperor's stolen visit was reported... It was evidence that he was still thinking of those two women! She would take no chances.

Before the emperor had the opportunity to speak to her, she spoke to him. He had been to see the two convicts, she was told. Was it true?

The emperor quickly denied it.

"Oh, I'm glad you didn't."

The emperor had as good as admitted that he had been wrong to see them. Lady Wu gave orders to her servants to have the two women whipped a hundred lashes. Then she had their hands and feet cut off, and, with their arms and legs crooked behind them, had them thrown into wine vats.

"Let these wenches' bones and marrow melt in drunken ecstasy," she said. The phrase was a reference to sexual pleasure.

After a couple of days, the two women died, as was to be expected. Their death was reported.

"Have their bones and marrow melted in drunken ecstasy?" she asked with an idle smile.

"Yes, they have, Your Majesty," answered the servant. (Lin, 1957, pp.40-41)

The four authors from whose work I have quoted above can be said to be sympathetic to Chinese women characters. We can fairly safely assume—and here I am fully aware of the dangers of such assumptions—that they want to present their Chinese women characters in human terms to their readers. I think that if they fail to characterize but succeed only in creating caricature, then the failing lies in the difficulty of the task rather than in ill will.

In the presentation of direct speech in a novel, as distinct from drama, the author has the advantage of varying the proportion of dialogue, and complementary and supplementary information, description or comment. (Page, 1973, p.26) The writer of dialogue for Chinese characters often resorts to attributions to speakers which are accompanied by detailed specific references to indications of language or dialect used, nature of accent, together with the more usual "stage directions" as to facial expression, movement, gesture, volume. In other words the various forms of "he said", "he cried", "he mused", etc. are elaborated to give details, to help along the illusion. Robert Elegant, for example, makes use of this device of description of the linguistic characteristics before launching into an effort to suggest the type of discourse described.

Her sons Thomas and James were on their feet shouting insults at each other in the harsh Cantonese that was their childhood tongue.

"Liar and betrayer," the Nationalist General screamed at his younger brother. "You sold China to the Russians. You betrayed the Generalissimo. You've destroyed China's culture."

"Lackey of the imperialists," The Communist General shouted. "Running-dog of the Americans. Your corrupt lot of

thieves squeezed the people 'til blood ran from their fingernails."
(Elegant, 1977, p.137)

The attempt to suggest their "childhood tongue" is
reflected in the stilted and archaic diction and the specific loan
translation, *running-dog*, together with the rather ludicrous
metaphor intended no doubt to reflect Chinese torture
methods. In spite of the references to specific qualities of
speech either in the accompanying comments or incorporated
in the dialogue itself by deviant orthography, italics, and so on,
the writer is still throwing the major burden of reconstruction
on the reader.

Comparisons may be helpful here. Consider the
unusually long stage direction in Bernard Shaw's *Pygmalion*.
Shaw has been trying to represent in deviant spelling
Eliza Doolittle's Cockney speech when he inserts the
stage-direction-cum-comment: "Here, with apologies,
this desperate attempt to represent her dialect without a
phonetic alphabet must be abandoned as unintelligible
outside London." But *Pygmalion* is a play and the text
comes to life as "an auditory experience" for playgoers
because the guidelines are sufficient for any reasonable
actress playing the part. Let us, then, take a novel to make
the comparison clearer. Emily Brontë's sustained efforts
with Joseph's dialectal idiosyncrasies in *Wuthering Heights*
are well known. For her own novelistic effects it seems
insufficient for her to simply characterize Joseph's dialectal
deviance from the standard by a descriptive phrase like
"He spoke in broad Yorkshire". But, however precisely
she attempted to reproduce or at least suggest the dialect
in Joseph's speech from graphological conventions, the
many readers not familiar with the phonological features of
broad Yorkshire would not have the benefit of any sort of
"auditory experience" approximating to the experience of
hearing "the real thing". Such is the case, only to a much
more exaggerated degree, with the "guttural Cantonese" of
the two brothers, for the average Western reader. Sometimes
all deliberate "sinicizing" conventions are left out, and the

reader is left only with the descriptive attribution, e.g. "Miss Tsang said in Cantonese." (Davis, 1983, p.76)

It is relevant to elaborate this point vis-à-vis the absence of linguistic conventions as a convention. Chang Hsin-hai, a Shanghai-born Western-educated Chinese scholar with a Ph.D. from Harvard, wrote a novel, his first and apparently his only novel, called *The Fabulous Concubine* (Chang, 1956). He drew on his wide knowledge of diplomatic and official life. His central character is a gloriously beautiful former singsong girl who becomes an elderly Mandarin's concubine (the fabulous concubine of the title) and thence the toast of Germany, where her husband is posted as Ambassador. Chang makes no concessions to the Westerner's usual image of the Chinese as inferior pigtailed servants or subservient cringing worshippers of Western men. His style of narrative is formal and a little stilted. The dialogue is similar in style. No conventions are deliberately employed to pander to any illusions Western readers may have about Chinese speech, as can be seen from the extract given below:

Wen-ching was satisfied with the talk, and that evening he told Golden Orchid about it. She was glad Yung-kai was singled out for special attention, but Wen-ching was struck by one point she made.

"When the other members of the staff learn of this talk," Golden Orchid asked, "won't they say that you are bestowing more than usual favour on Yung-kai? They'll say that because he has a powerful and influential father you have been partial to him. This is just a thought on my part, Wen-ching dear."

The year of residence in Berlin, with its wide social contacts and knowledge of foreign customs, had so changed Golden Orchid that she began to discard the old way of addressing her husband. The new way, she thought, was much more affectionate and strongly appealed to her. Wen-ching, too, seemed to like it.

"It's a good thought, my treasure," replied Wen-ching. "However, they won't know of it. And even if they do, they cannot feel slighted, because I have had such meetings with them before. Frankly, they are an impossible lot. I have no use for them."

"That may be so, but still they will feel offended."

"Time and again I have found that they have no interest in international affairs. I have given them every opportunity to improve themselves. Now you have brought up this subject, I might as well let you know that I have subscribed to magazines for them, and newspapers from many countries, and have brought books for them in the hope that they would read them. But they do not even touch them."

"I suppose they even say that you have insulted them."

"Exactly. One of them, I was told, commented that this is not a school but an embassy. He said he was not a schoolboy!"

"Of course, he wants to be known as a bureaucrat, even though he may sit like a dummy through these diplomatic functions." (Chang, 1956, pp.108-109)

The lack of specific conventions to differentiate speech from narrative is also a characteristic of the later work, Bette Bao Lord's *Spring Moon* (1982). Mrs Lord was born in Shanghai, went to America when her father, an official in the Chinese government, was assigned to the United States. She graduated from Tufts with a Master's Degree in Law and Diplomacy. She returned to China with her husband, Winston Lord, an American diplomat, in 1973, and her reunion there with her relatives became the genesis of *Spring Moon*. Spring Moon is the name of her high-spirited, supremely intelligent and sensitive Chinese woman who, in the course of the novel, ages many decades. Mrs Lord clearly wants her readers to be impressed by the beauty and intelligence of Spring Moon. Her dialogue is marked in the sense that the author deliberately eschews slang expressions or contractions which would seem anachronistic on the lips of a Ching Dynasty Chinese woman. But a balance is struck between being outrageously archaic and outrageously racy. And, as the extract quoted below will show, the dialogue is not different stylistically from the narrative.

Spring Moon straightened and paused for a moment, her brow furrowed. Then, quickly pushing her clothbound feet into a pair of pink embroidered shoes and pulling on her ta chin p'ao, she stepped out onto the gallery that bordered the garden of the

Court of Wise Heart. The garden was a small one and contained no hiding place, so she walked from door to door, looking into each room of the three wings of her family's quarters. Plum Blossom was not in any of them. No one was.

Where could the girl be? A sudden fear quickened Spring Moon's heart. Only a two-headed snake could have sent Plum Blossom away. Unless... what if Fragrant Snow had needed her? Had not Fatso complained that morning of a headache? Perhaps Plum Blossom had been called to wait on Mother in Fatso's place.

Quickly the child slipped through the Fan Gate, past the Court of Silent Bamboos, which belonged to the family of Great-Uncle Number Three, past the several courts of the Venerable's nephews, to the Bridge of Coming and Going and the Court of Womanly Virtues. As she neared the tall red columns that marked the entrance of the Hall, she could hear the hum of gossip and the clatter of gaming tiles within. For a moment she hesitated. What if Mother was losing again to Great-Aunt Number Three? But she could also be winning, and in good spirits. Resolutely Spring Moon walked the few steps across the gallery to the open door.

At the threshold, she paused once more, trying to locate Plum Blossom or Fragrant Snow among the grandmothers, mothers, widows, wives, concubines, daughters, slave girls, and servants who lived together in the thirty courts beneath the ancestral roofs.

Finally she spotted the plum silk that, years ago, Fragrant Snow had decided was her best colour and now wore exclusively. She was embroidering by the west window where she could catch the last of the afternoon light. Spring Moon slipped through the crowd.

"Mother!" She tugged at Fragrant Snow's sleeve. "Mother!" Fragrant Snow slapped the offending hand. "What are you doing, naughty girl? Rushing in like a gust of wind, interrupting your elders without so much as a greeting! Everyone will think that I have neglected my duties. You will heap shame upon our ancestors!"

Spring Moon bowed her head. "A thousand pardons, my mother." She turned away and walked slowly towards the Matriarch.

The old woman's full attention was now given to Grandniece Number Five, who stared at the hem of her tunic while being instructed on the conduct proper during expectant happiness.

"...and remember, no hashed foods lest the baby have a careless disposition..."

Spring Moon waited to be acknowledged.

"...and no sad thoughts lest the baby be infected." The Matriarch nodded. "You may go now and take tea." She turned to Spring Moon.

Spring Moon blushed, remembering all at once that she had neglected to wash after her nap. Grandmother would know, of course. She always knew. But you could never tell what she was thinking, for the rice powder hid her expressions as completely as the opera mask hid the face of the doll Eldest Uncle had given her before he went away. With the Matriarch looking at her, Spring Moon always felt as small as a sesame seed. (Lord, 1982, pp.3-5)

In a sense, the narrative can be seen as discourse: a Chinese woman talking about other Chinese. The use of the translated names in preference to transliterated ones gives a very strong Chinese flavour which the Western reader may find "charming" but may well be off-putting to the Chinese reader. This, and the deliberately artificial metaphors. In a sense, the narrative can be seen as the discourse of the narrator also.

While on the subject of fictional characters speaking "Chinese", I ought here to state the obvious: the fact that Chinese is by no means a homogeneous whole. Writers in English are often aware of this and their recognition of differences in the dialects, phonetic and otherwise, is sometimes reflected in their presentation of Chinese dialect, although, as one may imagine, any conventions in the text itself would be hard to sustain. In *The Fabulous Concubine*, Chang Hsin-hai describes a meeting of speakers from many different parts of China. The dialogue itself shows no markers of differences, but we are given descriptive information in the narrative: we are told that one of the characters speaks "with a strong Hunan accent", and of another the author writes that he "spoke slowly and with a gentle tone, for he was from Hangchow" (Chang, 1956, pp.18-19). I have already referred to Elegant's description of Cantonese as "harsh". All too aware of how different in sound as well as other aspects Putonghua is from spoken Cantonese, he uses the interesting but not altogether successful convention of resorting to romanization when he wants to suggest a change from Cantonese to the Mandarin dialect. For example:

Chin-tien ta chiang-lai, ming-tien mei chiang-lai! (Elegant, 1977, p.728)

One can easily see how this convention can only be one for creating a temporary illusion, not for sustaining the narrative through dialogue. The brief example I have quoted is followed immediately by the translation, "Today a big future, tomorrow no future."

In the characterization of Chinese women, place of origin plays a part. Different regions are believed to produce very distinctive characteristics; for example, women from Tung Koon County are supposed to be very fierce. But while some of these beliefs are without foundation, other ascriptions are true in a very general way. Shanghainese women are generally considered stylish, sophisticated and desirable. We see that as unlikely a writer in this context as J. D. Salinger has got hold of this idea. In *The Catcher in the Rye*, a conversation takes place between the know-it-all Columbia undergraduate, Luce, and the narrator, adolescent Holden Caulfield. Luce boasts of the girl he is going around with. Surprisingly she is a Chinese sculptress in her late thirties, clearly a very sophisticated lady who lives in the Village. One does not expect a reference to the Chinese and their sexuality in what is essentially such an "American" novel. What is more, Salinger adds the detail that the lady is originally from Shanghai, thus reinforcing the idea of her cosmopolitan sophistication and desirability (Salinger, 1958, pp.151-152). Other Western authors have chosen to capitalize on the alleged equation between Shanghai and sexy sophistication. Suzie Wong herself is from Shanghai, but is only through authorial comment and her own deprecatory remarks about Cantonese women, and not through any formal linguistic markers, that her regional origins are indicated.

Sumei in Christopher New's *Shanghai* is a Shanghainese singsong girl whom the English hero, Denton, marries. But again, no concessions are made to this "Shanghainese-ness" in her dialogue, either in English or in Chinese.

So far I have dealt with conventions used by authors writing dialogue for Chinese characters speaking in Chinese. What of the situation when the Chinese characters are speaking in English? It is usually when they speak English that the characters are seen in their relationships to native English speakers. It is then that the conventions used are usually more directly related to how the author perceives his Chinese characters and how he wants his readership to respond to them. A more important issue is how his readership does respond to them, because this response can be quite independent of authorial intention. Linda Wai-Ling Young has done a very interesting study on discourse strategies of Chinese speakers of English (Young, 1982, pp.73-84). The data she analyses are derived from a variety of formal speech encounters, including an academic conference and a number of business meetings involving Chinese speakers of English as active participants. Her study is guided by the assumption that these speakers will have transferred some of the mechanisms of their native speech patterns and discourse expectations into English. She is mainly interested in differences in basic sentence type and discourse strategies between these Chinese speakers of English and native English speakers, but her material also exemplifies some of the so-called "common errors" of Chinese speakers. This analysis is limited in that it concentrates on formal discourse of a limited type. And indeed for many Chinese speakers of English, the use of English is restricted only to very limited situations, and is by no means interchangeable with Chinese as a medium of communication. K. K. Luke and J. C. Richards provide an illuminating analysis of the essentially functional nature of English. They write, "The status of English in Hong Kong is unique. It is neither second nor foreign language... we would therefore suggest the term auxiliary language to describe it" (Luke and Richards, 1982, pp.47-64). In general it would be true to say, then, that discourse in English by Chinese people would not in almost all instances be naturally occurring talk. And what is more, as I have posited in the case of the representation in English of dialogue supposedly in Chinese, even if it were possible to produce descriptive models of all kinds of discourse in English of Chinese speakers, would strict adherence to these models result in an illusion of "the real thing"? I think not.

The use of comment and description either with or without varying degrees of exemplification in the dialogue is a technique used in the representation of Chinese-speakers' discourse in English. I have already noted this in connection with "Chinese" dialogue written in English. In Robert Elegant's *Dynasty* (1977), for example, the author shows his awareness of the different modes of speech being used by his English, Eurasian and Chinese characters of different backgrounds and levels of society. In the narrative there are quite a number of detailed descriptions of these varied accents and modes of speech. The patriarch of the Shekloong family, founder of the "dynasty", Eurasian, bilingual but more at home in Cantonese, is described as having a distinctive way of speaking English. "His accent might have been Welsh, except for the slurred s's, incomplete vowels, and stilted diction characteristic of Hong Kong's English-educated Chinese" (Elegant, 1977, p.77). But when he and the other Eurasian characters speak in English their "stilted diction" is usually not so marked as to set their speech apart from that of the English characters.

The English-speaking characters in such novels are generally bilingual, and it is interesting to note how novelists attempt to show the switch from one language to another. The inherent difficulties are evident: deviance from the norms of discourse in standard English would seem to be called for in the representation of speech in both English and Chinese. But conventions adopted vary. The Eurasian novelist Timothy Mo provides an interesting case study. He is clearly interested in dialogue as a tool of characterization, and in his two earlier novels, *The Monkey King* (1978) and *Sour Sweet* (1982), the use of the two languages, English and Chinese, plays a significant part in his thematic concerns. In his first novel, *The Monkey King*, Timothy Mo writes about a group of Hong Kong and Macanese characters, among them the hero, Wallace Nolasco, ethnically mostly Chinese. I say "mostly" because this is the author's explanation of Nolasco's origins:

> The Nolascos called themselves Portuguese, a courtesy title and thanks to the unremitting clannishness of the Chinese were so known. But physically, it would have been difficult to tell them apart from their Chinese neighbours. (Mo, 1978, p.9)

Right from the beginning of the novel Timothy Mo makes it clear that Nolasco "possessed the impeccable Cantonese of most of his compatriots but affected not to understand the vulgar, braying dialect" (Mo, 1978, p.8). For simple reasons of survival, because it was marriage or starvation, Wallace marries May Ling, youngest daughter of Hong Kong Cantonese merchant, Mr Poon. He moves into Mr Poon's ramshackle household, and for the rest of the novel the author switches supposedly between dialogue in English and in Cantonese. This constant code-switching is indicated only in the descriptive comments and attributions. The convention used in this novel for the presentation of dialogue is unusual in that for dialogue both in Cantonese and in English the author uses a sort of unauthenticated China coast pidgin. He claims to have had a definite motive in choosing this device: he wanted to use this stylized dialogue to give an impression of decay. While Mo himself is pleased with the result, he has found that his purposes tend to be misunderstood, especially by Chinese readers, many of whom think the use of pidgin is a form of denigration since they are unfamiliar with the satirical tradition.[6] What strikes me as unsatisfactory is not even his decision not to differentiate in any substantial way the two languages but the restricted effects that the sustained use of China coast pidgin is capable of; as, for example, in the following passages:

> Wallace was teaching May Ling how to play Chinese checkers, with dice, in the reception room when Ah Lung joined them...

Ah Lung stood close to the seated couple, trawling a comb through his quiff, using his reflection in an antique cabinet...

"Once you were reaching my side, you could crown your checker and make him king." Wallace competed with Ah Lung for her attention. May Ling's eyes flickered uneasily from side to side. Her husband's last remark gained her attention.

"Why not queen?" she demurred. "It should be queen if I was woman."

"That was just the way it was. You want to learn this game or what?"

"So the two love-bird quarreling already," Ah Lung broke in mockingly. "He go and beat the hell out of you later, May Ling. You better had watch out."

"Don't notice him, May. Stick and stone could be breaking my bone but word never could harm me."

"That was what you thought, Nolasco." Ah Lung went into the corridor where they could hear him rummaging among the piled newspapers by Mr Poon's desk. He continued round to his mother's room.

"Now, May, you didn't pay attentions. I tell you that if you were forgetting to take my piece then I could huff you. Look, huff, huff, huff." Wallace threw the wooden pieces back into their box.

May Ling swept the remaining pieces off the board. "Silly games! You tell me all the wrong thing, so you could win. It not fair."

Wallace sucked his teeth in exasperation. "OK, we start again and this time I would give you a start of three king. How about that, hah?"

May Ling pouted. "How about you gave me four king?"

The staccato exchanges of an argument in Cantonese had been registering as a peripheral distraction while Wallace administered the coup de grace to his wife. The high voices grew clearer. There was the crash of a heavy weight falling, the impact causing the glass in the cabinet to vibrate sympathetically. Ah Lung burst in with his newly greased hair now sticking up in spikes and tufts. He was hobbling on one shoe, pursued by Mr Poon who was brandishing a golf club which he swung in wide arcs at Ah Lung's legs, striking with the wood end.

"Eiyah! Eiyah! He go and kill me, Wallace! Save life! Save life!" Ah Lung fell on his knees, supplicating his father with clasped hands.

Mr Poon reversed his grip on the club and rained blows on his son's shoulders, carefully avoiding his head and landing with the handle.

Ah Lung wept, making no attempt to avoid the heavy strokes. "Give face. Give face."

A few days later Wallace was reading in the bedroom when Fong entered with a summons to assembly in the front room. The others were waiting for him. At last Mr Poon entered with Mrs Poon, serious-faced, behind him. He launched straight into a harangue in clipped, energetic Cantonese.

The flow stopped. Mr Poon began again in English. He stared at Wallace throughout. "A viper in our bosoms," he concluded, pronouncing it "wiper". "Now we would make search."

Ah Lung was genuinely mystified. "What the hell was going on, Nolasco, hah?"

Wallace protruded his lower lip. "You could search me."

Mr Poon clapped his hands. "There would be silence."

They returned to their rooms in Indian file. (Mo, 1978, pp.29-30, 40.)

Nolasco's brother-in-law, Ah Lung's switch to Cantonese is signalized by first the authorial comment: "The staccato exchanges of an argument in Cantonese had been registering as a peripheral distraction...", then by his use of *Eiyah*, a phonetic rendering of the Cantonese interjection and two direct translations of Cantonese expressions into English, namely "Save life" 救命 and "Give face" 俾面. I have included the second extract to illustrate once more the use of authorial comment to indicate code switching. Mr Poon is described first as launching "straight into a harangue in clipped, energetic Cantonese", and then beginning again in English. A cursory attempt at suggesting one of the common errors of Cantonese speakers speaking English is made in the comment on Mr Poon's pronunciation of viper as "wiper".

In writing dialogue for his second novel, *Sour Sweet*, which deals with Hong Kong immigrants learning to cope with a new life in Britain, Timothy Mo abandoned the stylization of his first effort. Mo's father is a local Cantonese solicitor, and he lived the first 10 years of his life in Hong Kong. His stepmother is from Shanghai and his half-brothers and sisters speak Cantonese. Mo lives in London, but returns regularly to visit his family in Hong Kong. He says he does not write Chinese but his "Chinese" dialogue for the *Sour Sweet* characters suggests strongly his knowledge of spoken Cantonese. By this second novel he seems to be more assured of his conventions. He does differentiate the dialogue in Chinese and the dialogue in English of his Chinese characters, and the dialogue in English is, paradoxically and yet aptly, usually in much poorer, less expressive English, as in the following extract:

> "Handsome boy," the strange woman complimented Lily in Cantonese. As Lily merely smiled without saying anything, she repeated her remark in English: "The boy good-looking."
>
> "No. Not at all. He's a very plain child."
>
> "Ah, so you are Chinese. I thought you might be Filipino." The woman used the idiom 'Person of Tang', a peculiar southern idiom. "But not from Hong Kong. Singapore, maybe?"
>
> "Kwangsi." Lily smiled.
>
> "I thought your accent was strange. Yes, you don't have the appearance of a Hong Kong person. Too independent-looking." She laughed at her own joke. (Mo, 1982, p.38)

Here two Oriental women meet in an alien land. First Cantonese dialogue, then English, then Cantonese again. There is a reference to the Kwangsi accent. It will be noticed that the author has taken some pains to differentiate the one sentence spoken in English from the rest of the dialogue. Structurally it is based on a Cantonese sentence pattern: subject+stative verb, without the English "be" form. The convention with regard to the Chinese is a lack of obvious sincizing conventions. What in the dialogue is written as the word "Chinese" is "re-written", as it were, in the author's comment as "Person of Tang", which is then glossed. The assumption is that the speakers' Chinese is non-deviant; it is their English which is deviant.

In the extract below, we are given a long stretch of Chinese utterances written in English.

–Husband, are you awake?

–I am now.

–You should talk more to Mui, Husband.

–What things do I have to say to her?

–You might talk to her, Husband. She feels she is in our way.

–How can she be in our way? She lived with us in the flat, didn't she?

–You hardly ever saw her then.

–She was welcome in our household then and she is welcome now. She isn't a guest; she's part of our family. She does more work than I do.

–Speak to her, Husband.

–What do I say? Good morning, young mistress? Have you eaten evening rice yet, Miss Tang?

–Speak to her, Husband.

–Husband!

–What is it now, Lily? I'm busy with these extra benches.

–A treat. Close your eyes.

–Sweet red-bean stew!

–Mui, bring the best bowls and spoons, the finest one for Husband.

–Girls, you must eat some too.

–We have eaten ours already, Brother-in-law.

–Get a bowl, Mui. I don't start until I see you eat yours.

–Brother-in-law, you give me so much!

–Not another word, Mui. And you, Lily, give me your bowl. Right, all together now. Wonderful! Nice and thick! What are you laughing at, Mui?

–Nothing, Brother-in-law.

–Come on, what is it?

–I hope you won't be offended, Brother-in-law, but you make such a loud noise, like a dragon putting his fire out in a big lake.

–That must show I'm enjoying it anyway. The red water shows

it's good for the blood. I should take this for colds instead of that bitter medicine, Lily...

–Son spoke to me this morning, Mui.

–Yes, he's getting quite talkative really. I was a bit worried for a while, he was such a silent little boy.

–Yes, but Mui, he spoke in English!

–Eiyah! In English! But where would he learn that?

–It's as mysterious to me as it is to you.

–What did he say, Lily?

–He said: "Hello, Dah Ling." But that's just nonsense; it's only the name of our village. Mui, why are you laughing?

–I'm not, I'm not...

–Lily, the ground has turned quite white! Look out of the window!

–Of course, this must be the first snow you have seen, sister. Apart from on television.

–How beautiful it is!

–But then it gets dirty and melts and gets in your shoes. Yes, it's beautiful now, all right.

–Ah, but like this it seems beautiful. And when the trains go by the blue flash lights up the whole horizon. (Mo, 1982, pp.100-102)

The only conscious and consistent device used here to "sinicize" the dialogue is the use of "names" to suggest direct translation from the Chinese with its emphasis on kinship relationships— *Husband, Brother-in-law, younger sister, elder sister*. Other instances of this type of linguistic colouring are in evidence but are rare. "Have you eaten evening rice yet?" Cantonese speakers, in particular, will be familiar with this question as a form of polite greeting, usually unaccompanied by any real curiosity. The words *evening rice* are directly translated from Chinese 晚飯. In the rest of the extract, only the simile used to describe Brother-in-law's cough—like a dragon putting his fire out in a big lake—and the interjection *Eiyah* can be said to be contrivances which are deliberate markers of foreignness and more specifically, Chineseness. The overall effect of the free direct speech without the reporting clause gives the reader the usual sense of more immediacy since the narrator is removed as an intermediary. What is more significant here is that the characters are perceived as vivacious and vocal people, well able to articulate their feelings in their native tongue.

It is interesting to compare the same set of characters speaking English to aliens, strangers whom they feel are intruders.

The tax man spread the assortment of papers on the counter in an intimidating silence. He had already asserted himself by refusing to allow customers in, not one, and making Mui turn the TV off. Otherwise they would have to come to the tax office with him, way up in another part of the country.

That would have been terrible, they preferred to confront authority on home ground. For some reason this seemed to have won them favour with this official. This good start was quickly lost. The tax man, who had been given Lily's stool, held a gas bottle's creased tag by its string with the same distaste as one might convey a dead rat to the dust bin by the tip of its scaly tail (always assuming the necessity). He poked the pile of papers—a heap of rubbish, the gesture implied—with the butt of his Bic biro.

"Are you seriously telling me that this is all you have to show the Inland Revenue?"

Lily nodded. She and Husband were on the customer side of the counter. How humiliating! Would their business be taken away from them? At least Husband had never sunk to drawing unemployment benefit, a disgraceful surrender which instantly and forever disqualified you from running a business of your own...

Lily smiled serenely but was inwardly frightened and, forgetting herself, nervously depressed one of the keys of the... till... The drawer slid out with a *ting!* and, on cue, Mui entered with a small apparition. Not content with the beggar's fancy-dress contrived by Lily, Mui had also smeared her nephew's face and hands with soot.

This is going too far, Lily thought.

But incredulity was not among the things registered on the tax man's surprisingly expressive currant-bun of a face. He watched Man Kee run in his peculiar way over to his father before putting

on his spectacles again. "How many children do you have, Mrs...
Mrs Chen?" "This son only."

"Well, you can claim child allowance for him."

"Hah?"

Mui came over. She said to Lily: "Because you have children
you pay less tax."

"Ah!"

"Any aged dependants?"

Chen shook his head vigorously and the girls, puzzled but
quick-thinking as well as obedient, kept blank faces.

The tax man produced a form from his tattered black plastic
briefcase. "This is a tax return, like the ones we sent you. Do you
know how to fill it in? No." He took his spectacles off again. His
eyes looked tired to Mui. "All right. Now listen closely."

Mui crossed to the owner's side of the counter, while Lily took
Man Kee away from Chen.

"You must put a roll in your till and keep it. You must also keep
receipts for purchases. Do you have a wholesaler?"

"Buy from Co-op."

"Well, it's not for me to tell you but you would get a much
more advantageous price from a wholesaler. Never mind. Just
keep all your bills in order in a file, or even a box would do. No
bank account? No. Now let me explain about a cash book, you
won't need a day book.

Mui's earlier suspicion about the simplicity of the procedures
was officially confirmed. She felt she had a natural, untutored flair
for these things. Finally, the tax man said: "The inspector of taxes
will have to make an assessment on what I recommend, which
you will pay in two parts in the next twelve months. We can make
some estimate from similar businesses in your area. It may be
higher than if you had kept a record but that will be your own
fault."

"You do our tax from Kebab House tax?" Lily asked hopefully,
remembering how empty that establishment always was.

"I can't speak for the inspector, I'm afraid."

Mui saw him personally to the door. (Mo, 1982, pp.147-149.)

Timothy Mo deliberately makes Lily and Mui speak pidgin,

their pretext of ignorance is their protection against these foreign and potentially hostile forces. The English the women use here is strictly of the type that is associated with the speech of Chinamen which lives in the imagination of a great many Westerners. Lily and Mui, armed with a great deal of native intelligence and strong survival instincts, make use of an established illusion to create the illusion of innocent stupidity. Dialogue in Chinese written in English, no less than dialogue in English written in English, plays a part in the author's characterization of the different, often comic, but always sympathetic Chinese women in his novel.

It is an unfair fact of life that, generally speaking, inability to speak an acquired language well suggests inferiority or lack of intelligence in a community or indeed in a situation where the acquired language is the dominant one. It is much more a "fact" or, let us say, an illusion of fiction. The recent authors who write about Chinese women do make use of this fact-cum-illusion, and in many cases an index to the respect with which the author wishes the reader to regard the character resides in the degree of proficiency of her English. I have referred to this in the preceding chapter in the character of Mrs Coomb, in Christopher New's *Goodbye Chairman Mao* (1979). Christopher New's Chinese heroine is her English husband's equal: not for her the obsequious bow and servile demeanour. Daughter of a wealthy industrialist, she studied in America and worked in an atomic energy plant. Cosmopolitan and still attractive, in spite of years of anxiety and suffering, her dialogue in English is perfectly correct and idiomatic. The reader is told "she spoke with an American accent". The author takes care to comment on this fact more than once:

> Her American accent sounded incongruous, coming from that Chinese face.

Then "Again the incongruity of the perfect American idiom and the Chinese face" (New, 1977, pp.46, 47-48). In the course of the extract Mrs Coomb displays tact, authority and courtesy in her dialogue. The author would probably detract from her stature if she were to speak the sort of English suggested by the dialogue assigned to May-may in *Taipan*.

The Chinese heroine of James Clavell's *Taipan* (1966) is a very far cry from Mrs Coomb. From the perspective of the emancipated Chinese woman of today she is a disgrace to our sex and race. She is clearly used by her creator to pander to the illusion of the superiority and irresistible attraction of Western men, here in the person of the uncouth Struan, the first taipan of the Noble House. The extract given below shows that she clearly sees herself as no more than a sex object. Clavell is also interested in presenting through her naïve obsequiousness the "barbaric" Chinese custom of concubinage, and Struan's justifiably shocked disbelief, then patronizing response to her attempt to please him. Clavell uses a form of "eye dialect" to present May-may's discourse which reflects to any discerning reader a status inferior to that of her lord and master.

The chills convulsed May-may. The fires consumed her. During the delirium May-may felt her womb rip asunder and she screamed. The life-to-be passed out of her, and in the passing took all but the merest spark of her soul and strength. Then the fever broke and the sweat released her from the nightmare...

"Hello, Tai-Pan." She could feel the continuous seeping from her womb. "Bad joss to lose baby," she whispered.

"Dinna fash yoursel'. Just get yoursel' better. Any moment the cinchona bark'll arrive. I know it will."

May-may summoned her strength and shrugged with a trace of her old imperiousness. "Pox on the longskirts! How for can the man hurry in a skirt, heya?"

But the effort depleted her and she slipped into unconsciousness. Two days later she seemed much stronger.

"Morning, lass. How do you feel today?"

"Fantastical good," May-may said. "It is a pretty day, heya? Did you seen Ma-ree?"

"Aye, she's looking much better. A tremendous change. Almost miraculous!"

"Why for so good change, heya?" she asked innocently, knowing that Elder Sister had gone to see her yesterday.

"I dinna ken," he said. "I saw Horatio just before I left. He brought her some flowers. By the way, she thanks you for the things you sent her. What did you send?"

"Mangoes and some herb tea my doctor recommended. Ah Sam went two, three days ago." May-may rested a moment. Even talking was a great strain for her. She must be very strong today, she told herself firmly.

There is much to do today, and tomorrow there is fever again. Oh well, at least now no problem for Ma-ree—she's rescued. So easy now that Elder Sister has explained to her what all young girls in houses are taught—that with care and meticulous acting and tears of pretended pain and fear, and the final modest telltale stains cautiously placed, a girl can, if necessary, be virgin ten times for ten different men.

Ah Sam came in and kowtowed, and muttered something to her. May-may brightened. "Oh, very good, Ah Sam! You may go." Then to Struan, "Tai-Pan, I need some taels of silver, please."

"How many?"

"Lots. I am impoverished. Your old mother's very fond of you. Wat for you ask such things?"

"If you hurry up and get better, I'll give you all the taels you need."

"You give men great face, Tai-Pan. Hugest face. Twenty thousand taels for medicine cure—ayeee yah, I am worth like an empress lady to you."

"Gordon told you?"

"No. I was listen at door. Of course! Do you think your old mother likes not to know what doctor says and you say, heya?" She glanced at the doorway.

Struan turned to see a lovely young girl bowing gracefully. Her hair was coiled in a thick, dark snake atop her exquisite head and adorned with jade ornaments and flowers. Her almond-shaped face was like purest alabaster.

"This is Yin-hsi," May-may said. "She is my sister."

"I did na ken you had one, lass. She's very pretty."

"Yes, but, well, she's not really sister, Tai-Pan. Chinese ladies often call each other 'sister'. It's politeness. Yin-hsi's your birthday present."

"What?"

"I bought her for birthday."

"Have you taken leave of your senses?"

"Oh, Tai-Pan, you are very trying sometimes badly," May-may said, beginning to cry. "Your birthday is in four monthses. At that time I would have been heavy with child so I arranged search for a 'sister'. It has been difficult to decide bestest choice. She is bestest, and now because I am sick I give her now and na wait. You dinna like her?"

"Good God lass! Dinna cry, May-may. Listen. Dinna cry… Of course I like your sister. But you dinna buy girls as birthday presents, for the love of God!"

"Why not?"

"Well, because you just dinna."

"She's very nice—I want her for my sister. I was going to teach her for the four monthses, but now…" She broke out sobbing again.

Yin-hsi hurried from the doorway and knelt beside May-may and held her hand and dried her tears solicitously and helped her to drink a little tea. May-may had warned her that barbarians were sometimes strange and showed their happiness by shouting and cursing, but not to worry.

"Look, Tai-Pan, how pretty she is!" May-may said. "You like her, surely?"

"That's na the point, May-may. Of course I like her."

"Then that's settled, then." May-may closed her eyes and lay back in her nest of pillows.

"It's na settled, then."

She summoned a final broadside. "It is, and I'll na argue with you any more, by God! I paid huge monies and she's bestest and I canna send her away for she'll lose all face and she'd have to hang herself." (Clavell, 1966, pp.598-600.)

Christopher New's Mrs Coomb is seen as a thinking and feeling entity independent of her husband. Her independent status is highlighted by her American accent, acquired independently of Coomb and still distinct from Coomb's after years of marriage. May-may's English speech, on the other hand, contains markers which indicate that she has picked her English up entirely from Struan. Clavell makes her speak a hodge-podge of presumably mildly Scottish-accented pidgin interspersed with Chinese-sounding interjections like *heya* and direct translations and "disarmingly endearing" malapropisms like *cleveritious*.

It seems fairly evident that authorial attitudes can be seen as being mirrored in the use of dialogue. But readers' responses to the clues in the dialogue may not be infallible, simply because of their own differences and prejudices. In judging or, if not judging, at least commenting on the effectiveness of dialogue for Chinese women, I have been guided essentially by my own judgment, coloured as it is by strong defensiveness and "protective instincts". Since Western readers too vary in degree of knowledge and sympathy, intelligence and sensitivity of response, the whole subject is fraught with imponderables.

Epilogue:
Towards Seeing Face to Face

As I was working on this project a colleague (and a very good friend) drew my attention to the extract, discussed in the previous chapter, from Salinger's much read *The Catcher In the Rye*. It was the very unexpected nature of the context that struck him—and me. As I have said one does not expect a reference to the Chinese and their sexuality in what is essentially such an "American" novel. But here we do find such a reference, and the Chinese woman image given has the usual associations of desirability and sexuality: the familiar "forbidden fruit" motif. The introduction of *Shanghai* has a familiar ring—Shanghai had the reputation of being the centre of exotic cosmopolitan delights. Salinger has added a touch of profundity to the image. The lady is a woman of the world at thirty-nine, not a nymphet. She is a sculptress living in the village. The Oriental exotic image coupled with the unconventional Bohemian one. Her attraction is spiritual as well as physical. She has just arrived in America a few months ago and, if one believes Luce's testimony, already quite at home in a liaison with an intellectual young man half her age! No May-may or O-lan, this Shanghainese sculptress. Still the stereotypical outlines remain, and the Western reader would not get far beyond seeing the image of Chinese women as in a glass, darkly.

I started off this collection with the obvious observation that, while the human mind tends towards stereotyping of fellow human beings outside the immediate circle of friendship, people tend to be distinctive individuals, even though they may fall into types. Dennis Bloodworth, in his 1967 work, *The Chinese Looking Glass*, argues for the idea of a "Chinese woman", characterized by a cultural heritage shared with other Chinese women. (See Bloodworth, London, pp.24ff) Even if we accept the premise of a common cultural heritage and behaviour conditioned to some extent by that heritage, we would be disappointed if Chinese women characters in literary works are presented as one-dimensional stereotypes. It is extremely difficult to make dogmatic pronouncements about verisimilitude in art: not every author who attempts to delineate characters of his own race succeeds equally in presenting characters who are "real". Apart from anything else, there is the vexed question of readers' response. When I talk of "seeing face to face" and a fairer deal for Chinese women I am setting up only the criteria of multi-dimensional characterization and variety of conception. If we now have characters with whom Western readers can identify as having the same flesh and blood as they, capable of human feelings, love, hate, disappointment, sacrifice as well as a sense of self-preservation, then we will have come some way from Thomas Hood's Hyson or the Dragon Ladies of Sax Rohmer's work. There is the question also of attitude and motivation on the part of the author, which is partly dictated by the social and political climate of the times in which he or she is writing. Maugham's portraits of the Chinese are coloured at least in part by the Colonial times in which he lived. Christopher New, while clearly with an eye to the financial rewards of a potboiler, wrote *Shanghai* in more "enlightened" times and the Chinese heroine, Sumei, is treated with much greater sympathy, so that, apart from the stereotypical traits which have for better or for worse come to be associated with Chinese woman characters, the reader can accept her as a *woman* who happens to be Chinese. At least some—as it turns out many—of her preoccupations and concerns are universal.

At least four factors have, I feel, brought about more optimistic prospects for a sharper focussing of images of Chinese women in Western literature. I have already mentioned the more enlightened tenor of the times. International travel has made the world smaller; direct contact with the reality from which images have been drawn has certainly helped to sharpen, and to make more just, the images drawn. We have still a long way to go, but once a large percentage of the world ceases to regard China and the Chinese as mysterious and totally out of reach, then writers even of potboilers will have to aim for multidimensional portrayal and only fall short through lack of skill and or knowledge rather than lack of caring. Approaching the end of the twentieth century, a multiplicity of works on Chinese history appeared, the products of different levels of scholarship, but many enjoying popular success. Examples are Jonathan Spence's excellent works, *The Dream Palace of Matthieu Ricci* (London, 1985), dealing with the Ming period, and his *The Gate of Heavenly Peace* (New York, 1981), dealing with contemporary China, which have generated an interest even in Western readers who are not essentially sinologues, or even sinophiles. Christopher Hibbert's *The Dragon Wakes* (London, 1970), Ross Terrill's *White Bone Demon* (London, 1984) and David Bonavia's popular works on the Chinese and recent Chinese history are books of this type. Oxford University Press reprinted, with new introductions, books about China and Chinese history, for example, Peter Fleming's *The Siege at Peking* was reissued as a paperback by Oxford in 1983, with an introduction by David Bonavia. And in real terms China has made spectacular advances as a power to be reckoned with politically and economically and, this, together with the growth of international contacts, has helped to make less possible the dismissal of Chinese women characters in works of Western writers who choose to write about them. The alternative is, of course, not to write about them. This course was chosen by Anthony Cooper in writing his *The Sanctuary*. What his hero alter ego says about them suggests he made a wise decision— not that this judicious avoidance of what he could not in his insularity understand has made his book a work of literature. Timothy Mo who had delineated Chinese women with degrees of eccentric success in his two earlier novels, concentrated on his American heroes in his third, and as yet most critically acclaimed novel, *An Insular Possession*. (London, 1986)

The much greater effectiveness of the communications media, especially television and home video systems, as disseminators of images in recent years, is a second factor which has made the images of Chinese women more multidimensional or at least more varied and more familiar. In the 1930s films made popular images of Dragon Ladies in the style of the villainesses in Fu Manchu films. The peasant images of Pearl Buck characters also became impressed on the minds of earlier generations of filmgoers. *Dragon Seed*, and especially *The Good* Earth have been shown periodically on television reintroducing the images to many generations after the 1930s. Since the 1950s two important additions were made to the Western popular culture vis-à-vis its perception of Chinese womanhood. One was the image of Jennifer Jones, elegantly clad in a cheongsam in *Love is a Many-Splendoured Thing*, the film version of Han Suyin's Novel *A Many-Splendoured Thing*. The other was of Nancy Kwan as the saucy, memorable prostitute with the heart of gold, Suzie, in *The World of Suzie Wong*. It did not matter that Jennifer Jones was not Chinese at all and Nancy Kwan only half a one because of her Scottish mother. For a couple of decades rightly or wrongly European men saw them, particularly Nancy Kwan, as the epitome of all that is delectable and desirable in Chinese women. Indeed, for some, in all women. I pass no moral judgments here; I am just tracing the proliferation and familiarization to international audiences of more varied and more in-depth images of Chinese women. Perhaps I ought to consider one point here. Louise Rainer, Jennifer Jones, Nancy Kwan, France Nuyen were chosen to play starring roles in important films featuring Chinese or at least (in the case of France Nuyen) Eastern characters. The fact that the film-makers in each case did not choose "real" Chinese actresses seems significant. They were probably playing it safe and did not want to put their productions at risk by asking their international audience to accept an unfamiliar type of beauty; that is, beauty based on a set of premises which would be different from those film audiences would be used to. This hedging of one's bets can also be detected, as I have remarked in my Chapter V, in the "Westernizing" of the appearances of some of the heroines in "Hong Kong fiction." Of course an exception that comes easily to mind is the stereotypical Oriental vamp, Anna May Wong, but she was not called upon, like Louise Rainer, to play the sympathetic central character.

Steps forward can then be said to have been taken towards giving the West a chance to see Chinese women face to face at least on the big or small screen. When casting was underway for the lush-budget film version of *Taipan* every effort was made to secure a Chinese actress to play the part of Struan's compliant mistress, May-may. Other Chinese women were needed for less important parts. The media coverage generated by the search in Hong Kong, the Chinese mainland and Taiwan was, of course, part of the publicity campaign for giving advance publicity to the film, which in fact turned out to be a colossal flop, both in artistic and box-office terms. Patty Toy, an American-born Chinese secured the minor role of a syphilitic prostitute in *Taipan*, while another American Chinese, Joan Chen, who has gone on to dozens of leading roles in other Western and Asian productions, landed the coveted role of May-may. The film was generally badly received; local feelings ran high against the servile representation of Chinese womanhood. But here I must return to the main point of my argument. Joan Chen was chosen for a starring role, not a Caucasian or Eurasian lady who would be made up with slanty eyes to defer to the idea of Chinese-ness; viewers could be trusted to appreciate Chinese beauty in its own form. The American Chinese woman reporter in the controversial film on drug trafficking carried on by the Chinese community, Michael Cimino's *The Year of the Dragon*, based on the book, was played by American Chinese fashion model, Ariene, whose unsylph-like physical attributes are very atypical, and whose facial features strike the Chinese viewer as Japanese or Korean rather than Chinese. The film caused great offence to Chinese communities all over the United States, and protest meetings and demonstrations were held in front of theatres screening it. Let us hold our moral and artistic judgment in abeyance for the moment, and concentrate on the apparent intentions of the film-makers. The intention was, presumably, to create a heroine on the right side of the law, determined to ferret out the truth in the tradition of the good investigative reporter. She is beautiful, desirable, powerful, rich, independent *a la* Barbara Walters, or at least the successful West Coast broadcaster, Connie Chung; she is the unwilling supplanter of the "good", loyal, long-suffering worn-out Italian-American wife. Here we have a reversal of the cliché Caucasian man-Oriental woman roles: she is superior in education, wealth, degree of sophistication. The ultimate irony is the ego-boosting (for Caucasian male fantasizers) finale when she runs into the arms of the loud-mouthed and uncouth "hero". The joke is perhaps, after all, at the expense of Chinese women (and men). Thus the depiction of the investigative reporter is a neat bit of fantasy feeding which has the side effect of glamourizing, though not really improving or giving sharper focus to, the image of Chinese women to a popular film-going market. One can only say, as in the Virginia Slims ads, "You've come a long way, baby." But perhaps not long enough. The heroine's Chinese-ness meets the demands of the plot, but apart from the frequent racial slurs and name-calling by the unsympathetic characters in the film (and these are legion) there are few concessions made to the fact of her race. Still, because of the nature of the medium, the impact of the visual image comes into play.

American-Chinese film-makers, some of whom have originated in Hong Kong and Taiwan, have possibly done a better job in giving international audiences an opportunity of seeing Chinese women "face to face" if only by means of celluloid. The names Wayne Wang, based in San Francisco and Po-Chih Leong, born in England, come to mind. Wayne Wang's films are about immigrant life in America, the cultural gap between generations, and are essentially an extension into film of the literary genre Asian-American literature. Films like Wang's *Chen Is Missing* and *Dimsum* have enjoyed a certain degree of international success, as has Po-Chih Leong's *Ping-Pong* but certainly nothing on the scale of *The Year of the Dragon* or Bertolucci's *The Last Emperor*. An unexpected box-office success in relative terms was *A Great Wall* (Orion Picture Corporation, directed by Peter Wong, produced by Shirley Sun), which deals with the barriers initially encountered and ultimately overcome by an American Chinese family returning for their first time to Peking for a reunion with their relatives. The cast of films like *Chen Is Missing*, *Dimsum* and *A Great*

Wall is Chinese, chosen from quite ordinary Chinese people, and the international distribution means the opportunity for an international audience to see ordinary Chinese men—and women—"face to face", as it were.

Another such landmark in terms of projecting and disseminating images of Chinese women occurred with the release of the British film production of Timothy Mo's novel about Hong Kong immigrants to Britain, *Sour Sweet*. Directed by Mike Newell, produced by Roger Randall-Cutler and released internationally in 1988, it featured a "superstar" of Taiwan and Hong Kong films, Sylvia Chang, cast in the lead role, that of Lily Chen. The film had an all-Chinese cast, except for the part of the immigrant family's neighbour, a Greek garage owner and some other bit parts. Sylvia Chang is an award-winning producer and director of Hong Kong and Taiwan films as well as an actress who, in 1987, won the Hong Kong Film Awards Best Actress award. She has a reputation for being intelligent, sensitive and knowledgeable. In an interview prior to the release of *Sour Sweet*, she talked about the spate of films on Chinese subjects then on offer or shortly forthcoming. She was speaking as a woman who had turned down offers to appear in Cimino's *The Year of the Dragon* and Bertolucci's *The Last Emperor*. She felt that the then-current crop of overseas pictures on Chinese subjects had not been well done.

Most have been pretty disastrous. After a while I stopped auditioning for roles. You could see after a few pages of the script that the film-makers didn't know about Chinese people, the way they think or how they behave. The stories were written only for Western people and for what they want to see. I was uneasy about *Sour Sweet* initially. But when Mike Newall (the director) asked me whether I felt comfortable with the script and I pointed out some things that were not right, he agreed and said in coming to Hong Kong and Taiwan he realised that certain things were totally different from how they originally thought...

I do think it strange that it's a British crew with a Chinese cast but then they are not trying to make a film about Hong Kong. The picture is about life in London and the film-makers know how to reflect the English environment...

Chinese people keep their own characters wherever they are. So though Lily lives in a different environment, the cultural characteristics will still be the same. (*South China Morning Post* July 5th, 1987, "Guide" p.1)

The film was made entirely in English. The convention was that Chinese actors converse amongst themselves in articulate English but speak with a stronger accent when in conversation with outsiders. The novel *Sour Sweet* was short-listed for both the Booker and Whitbread Prizes in 1982 and won the Hawthornden Prize of the same year. Lily Chen and her sister Mui are a pair of rather unconventional Chinese heroines. The film was an international success and the images of Sylvia Chang and Jodi Long, the Chinese-American actress chosen to play Mui, giving sympathetic and intelligent portrayals of their compatriots, was viewed worldwide. Books as a medium for conveying images leave a great deal to the readers' imagination, and when the imagination has little concrete to work with through total ignorance, films or television or video can come to the rescue. The result may be a fossilizing of certain images, a stifling of the capacities of the imagination. But if the images are many and varied and multidimensional, then they may have their usefulness in dispelling the ludicrous or unfair stereotype. The celluloid images in turn shape images in the Western mind in subsequent reading.

A third factor which has helped in making the Chinese women less chimerical in the Western mind is the increasing number of Chinese women who write, and write successfully in English. I have mentioned Maxine Hong Kingston, whom one could view as the doyen of Chinese American fiction; if not the first, the first to be known internationally. Her autobiographical novels, *The Woman Warrior* (first published in Great Britain by Allen Lane, 1977) and *China Men* (Pan, 1981) became award winning best-sellers and caught the imagination of a large international, especially American, readership. She continues to publish primarily non-fiction and poetry to the present day, but these two earlier autobiographical works received a great deal of media coverage worldwide. Within their pages,

Americans in particular were given the opportunity of seeing and hearing, as well as reading the work of, an intelligent and sensitive Chinese woman well able to articulate the feelings of Chinese immigrants adapting to an alien society. In *China Men* she turns her attentions to her patriarchal forebears, whose lives she reconstructs out of memories and imagination into a saga of magic and history. It is the succeeding generations of these forebears who journey from China to "the Gold Mountain". Her literary style, especially her use of symbolism and her effective use of dialogue, received critical acclaim. Confronted by this Chinese woman writer writing in English, Westerners had to rethink their ideas about Chinese women. They would have to replace the simple Anna May Wong/"Dragon Lady" image with a more complex one. But Maxine Hong Kingston was born in the United States; she speaks little Chinese and is unable to write it. The daughter of very poor working-class immigrant parents, she hardly presented the image of the polished, patrician Chinese lady in the Madame Wu mode. Then came the work of Bette Bao Lord. Bette Bao was born in Shanghai in 1938. She first went to America in 1946, when her father, an official with the Chinese government, was assigned to the United States. After 1949 and the establishment of the People's Republic, the family decided to stay in America. She is a graduate of Tufts University and has a Master's Degree from the Fletcher School of Law and Diplomacy. She married American diplomat, Winston Lord, who was appointed United States Ambassador to China; as a result the Lords resided in Beijing from 1985 through 1989. She wrote an account of her younger sister Sansan's life in China from 1946 until her reunion with her family in the United States in 1962. The book is entitled *Eighth Moon* and is "by Sansan as told to Bette Bao Lord". The book, which depicts the hardships of Sansan growing up without her parents and sisters in the China of the 1950s and 60s, was first published in Great Britain by Robert Hale in 1966, but it was not until the publication of Bette Bao Lord's novel *Spring Moon* by Victor Gollancz in 1982 that she gained international recognition as a writer. The envious attributed her popular success to her husband's political and social clout. But whatever ancillary aid, if any, was at work, *Spring Moon* is a well-written, if in places melodramatic, novel. A return to China in 1973 with her husband, then principal advisor to Henry Kissinger for the China opening, and a reunion with her relatives "became the genesis of *Spring Moon*" (blurb, *Spring Moon*, Sphere Books ed'n, 1982) However Chinese readers may respond to the often unconventional behaviour of the heroine, who, in the course of the novel, has a passionate affair with her uncle, the intentions of the author are not in doubt. I think she is sincere in her efforts to present a charming, intelligent, strong-willed and independent Chinese woman growing up and growing old in times of restless change, from the days of mandarin rule during the declining years of the Ch'ing Dynasty to the Cultural Revolution. But at this stage of my discussion I have not set myself the task of analysing the literary merits of the work. There is no doubt that, as a bestseller, *Spring Moon* enhanced the image of Chinese women through its heroine. But my point here is that the author herself, by being herself, has also contributed towards making the chimerical more tangible to the West. Like Maxine Hong Kingston, she also received considerable media coverage, and the image she presents is one of impeccable poise and elegance, quite different from the casual, rather unkempt image presented by Maxine Hong Kingston, with her flowing long hair and simple clothes. On the frontispiece of the hard-cover edition of *Spring Moon* Bette Lord's picture appeared with not a hair out of place and immaculate in traditional Chinese clothes. The daughter of a "Mandarin", the wife of a contemporary "Mandarin", the lady presented a formidable image. Barbara Walters interviewed her in Beijing for American television in 1987, and she was vocal and articulate as well as impeccably groomed. We have indeed come a long, long way from Pearl Buck's O-lan and "The Mother".

A short time later, another elegant image of a Chinese lady impinged on the consciousness of the West; her serene, composed and delicate countenance adorned the dust cover of her book *Life and Death in Shanghai* (New York, 1987), and the same placid, elegant face was seen in *Vogue* and *Newsweek*. She is Nien Cheng, author of the much acclaimed account of life during the Chinese cultural Revolution.

> *Life and Death in Shanghai* is the deeply moving memoir of Nien Cheng's personal struggle for justice in China between 1966 and 1980. The book has been compared to *Darkness at Noon*, Arthur Koestler's classic novel about Stalin's terror and the Moscow show trials of the 1930s. But the comparison is misleading. Koestler wrote as a former communist who had suffered a crisis of conscience. Nien Cheng by contrast writes as a devout Christian. Her account of her imprisonment is a tale, not of disillusionment and moral conversion, but of unwavering religious faith. Though the details are often grim, the effect is finally uplifting. (Jim Miller, *Newsweek*, July 6, 1987, p.44A)

The bare facts of Nien Cheng's case were simple. Educated in England and fluent in English, she had been an adviser to the management of Shell Petroleum and one of perhaps a dozen people in Shanghai wealthy enough to maintain her old home and employ a maid and a cook. All this changed with the Cultural Revolution. She was charged with being "a running dog of imperialism" and a "foreign spy". In the early 1970s the political winds blowing from Beijing shifted. In 1972 Nien Cheng was released from prison, and in November 1978, after the death of Mao and the downfall of the "Gang of Four" she was officially rehabilitated. Upon her release she discovered that her daughter and only child, Meiping, had been murdered by the radicals. Unforgiving and unwilling to risk more suffering through another change in the party line, Nien Cheng resolved to leave China. On September 20th, 1980 she finally left Shanghai for Hong Kong. She lived the remainder of her life in the United States, passing away in 2009. Her articulate, indeed as *Vogue* put it, moving and yet apparently objective narration of events, the very elegance of her style, with its emphasis on concrete settings and objects, and the fact she was dealing with an important segment of history, all helped to make her book a bestseller. The work is autobiographical: author and protagonist are one, and the English reading public felt they had been brought closer to the heart and mind and soul of a Chinese woman. The image became better focussed. More and more it continues to become evident that there is not just one stereotypical Chinese woman. Chinese women are human, individualized and can be highly sympathetic. Maxine Hong Kingston, Bette Bao Lord, Nien Cheng as much by being themselves Chinese and women, as by the works of art they created, gave sharper and more varied images of Chinese women. There are now legions of educated and intelligent Chinese women who could add to the ranks of apologists for their fellow Chinese women, as yet mute inglorious Miltons who might some day write eloquently of their race and sex. The variety of Chinese women as manifested in Chinese women authors was further attested to by the then little known (in an international sense) efforts of Lucy Ching, Hong Kong's best known blind author. In 1980 she finally gained publishing rights to a book, *One of the Lucky Ones* she had written seven years ago. Miss Ching was inspired to write the book through her friendship with the late American author, Helen Keller, who was deaf, mute and blind. Blinded at six mouths by an eye lotion prescribed by a Guangdong countryside herbalist, Miss Ching has been completely without sight since. Ms Ah Wor, her childhood *amah*, was credited with providing all forms of support during Miss Ching's ordeals and the book was dedicated to her. In 1959 she was the first blind social worker in Hong Kong, and found it important to tell others of her rise above the life that was usually expected among the Chinese sightless. She attended the Perkins School for the Blind in Massachusetts and went to Leeds University for training in social work. She wrote her 290-page account in her second language, English, because she could not cope with the mechanical difficulties of a Chinese typewriter. The book was subsequently translated into several other languages, and was the basis of a 1994 film directed by Clifton Ko, a prolific Hong Kong director. In a very minor way, Lucy Ching also contributed yet another image to the collection of images that was becoming more available to the Western public.

The four Chinese women authors I have cited as examples of how the author as well as the book can help to enhance, broaden and deepen impressions of Chinese women are all women who have been educated in the West. Let us leave aside Lucy Ching for the moment. Maxine Hong Kingston, Bette Bao Lord and Nien Cheng may be seen by the most traditional Chinese as "Westernized Chinese". And Westernized Chinese are perhaps a breed apart. Dennis Bloodworth has this to say about them in his attempt to write about "the Chinese":

> Many westernized Chinese may... feel that I have painted a picture of their people that is quite unrecognizable. But I have not really been writing about them. There is no point in explaining westernized Chinese to the West: someone should write a book that explains them, rather, to the Chinese. (Bloodworth, op.cit., p.14)

This brings me to what I think is a fourth factor which is contributing, and, hopefully, will contribute further towards the understanding of Chinese women among Westerners, provided always they have the desire, the willingness to know, to understand. Feminism as a militant movement may be a spent force but one very commendable by-product is the interest it generated in women in literature, women as writers and as literary creations. "Women in Literature" courses have grown in popularity in English-speaking countries, and presses have been established to publish new or unavailable work by woman writers, publishing houses like Virago or Feminist Press or Pandora Press. In the desire to understand and give a sympathetic hearing to women of all races, nationalities and persuasions, works of Chinese women writers are more and more available in English translation. Some of these works are finding their way on to the syllabuses of "Women in Literature" courses in the United States. Panda Books (distributed by China Publications Centre) and Joint Publishing Company have been responsible for translations of the collected works of women writers, particularly those who wrote in the 1920s and 1930s, after the May 4th Movement of 1919. The May 4th Movement takes its name from a massive student protest in China and refers to a period of enormous political, social and cultural change. "Prime target of the intellectual-idealists was Confucianism, the age-old philosophy which sanctioned so much that was cruel and self-destructive in Chinese society, such as arranged marriages, scorn for manual labour and the hierarchical power structure. The most obvious victims of the Confucian patriarchal code of morality were women, who continued to suffer from the institutionalized practices of footbinding, concubinage and the chastity cult. It was on these oppressive institutions that the newly fostered women's liberation movement initially focused its attention." (J. Anderson and T.F. Munford, *Chinese Women Writers*, Hong Kong, 1985, p.xi) Chinese women started to find a literary voice, to give expression, in the form of novels but more often short stories, to their individual struggles to come to grips with the problems of a changing society and their changing roles in that society. Many were preoccupied in particular with the problems of love, marriage and sexual relations. More contemporary women writers are now also available in translation. I was surprised to learn from a Hong Kong student doing a literature course in a Midwestern American University that among the books he had had to read his previous semester was *Selected Stories of Xiao Hong*, translated by Howard Goldblatt and published by Panda Books (Beijing, 1982). Xiao Hong wrote during the 1930s; she died in 1942. Her main theme was the oppression of women from the underprivileged classes. Her stories are almost always tragic, offering little hope for the future. (See Howard Goldblatt's Introduction.) Other collections in translation of the work of Chinese women writers of the 1930s and much later have also become more available.[1] It was significant that Pandora Press, which was also responsible for the reissue of Agnes Smedley's *Battle Hymn of China* as *China Correspondent* in 1984, also published in 1986 a new edition of Hsieh Ping-ying's *Autobiography of a Chinese Girl*, translated into English by

Tsui Chi, with a new introduction by Elizabeth Croll, a Fellow of Wolfson College, Oxford and of the Oxford Queen Elizabeth House Centre for Cross-Cultural Research on Women. Hsieh Ping-ying was born at the beginning of the century and she rejected the traditions of the old order, leading a turbulent life as student, soldier and writer; her autobiography was first published in 1936. In her introduction to the new edition of the English translation Dr Croll wrote,

> It is the distinctive contribution of such personal documents as autobiographies and diaries that they record one person's individual and often intimate perceptions of their times and thus greatly add to our knowledge and understanding of past events. For those whose gender and class have excluded them from the formal histories, they may be the chief means of documenting the details of their lives. For women, they offer an opportunity to make sense of the ways in which they perceive their own opportunities and choices, and expect these to be bounded by their families and by society… (p.9)

The acknowledgement of the value of Hsieh Ping-ying's autobiography in these terms is the acknowledgement of the common bond between women of all cultures and races. As Chinese women writers are given a chance to speak for themselves, if only through the medium of able and sympathetic translators, then they can perhaps help project to the West with greater fidelity their own images.

Endnotes

Preface:

1. See Boswell, James; *The Life of Samuel Johnson*, 1791.
2 & 3. The italics in this sentence are my own.

Chapter I:

1. See quotation from James Legge's translation of *The Book of Rites*, preface.
2. Also known as *A Dream of Red Mansions*, translated by Yang Hsien-yi and Gladys Yang, published by Foreign Languages Press, 1978, 1980; David Hawkes' translation is entitled *The Story of the Stone*. The first eighty chapters are by Cao Xueqin, the last forty by Gao E. Xueqin was born in Nanjing in about 1715 and died in Beijing in 1763. Gao E's dates are uncertain, but he must have written the sequel to *A Dream of Red Mansions* in about 1791.
3. *Décadence Mandchoue* was finally published for the first time in an unexpurgated edition in 2011, by Earnshaw Books, Hong Kong, using a combination of Backhouse's three original manuscripts now held in the Bodleian Library, London. A heavily censored edition in Chinese was released concurrently by New Century Press, Hong Kong.

Original Footnotes to Giles' Translation of Po Chu-i's *The Everlasting Wrong*:

1. Referring to a famous beauty of the Han dynasty, one glance from whom would overthrow a city, two glances an empire.
2. Referring to A-chiao, one of the consorts of an emperor of the Han dynasty. "Ah," said the latter when a boy, "if I could only get A-chiao, I would have a golden house to keep her in."
3. A fancy name for the women's apartments in the palace.

4. The mandarin duck and drake are emblems of conjugal fidelity. The allusion is to ornaments on the roof.
5. Each bird, having only one wing, must fly with a mate.
6. Such a tree was believed to exist, and has often been figured by the Chinese.

Chapter IV:

1. Simon Leys (Pierre Ryckmans), the well-known sinologist, wrote a scathing attack on Han Suyin's lack of respect for the truth and her conveniently changing political convictions in what is essentially a review of her book, *My House Has Two Doors*, London: Jonathan Cape, 1980, published in *The Far Eastern Economic Review*, December 26th, 1980. I quote:

Madame Han Suyin is very popular in the West. In China (except among some bureaucrats of the Propaganda Department) she is un-loved, and nowadays most Chinese intellectuals, artists and writers will frown if you so much as mention her name. Is this an excessively harsh response on the part of the survivors of the Cultural Revolution? The publication of her latest book, *My House Has Two Doors*, provides the opportunity to answer this question through a retrospective examination of her work.

Madame Han Suyin likes to take her imagery from the natural world, and many of her books have fine titles—*And the Rain My Drink* (1956); *The Mountain Is Young* (1958); *The Morning Deluge* (1972), and so on. In order to put her latest book into perspective I was inquisitive enough to leaf through a few of her other recent publications—*China In The year 2001* (London, 1967); *Asia Today* (Montreal-London, 1969); *and Wind In The Tower* (London, 1976). In the passages quoted below I have re transcribed the Chinese names into pinyin and abbreviated the references to 2001, *Asia*, and *Wind*, respectively. During those hours of reading I often found myself floundering, almost drowning, in the roaring tide of the author's powerful imagination, but at the same time I acquired a firmer grasp of the positively cosmic quality of her overall vision. It is a fertile chaos, a polyphonic coexistence of opposites, a lyrical alternance, a grand dialogue between Yin and Yang. After all, Madame Han Suyin has readily informed us that her house has two doors, and her work resembles those clothes you can buy with two different patterns and colours so that depending on your mood or the weather you can wear them with the outside in or the inside out. I believe that in the trade they are called "reversible models"; a useful notion, especially for people fond of turning their coats. Her work, thus, displays two different faces simultaneously, heads as well as tails; the subtle counterpoint can only be properly appreciated if one takes the trouble to put them into stereoscopic focus.

He then goes on to illustrate by quoting specific statements in *My House Has Two Doors* which blatantly and directly contradict statements made in *China in the Year 2001, Asia Today* and *Wind in the Tower*.

2. Just as Leys attacked Han Suyin's lack of respect for the truth with regard to political events, so Lydia Dan Li-t'i, in a Letter to the Editor of the *Far Eastern Economic Review*, May 8th, 1981, attacked her veracity with respect to her personal life. The letter casts such severe doubts on the author's integrity and the validity of her "memoirs" that I have decided to quote it in full.

Suchen speaks out—It was the greatest pleasure I have had for years to read the article by Simon Leys on Han Suyin's writings [Review, Dec. 26, '80], her inventions and her amoral opportunism.

I was her neighbour and classmate at the École du Sacre-Coeur in Peking in the 1920s to the early 1930s—when she was called Mathilda Tcheou—and I am described in one of her autobiographical books as her longest childhood friend. Our house at 16 Ta Tsao Ch'ang was just around the corner from hers. I feel I have the right to break my silence of many years and point out some of the many falsehoods in her writings.

In one of her books she spoke of working at the Peking Union Medical College in 1931 at 14 years of age. I am 66 this year and certainly do not remember that she was younger than I: rather I thought she was about the same age and her sister Za-Za about two years younger. (Za-Za was the nick-name for Therese. She is referred to as Tiza in Han Suyin's books.)

De-De (the nickname for Mathilda) was very proud of her European mother and, contrary to the impression in her books, not friendly with us Chinese girls.

Her first book published in 1941 (*Destination Chungking*) was a patriotic one and, when I read it in Boston, I did not realise that the writer was Mathilda. In 1952, I met other classmates of Sacre-Coeur in Hongkong and they told me that Han Suyin was Mathilda, that she was in town and was known as Dr Tong at the Queen Mary Hospital.

As it was, we met her on Queen's Road, and she invited us for tea at her place at the hospital. The party was enlivened by Mathilda reading us the manuscript of her famous book *A Many Splendoured Thing*. She was indeed very gifted with her pen; it is a beautifully written book. She then commented: "The Communists seem bent to destroy my life. My husband was killed near Peking, my fiance is killed in Korea, and now my future husband is fighting the terrorists in Malaya."

The success of her book and the film filled me with pride for having been her classmate. In the intervening years, I lived in a country where books were expensive and hard to get, so Han Suyin was not on my mind. I heard however that she had climbed on to the Peking bandwagon and was rather surprised when the SEATO cultural attache arranged for her to give a lecture at the Alliance Française in Bangkok. I went to speak to her after the meeting, but she gave the impression of having forgotten me. That was in the early 1960s.

Several years later a friend asked me whether I had read the series on her life including *The Crippled Tree*. I had not. However, in 1971, I borrowed the book from the public library and, to my horror, I read the references to my mother, Mme Dan. She is described as being "very cruel, capriciously cruel, like so many lovely, fragile-looking women are".

There is a description—like something out of a cheap Hollywood production—of her playfully throwing handfuls of diamonds, pearls and precious stones on to the floor, giving an impression of limitless wealth and of callous indifference to money.

The book claimed of my mother and Suchen (the name she invented for me). "Her mother beat her, made her kneel on the courtyard stones with a big stone poised on her head. If the stone fell off, she was beaten again. 'That is because my mother is a princess. She wants absolute obedience,' said Suchen."

Han Suyin went on to concoct the story that I had been "bought" by my mother from a "poor peasant family" because the Manchus were "effete and degenerate with sloth and disease" and my mother wanted me to marry a Manchu nobleman to "improve the breed of her family".

My mother was a princess and a Manchu. But she never used the title. My father was Cantonese—Dan Paotchao. He was a career soldier who went to St. Cyr and Saumur, the French military academies. He was never a warlord. Dan is a French transliteration and corresponds to Tong, or T'ang.

Determined for some reason to create fictions about her childhood friends, Han Suyin asserts not only that Suchen was "not happy" but was "never to know" any love or tenderness. No wonders she did not want to talk to me in Bangkok. I was quite successful then, married and the mother of three children—she saw me with my elder daughter in Hong Kong in the early 1950s.

As a converted communist propagandist, Han Suyin has no hesitation about living with her fortune in tax-free Switzerland. "Readers don't remember"? You are very right, Mr Leys. One cannot but regret that, given the gift for writing, Mathilda did not use it for novel writing rather than making fantasies of her need for autobiography, or publishing cheap double-talk as current history.

Lydia Dan Li-t'i

3. Dr C.Y. Sin, Chinese etymologist, lecturer, Department of Chinese, University of Hong Kong, cites scholarly evidence to support the idea of the cross bars suggesting hard work but it is the character for *mother* which has the two dots to indicate breasts.

Chapter V:

1. For studies of the image of women in literature, see Mary Anne Ferguson (ed.), *Images of Women in Literature*, New York, 1973; Susan Koppelman Cornillon (ed.) *Images of Women in Fiction*, Ohio, 1972; Arlyn Diamond and Lee R. Edwards (eds) *The Authority of Experience: Essays in Feminist Criticism*, Amherst, 1977.
2. See Sharon Spencer, "Feminist Criticism and Literature", *American Writing Today*, Richard Kostelanetz (ed.), Washington, D.C., 1982, p.159.

Chapter VI:

1. A variant of this chapter was previously published as "Chinese Women's Speech in English Fiction" in *Language & Communication*, Vol. 10, No. 4, 1990, pp.231-253.
2. For a more detailed discussion of this subject see Page (1973), p.3ff.
3. An insightful analysis is given of the relationship between modern drama dialogue and naturally occurring conversation in Burton (1980).
4. An example of work in this area is that of Li and Thompson (1976).
5. Nida and Taber (1969) in *The Theory and Practice of Translation*, p.88, claim that the fox is considered cunning only in the Western world. I notice, however, that the characteristic most often associated with the fox among Chinese speakers is also cunning.
6. Timothy Mo made these comments in an informal discussion in London, March 1983.

Epilogue

1. For example, *Chinese Women Writers; A Collection of Short Stories by Chinese Women Writers of the 1920s and 30s* translated by Jennifer Anderson and Theresa Munford, Hong Kong, 1985; *Seven Contemporary Chinese Women Writers*, Beijing, 1982, second edn. 1983.

Bibliography

Abercrombie, D. "Conversation and spoken prose" in *Studies in Phonetics and Linguistics*, pp.1-9. London: Oxford University Press, 1965.

Anderson, J. and T. F. Munford. *Chinese Women Writers*. Hong Kong: Joint Publishing Co., 1985.

Ayscough, Florence. *Chinese Women* Yesterday and Today. London: Jonathan Cape, 1938.

Backhouse, Edmund. *Décadence Mandchoue: The China Memoirs of Sir Edmund Trelawny Backhouse*. Hong Kong: Earnshaw Books, 2011.

Barrow, John. *Travels in China*. London: printed for T. Cadell and W. Davis, 1806.

Bland, J.O.P. and Edmund Backhouse. *China under the Empress Dowager*. London: Heinemann, 1911.

Boggs, Lucinda Pearl. *Chinese Womanhood*. Cincinnati: Jennings and Graham, 1913.

Bloodworth, Dennis. *The Chinese Looking Glass*. London: Secker and Warburg, 1967.

Buck, Pearl. *East Wind, West Wind*. New York: John Day Co., 1930.

———. *The Good Earth*. New York: John Day Co., 1931.

———. *The Pavilion of Women*. New York: John Day Co., 1946.

———. *Imperial Woman*. London: Methuen, 1956.

Burton, D. *Dialogue and Discourse*. London: Routledge & Kegan Paul, 1980.

Cao Xue-qin. *A Dream of Red Mansions*. Translated by Hsien-yi and Gladys Yang. Beijing: Foreign Language Press, 1978.

Carl, Katherine. *With the Empress Dowager of China*. London: Nash, 1906.

Chang, Hsin-hai. *The Fabulous Concubine*. New York: Simon and Schuster, 1956. Reprinted Hong Kong: Oxford (Far East), 1986.

Chang, Jung. *Wild Swans: Three Daughters of China*. New York: Simon and Schuster, 1991.

Chang, Leslie T. *Factory Girls*. New York: Spiegel and Grau, 2008.

Chao, Y. R. *A Grammar of Spoken Chinese*. Berkeley: University of California Press, 1968.

Chua, Amy. *Battle Hymn of the Tiger Mother*. New York: Penguin Press, 2011.

Chen, Fan Pen-li. Changing *Images of a Historical Beauty in Chinese Literature*. Ph.D. dissertation, Columbia University, 1984.

Cheng Nien. *Life and Death in Shanghai*. New York: Grove Press, 1987.

Clavell, James. *Noble House*. London: Hodder and Stoughton, 1981.

———. *Taipan*. London: Hodder and Stoughton, 1966. Reprinted Philadelphia: Coronet Books, 1984.

Coates, Austin. *Myself a Mandarin*. Singapore: Heinemann (Asia) Ltd., 1974.

Collis, Maurice. *The Motherly and the Auspicious*. London: Faber & Faber Ltd., 1943.

Cooper, Anthony G. *The Sanctuary*. Hong Kong: Communication Management Ltd., 1984.

Cusack, Dymphna. *Chinese Women Speak*. London: Century Hutchison Ltd., 1958.

Defoe, Daniel. *Robinson Crusoe*. Oxford University Press, 1910.

Davis, John Gordon. *The Years of the Hungry Tiger*. London: Corgi, 1983.

Der-ling or Te-ling. *Two Years in the Forbidden City*. London: Fisher Unwin, 1912. First published New York: Dodd Mead, 1911.

Edkins, Joseph. *China's Place in Philology*. London: Trubner, 1871.

Elegant, Robert. *Dynasty*. New York: Fawcett Crest, 1977.

———. *Manchu*. Harmondsworth, Middlesex: Penguin, 1981.

———. *Mandarin*. London: Sphere Books Ltd., 1984.

Evelyn, John. *Diary*. London: Gibbings and Company, 1895.

Fitzgerald, C.P. *The Empress Wu*. Melbourne: F .W. Cheshire for the Australian National University, 1955.

Fleming, Peter. *The Siege at Peking*. Reissued by Oxford (Far East), 1983.

Fung, Sydney S.K. and Lai, S.T., comp. *Twenty Five T'ang Poets; Index to English Translations*, Hong Kong: Chinese University Press [A Renditions Book], 1984.

Giles, Herbert A. *A History of Chinese Literature*. New York and London: D. Appleton and Co., 1901.

Goldsmith, Oliver. *Citizen of the World, Works*. London: Macmillan, 1912.

Greene, Graham. *The Quiet American*. Harmondsworth, Middlesex: Penguin, 1917.

Hahn, Emily. *The Soong Sisters*. London: Hale, 1942.

———. *China to Me*. Philadelphia: The Blakiston Co., 1944.

———. *Hong Kong Holiday*. New York: Doubleday, 1946.

Haldane, Charlotte. *The Last Great Empress of China*. London: Constable, 1965.

Han, Suyin. Destination Chungking. London: Jonathan Cape, 1942.

———. *A Many Splendoured Thing*. Triad Panther, 1978. First published London: Jonathan Cape, 1952.

———. *The Crippled Tree*. Triad Panther, 1982. First published London: Jonathan Cape, 1965.

———. *A Mortal Flower*. Triad Panther, 1982. First published London: Jonathan Cape, 1966.

———. *Birdless Summer*. Triad Granada, 1982. First published London: Jonathan Cape, 1968.

———. *My House Has Two Doors*. Triad Grafton, 1982. First published London: Jonathan Cape, 1980.

———. *Phoenix Harvest*. Triad Panther, 1982. First published London: Jonathan Cape, 1980.

———. *Till Morning Comes*. London: Bantam Books, 1982.

Harris, Theodore F. *Pearl S. Buck, a Biography*. London: Methuen, 1970.

Headland, I.T. *Court Life in China*. New York: Revell, 1909.

Hibbert, Christopher. *The Dragon Wakes*. London: Longman, 1970.

Hood, Thomas. "Fancies on a Tea-cup", *Works*. Edited by his son and daughter. London: B. Moxton, 1870.

Hsieh Ping-ying. *Autobiography of a Chinese Girl*. Translated by Tsui Chi. Reissued by London: Pandora Press, 1986.

Hsiung Shi-i. *Lady Precious Stream*. London: Methuen, 1949.

Isaacs, Harold. *Scratches on Our Minds: American Images of China and India*. New York: John Day Co., 1958.

———. *Re-encounters in China*. Hong Kong: Joint Publishing Co. and New York: M.E. Sharpe, 1985.

Jenyns, Soame. *Selections from the Three Hundred Poems of the T'ang Dynasty*. London: John Murray, 1948.

Jones, Dorothy. *Portrayal of China and India on the American Screen 1896-1955*. Boston: Centre for International Studies, M.I.T., October, 1955.

Johnston, Reginald. *Twilight in the Forbidden City*. London: Victor Gollancz, 1934.

Kingston, Maxine Hong. *The Woman Warrior*. New York: Knopf, 1976.

———. *China Man*. New York: Knopf, 1980.

Kwok, Jean. *Girl in Translation*. New York: Riverhead 2010.

Kwok, H. *A Linguistic Study of the Cantonese Verb*. Hong Kong: Centre of Asian Studies, University of Hong Kong 1971.

———. *Sentence Particles in Cantonese*. Hong Kong: Centre of Asian Studies, University of Hong Kong 1984.

Lamb, Charles. "Old China". First published in the *London Magazine*, 1823.

Lee Ding-fai. *Running Dog*. Singapore: Heinemann (Asia) Ltd., 1980.

Legge, James. *The Four Books*. Oxford University Press, 1892.

Levy, Harold. *Harem Favourites of an Illustrious Celestial*. Tai Chung: Chung-tai Printing Co., 1958.

Leys, Simon. *Chinese Shadows*. Harmondsworth, Middlesex: Penguin, 1978.

Li, C. N. and Thompson, S. A., *Mandarin Chinese Reference Grammar*. Los Angeles: University of California Press, 1976.

Lin Yutang. *Lady Wu*. London: Heinemann, 1957.

——— . *My Country and My People*. London: Heinemann, 1936.

Lodge, D. *The Language of Fiction*. London: Routledge & Kegan Paul, 1966.

Lord, Bette Bao. *Spring Moon*. London: Sphere Books Ltd., 1982.

————. *Eighth Moon*. London and Sydney: Sphere Books Ltd., 1984.

Luke, K. and J. C. Richards. "English in Hong Kong: functions and status", in *English World Wide* 3(1), 47-64, 1982.

Malraux, André. *The Conquerors*. Translated by Stephen Becker. New York: Grove Press, 1977.

————. *Man's Estate*. Translated by Alastair MacDonald. Harmondsworth, Middlesex: Penguin, 1975.

Mason, Richard. *The World of Suzie Wong*. London: Fontana Books, 1959.

Maugham, W. Somerset. *The Painted Veil*. Harvard Classics, Pan Books, 1978. First published London, 1925.

Mill, J .S., "On Liberty". New York: P.F. Collier & Son Co., 1909.

Mo, Timothy. *The Monkey King*. London: Andre Deutsch, 1978.

————. *Sour Sweet*. London: Andre Deutsch, 1982.

————. *An Insular Possession*. London: Chatto and Windus, 1986.

Morrison, Robert. *A View of China*. London: Black, Parbury and Allen, 1817.

New, Christopher. *The Chinese Box*. London: Allen, 1975.

————. *Goodbye Chairman Mao*. London: Coward, McCann and Geoghegan, 1979.

————. *Shanghai*. London and Sydney: Futura, 1985.

————. *A Change of Flag*. Hong Kong: Soho Press, 2002.

Nida, E. A. and C. R. Taber. *The Theory and Practice of Translation*. Leiden: United Bible Societies, Brill, 1969.

Page, Norman. *Speech in the English Novel*. London: Longman, 1973.

————. *Dialogue in the English Novel*. London: Longman, 1982.

Po Chu-i. "Song of Everlasting Grief". Translated by M. Chan and P. Gray. *Renditions*. Hong Kong, autumn, 1980. Translated by H. Giles. *A History of Chinese Literature*. New York: D. Appleton and Co., 1901.

Polo, Marco. *The Travels*. Harmondsworth, Middlesex: Penguin, 1982.

Pratt, Annis. "The New Feminist Criticism", *Essay in Feminist Criticism*. Amherst: University of Massachusetts Press, 1977.

Ricketts, Harry. *People Like Us: Sketches of Hong Kong*. Hong Kong: Eurasia Publishing Corporation, 1977.

Seagrave, Sterling. *The Soong Dynasty*. New York: Harper and Row, 1985.

Salinger, J .D. *The Catcher in the Rye*. Harmondsworth, Middlesex: Penguin, 1958.

Shu Chiung. *The Most Famous Beauty of China*. London: Bretano's, 1924.

Smedley, Agnes. *Daughter of Earth*. New York: Coward McCann, 1935. Virago (U.K.) and Feminist Press (U.S.A.), 1973.

———. *Chinese Destinies*. New York: Vanguard Press, 1933.

———. *China Fights Back*. Westport, Connecticut: Hyperion Press, 1977. Reprint of original edn., published New York, 1935.

———. *China Correspondent*. First published as *Battle Hymn of China*. London: Victor Gollanz, 1944. Pandora Press, 1984.

———. *Portraits of Chinese Women in Revolution*. New York: Feminist Press, 1976.

Smedley, A. *Chinese Destinies*. New York: Vanguard Press, 1933.

Snow, Helen Foster, (Nym Wales). *Women in Modern China*. The Hague, Mouton, 1967.

Spence, Jonathan. *The Death of Woman Wang*. London: Weidenfeld and Nicolson, 1978.

Stilwell, Joseph. *The Stilwell Papers*. Arranged and edited by Theodore H. White. London: Macdonald, 1949.

Terrill, Ross. *The White Boned Demon*. London: Heinemann, 1984.

Thursby, Geoffrey. *Miller*. Hong Kong: Communication Management, 1983.

Trevor-Roper, Hugh. *Hermit of Peking: The Hidden Life of Sir Edmund Backhouse*. Papermac, 1986. First published London: Macmillan, 1976.

Venne, Peter. "Pearl Buck's Literary Portrait of China and the Chinese", in *Fu Jen Studies*. Taipei, No.1, 1968, pp.77ff.

Waley, Arthur, trans. *One Hundred and Seventy Chinese Poems*. New York: Knopf, 1919.

Warner, Marina. *The Dragon Empress*. Papermac edn. 1984. First published London: Macmillan, 1972.

Wu, William F. *The Yellow Peril: Chinese Americans in American Fiction 1850-1940*. Connecticut: The Shoe String Press, 1982.

Xiao Hong, *Selected Stories of Xiao Hong*. Translated by Howard Goldblatt, Beijing: Panda Books, 1982.

Young, Linda Wai-Ling "Inscrutability revisited" in Gomperz, J.J. (ed.) *Language and Social Identity*, pp.73-84. Cambridge: Cambridge University Press, 1982.

Index

About the Author

Mimi Chan was born in Hong Kong during the Second World War. Indeed the War—and not human choice—dictated her place of birth since her family had for generations lived in southern China.

After the War Ms Chan's father assumed a diplomatic post with the Chinese government and the family went to live in New York where the author learned English and began her education. Life as a child in the United States came to an end not long after 1949. Mimi Chan returned with her family to continued studies in Hong Kong, there to learn to read and write Chinese, a language which she had virtually forgotten in her American years. She read English language and literature at the University of Hong Kong and was awarded the M.A. degree on Chaucer; thereafter, under a Commonwealth Scholarship, she proceeded to research on Shakespeare at University College, London.

She returned to the Department of English Studies and Comparative Literature at the University of Hong Kong after completing her studies in London and was appointed to the post of Senior Lecturer in 1976, retiring as professor in 1997. Mimi Chan is currently Honorary Professor and Senior Consultant to the University of Hong Kong, School of Professional and Continuing Education ('SPACE').

Ms. Chan has published articles on Shakespeare, Chaucer, English-Chinese translation and on bilingualism. Her published work includes two monographs on lexical borrowing, the first from English into Chinese and the second from Chinese to English. She published her first work of historical fiction, *All the King's Women*, in 2000.

Mimi Chan is married with two children.

www.ingramcontent.com/pod-product-compliance
Lightning Source LLC
Chambersburg PA
CBHW060226030726
47499CB00004B/1200